THE
DARK
HEART

THE

DARK

HEART

A True Story of
Greed, Murder, and
an Unlikely Investigator

JOAKIM PALMKVIST

TRANSLATED BY AGNES BROOMÉ

amazoncrossing

Previously published as *Hur man löser ett spaningsmord: Therese Tangs berättelse* by Albert Bonniers Förlag in Sweden in 2017. Translated from Swedish by Agnes Broomé. First published in English by AmazonCrossing in 2018, by arrangement with Bonnier Rights, Sweden.

Published by AmazonCrossing, Seattle

www.apub.com

Amazon, the Amazon logo, and AmazonCrossing are trademarks of Amazon.com, Inc., or its affiliates.

ISBN-13: 9781503904804 (hardcover)
ISBN-10: 1503904806 (hardcover)
ISBN-13: 9781503904798 (paperback)
ISBN-10: 1503904792 (paperback)

Cover design by Rex Bonomelli

Printed in the United States of America

First edition

To my wife, Cecilia.
Without you, there would be nothing.

PEOPLE

Therese Tang: Chief operating officer of Kalmar's branch of Missing People Sweden, 2012–2014. Security officer, hairdresser, model, stylist, mother of three.

Göran Lundblad: Multimillionaire, farmer, and property owner in Norra Förlösa. Reported missing in September 2012.

Sara Lundblad: Göran Lundblad's oldest daughter. In a relationship with Martin Törnblad.

Maria Lundblad: Göran Lundblad's youngest daughter.

Knut Lundblad: Göran Lundblad's grandfather, gold miner, and adventurer. Established the family fortune in the early twentieth century.

Gustav Lundblad: Göran Lundblad's father, engineer. Invented the Dollar Pipe. Added to the family fortune.

Irina Lundblad: Göran's ex-wife, Maria's mother.

Åke Törnblad: Farmer, Göran Lundblad's neighbor in Norra Förlösa.

Martin Törnblad: Son of Åke Törnblad, boyfriend of Sara Lundblad.

Anders Lindfors: Security officer, Therese Tang's colleague at Missing People Sweden.

Marie-Louice Strannemark: Therese Tang's colleague at Missing People Sweden.

Mats Råberg: Second-generation tenant farmer in Norra Förlösa. Rents land from the Lundblad family.

Britt-Marie Einarsson: Partner of Mats Råberg. Owns a house in Norra Förlösa, next to a forest pond.

Ulf Martinsson: Detective and lead investigator in the Göran Lundblad case.

Jonas Blomgren: Police officer, dog handler. Prepared the initial report regarding Göran Lundblad's disappearance.

PART ONE

MISSING WITHOUT A TRACE

1

THE END

It is the beginning of the end.

Therese's stomach tightens into a knot as she peeks out the kitchen window at the car turning into the yard. A champagne-colored Saab 9-5 with a young man behind the wheel inches toward the garage. Her mind is racing. She keeps back from the window so he won't catch her watching. This is it.

The car's paintwork sparkles in the sun. The man looks straight ahead through the windshield while the car slows down, then stops. It is eight in the morning on this chilly June day, and everything is happening much too quickly.

Over the past few days, she has been playing a dangerous cat-and-mouse game with this man in the car. Hours-long phone calls, text after text in the middle of the night. She has been waiting for him to tip his hand, for him to confess what she already thinks she knows but has yet to prove beyond a reasonable doubt.

This man has kept a dark secret for almost two years, resisting police interrogations and somehow holding up under intense psychological pressure. He clearly can't be forced to confess. But she believes she can break through his silence by making him feel safe, by inviting him into her life. She has to play along, to appear vulnerable and just a bit lost herself.

He must believe he is the one in charge.

The previous night, at twenty to midnight, she sent him a carefully worded text:

Can I trust you? I just don't know what your agenda is. What if you're just lying to me? You have to understand . . . I am drawn to the thrill, but how do I really know I can trust you?

It was all part of her game. But in this moment, with him sitting outside in his car, about to walk into the house, she is no longer pretending to be vulnerable. She is alone in the house, and he will soon be at the door.

Their meeting this morning is essential. She has grown tired of feeling that she is not in control of the situation; she wants to reclaim the initiative. She has come to accept that she is never going to be able to coax the decisive words out of him over the phone, so she has finally agreed to meet him in person.

Therese wanted the meeting to happen in a location of her choosing, at a time she requested, and in a context where she could have the upper hand, insofar as that is possible. She did not want to meet him back home in Oskarshamn, where her children live. This is better; Gamleby, fifty miles north from her home, where she sometimes uses the spare room in her colleague Anders Lindfors's house after her long and often late shifts at the detention center in Västervik.

Gamleby is neutral ground for a meeting with a murderer.

She would have preferred meeting in a public space, at the café in Gamleby, next to the supermarket, at the pharmacy or the corner shop. Or by the local liquor store—there would certainly be a crowd there today, stocking up on booze for the traditional Midsummer festivities that weekend. They could have found a quiet spot and spoken in private, yet with people around. The waitress at the café could, for example, have sounded the alarm if something were to happen. Meeting in public is always safer.

But it was not even seven in the morning when he called, already in his car, on his way to see her, and at that hour, everything in town is closed. The café she'd had in mind didn't open until nine.

Suddenly everything is on fast-forward. Instead of getting mentally prepared for the most important conversation of her life, the one that might finally bring everything to a close, Therese starts running around the unfamiliar house, collecting anything that can be used as a weapon, hiding every sharp thing she finds—kitchen knives, pairs of scissors—in case things spiral out of control.

The meeting will take place here, in this house. It must. She has run out of excuses. If she backs away now, it will raise his suspicions. Failing is not an option at this point. Especially not now, when he seems more ready to talk than ever before.

On the second floor, in the spare room she uses, she places one of Anders's pocketknives under the crime novel she is reading, *The True Story of Pinocchio's Nose* by Leif G. W. Persson. She double-checks to make sure the handle is hidden. She goes back downstairs to slip a second knife into the right-hand pocket of the jacket in the hallway.

She doesn't have a firm grip on what might happen, nor how a fight or an attack would play out. Therese has no experience with lethal force. All she knows is that it is better to have the means to defend yourself than to find yourself in need of a weapon and have nothing at hand. She is putting her life on the line in doing what she is doing. If you wield a weapon, you must be prepared to use it. You must be willing to follow through, otherwise you might lose the knife and be stabbed with your own blade.

While she moves quickly about the house, she gives a brief thought to Anders's firearms. He keeps several weapons in a locked cabinet down in the basement. She knows the code and has even used the guns, under supervision. She could probably hit a target.

But she has enough to worry about. Just keeping her breathing steady takes serious effort.

When Therese looks out the kitchen window, her colleague Anders's garage is to her left. Beyond it, his boat sits on a trailer, draped in a green tarpaulin on which drops of dew glisten like pearls in the morning sun. It is a damp morning here, in this house perched a quarter of a mile up from Gamleby Bay.

The man in the car has stopped in the yard midway between her black BMW and the front steps of the house. He stays in his seat for a while after killing the engine. She watches as he pulls the sun visor down and studies himself in the mirror. He fixes his hair and makes sure he is looking his best, preening, as if preparing for a romantic encounter. Something that might go his way, if only he plays his cards right.

At the same time, his fussing is an obvious sign of nerves on his part, which Therese chooses to believe might give her an edge.

He is young—not far off from the childishly rounded features of adolescence. Brown hair, cropped for practical reasons as any country boy would tell you. A lanky but strong young man with a wide forehead and deep-set eyes, also brown. They glow and blacken at the same time when he gets angry. But now, his gaze settles far off in the distance for a couple of seconds before he seems to pull himself together.

He climbs out of the car. She can see that he is not only younger but also stronger than she is. The kind of strength you get from working with farm animals and in the forest and fields. He is also impulsive, self-absorbed. Unreliable. What happens if everything goes wrong when they meet? Would she be able to outrun him? How far would she get?

The road is fifty yards away, and it is only another couple of hundred yards to the local technical college. There might be people there, but what if she trips, slips on the wet grass, falls over?

It takes about three minutes to die of asphyxiation, though it is only a matter of seconds before the circulation is affected. The brain's oxygen supply is cut off. The world goes dark. You kick and convulse while your life is slowly extinguished. Perhaps it feels like drowning, but with another person on top of you, fingers wrapped around your throat.

She brings her mind back to the present. She has to stay focused. He mustn't stop trusting her or start thinking twice about things. He has to stay trapped in his fantasies, lost in the world of his own creation, where everything is as it should be. Where he is going to get off scot-free, even if the police find the body. Where everything he has worried about will be fine, the money will roll in, his future will be secure. He mustn't stop believing. She must make him believe.

The top step of Anders's front stairs is loose. When the man outside walks up, she hears the slight wobble. Therese has been waiting for that signal, and now she pushes the door open and takes half a step out, smiling as brightly as she can.

"Not too hard to find, was it?"

She gives him a warm hug and gestures him inside, pulling the door shut, but not locking it. Getting out will be quicker if the door is unlocked. She averts her eyes from the jacket with its hidden knife.

On the other side of the closed door, the neighborhood is dead silent; even the birdsong from the birch trees at the end of the garden sounds muted. As if the world is holding its breath.

2

POLICE REPORT

Police report 0400-K35804-12 [excerpt]

Södermanland Police Authority

Criminal code: 9011

Missing person

Reporting party: Maria Lundblad

INCIDENT

The missing person, Göran Lundblad, has been missing since August 31, 2012.

On August 30, Göran was involved in a serious quarrel with his daughter Sara about Sara wanting access to and responsibility for land owned by Göran.

According to the reporting party's information, Göran's disappearance has been reported to the Kalmar police, who now suspect Göran might be the victim of a crime.

Göran resides in both Kalmar and Nyköping.

The reporting party wants the Nyköping police to investigate Göran's disappearance because the Kalmar police have not been in touch with her and because she feels the Kalmar police are too inactive.

It was a little after 4:30 p.m. on Tuesday, October 23, 2012, when Maria Lundblad, eighteen, called the Swedish police's nonemergency number. Since she was calling about an existing missing-person report, rather than a confirmed crime, she was put through to the K9 unit, which normally deals with disappearances involving potential terrain searches.

But Maria's concerns went beyond the missing person himself. She suspected her sister, Sara Lundblad, of foul play:

"I'm not sure Sara is being entirely truthful," she told the police. "I'm worried the Kalmar police are trusting too much in her version of events."

Maria didn't have anything concrete to point to, more a feeling that something was awry. A gut feeling. Not enough, in her opinion, to go to the police. Until now.

Before acting on her hunch, she had spoken to her mother, her older half sister Eleonora, and her school counselor, all of whom had advised her to report her suspicions. The counselor had also recommended contacting a new volunteer organization called Missing People Sweden, a group that assists the police in searching for people who have been reported missing.

The officer who took her call that afternoon, Daniel Augustsson of the Södermanland police, asked a number of routine questions. He learned that Göran Lundblad was wealthy, good for tens of millions of kronor, and that he made his living from, among other things, renting out arable land and housing property, both in Norra Förlösa, outside Kalmar, and in Stigtomta, located some 180 miles farther north, near Nyköping. Göran also ran a business that manufactured a certain kind of smoking pipe for which he had a patent.

The interview quickly zeroed in on two circumstances that appeared particularly interesting, at least from the police's point of view, two specific details that could potentially lead to a reclassification of the disappearance as something altogether more serious.

One was that Maria's older sister Sara had gotten into a big fight with her father before the disappearance. Sara wanted to get her hands on some land and properties, but her father resisted, in part due to his disapproval of her relationship with her boyfriend, Martin Törnblad. Göran felt certain he was only after Sara's money, as Martin's family had significant debt.

The other circumstance was more concrete. Less than a week after Göran's disappearance, Sara and Martin started renovating Göran's studio apartment in Kalmar. Maria was clearly concerned about this fact.

Shortly after Sara's fight with her father and his disappearance, she and Martin drove into Kalmar to start renovating Göran's apartment on Vasallgatan. Just a few days after Göran's disappearance, on September 5, 2012, they headed over with a tractor and trailer. Sara had called ahead to the housing company and had been given the go-ahead to throw things out the window, straight into the trailer, and to move new building material with their tractor bucket.

This started, in other words, only a few days after Sara called her half sister and stepmother in tears, asking for their advice and help because Göran was missing, and several days *before* she reported the disappearance to the police on September 10.

Their actions struck many people, including Maria, as insensitive and contradictory. When Sara was asked about this in police interviews, she said she and Martin were meant to move into the apartment together.

"Göran had approved the renovation," she said.

Martin, for his part, said they started working on the apartment because they didn't want to stay with his father.

"Sara talked to Irina a lot after Göran disappeared and she figured we should start making it homier. It was nice for both of us to have something to distract ourselves with," he said, referring to Göran's ex-wife, Irina.

During September and October, they cleared out the apartment, put up new wallpaper, laid down new floors, and moved all Göran's papers and accounting over from the farm.

Ställe Farm was, after all, empty and could potentially be broken into, or something else could happen to make all the important paperwork disappear. But Martin and Sara remained in Martin's family's home, and the renovation of the apartment on Vasallgatan was never completed.

According to Maria when she reported this to the police, there was no way the two of them could have obtained approval for the renovation. Göran would have been furious to find out Martin was even there and would have kicked him out immediately.

The officer could not help but raise his eyebrows at this statement. Renovating an apartment is hardly something you would do without the approval of the actual owner, unless, perhaps, you are completely sure he isn't coming back. Circumstantial evidence that raises eyebrows, though, is simply that: circumstantial. They would need much more to proceed with a criminal investigation.

The police officer asked Maria if she believed her older sister Sara was directly involved in Göran's disappearance.

"I think she might do him harm to get at the money, but there is no way for me to know for sure," Maria replied. "Sara is capable of hatred toward anyone going against her. She has an aggressive personality. Her boyfriend, Martin, is more withdrawn; he's hard to read."

Maria had no new evidence to give, but she wanted to alert police to her suspicions to make sure nothing was left to chance.

At 5:02 p.m., Daniel Augustsson ended the recording. The interview had lasted just under half an hour. It would prove to have a decisive impact on a six-week-old investigation in Kalmar that had recently ground to a halt.

3

GONE MISSING

Justice is a slow-grinding machine. The cogs and wheels of that same machinery had been clicking for over a month when Maria made her frustrated call to the local police in late October.

Six weeks earlier, on September 10, 2012, Detective Jonas Blomgren from the Kalmar police had knocked on the door of Göran's home, Ställe Farm in Norra Förlösa. Had he brought his police dog Ido into the house that day, things might have gone differently. But for Detective Blomgren, this was merely a routine visit. A young woman had called the police, saying her father had been missing for several days. In such cases, the police prepare a basic initial report and begin the standard investigatory process.

When Detective Blomgren stepped into Göran's house to meet with the missing man's daughter Sara, Ido stayed in his crate in the car. The detective shook hands with both Sara and her boyfriend, Martin, who was with her in the house that day. The couple did not live in the house; they resided together on the next farm over, which belonged to Martin's family. They hardly needed to explain this because it was obvious from the state of the house that the young couple didn't live there. Ställe Farm was dirty and neglected, lacking "a woman's touch," as the detective put it.

Once they had taken a seat in the living room, Sara told Blomgren that her father had been missing for several days. He had gotten into his car, a gray Chrysler, driven into Kalmar, left the car there, then disappeared entirely.

"The conversation was subdued and calm," Blomgren later recalled. "Sara seemed sad to me because her manner was reserved, and it was hard to get her to talk. She cried a little, I think, at the beginning of the conversation."

Sara provided most of the background information, but her boyfriend was helpful as well, answering as many questions as he could. But Blomgren did most of the talking, asking all the standard questions, as per procedure.

Police work always relies on historical knowledge based on information from previous cases; it operates from a baseline of circumstances and behavior it considers "normal." Consequently, anything that deviates from "normal" arouses suspicion and ought to be scrutinized. Call it what you will—cynicism, prejudice. But the police tend to call it experience.

Having the ability to quickly read people in an interview situation is one thing—not everyone has a talent for it—but police officers are trained both before being put into service and while on the job to identify contradictions in information and to recognize unusual behaviors and narratives.

Detective Blomgren had at this point been an officer of the law for over a decade and had thus seen most of what a uniformed officer in the Kalmar area was ever likely to see. He had been a dog handler for a few years at this point. The Swedish police have relatively few such specialists, only about four hundred in total, spread across the whole country. For that reason, they are often dispatched to provide support in other regions, to help to track suspects from the scene of a crime, for example, or to search for missing people.

During his career, Blomgren had worked on a lot of missing-person cases. In his experience, the family members were often very helpful, coming up with creative suggestions and useful information to aid the police in their investigation. But Blomgren noted quickly that Sara and Martin were not behaving at all as he would have expected. He felt he had to drag information out of the couple.

They told him about the fight between Sara and Göran, after which she said she left the house and did not return for a day or two. At that point, she told the detective, Göran and his Chrysler were gone. She later discovered the car outside her father's apartment in Kalmar when she and Martin went looking for him.

After that basic story had been told, Blomgren hit a wall. Sara and Martin's answers dwindled down to mostly yes or no responses for the remainder of the interview.

"I asked what they thought might have happened," Blomgren said. "We talked about Göran's habits and how he normally behaves. I had to be very proactive to get anywhere. It was hard to coax even basic information out of them. Given that very little came out unprompted, I got the feeling there was more to the situation than they let on."

The couple told Blomgren that Göran appeared to have taken his passport and briefcase, and that he had been traveling earlier in the summer and could have gone off again without telling anyone. Göran, he was told, mostly kept to himself and tended to withdraw in times of conflict, though not usually this abruptly. Sara told the detective of her suspicion that Göran's disappearance might have been his way of punishing his daughter. By making himself unreachable, he might be forcing her to get by on her own and perhaps to realize that she actually did need him.

At least that was what she had thought for the first few days, Sara said. But then she became increasingly worried and finally contacted her stepmother, Göran's ex-wife, Irina, who lived in Norrköping, for advice. Irina felt Sara could hold off on doing anything for a bit longer, that Göran would probably turn up. She suggested that Sara look around the neighborhood, or perhaps try the hotels in Kalmar. Göran had enough money to spend a few nights in a hotel. For that matter, he could also afford to get on a plane to anywhere in the world.

After that phone call, Sara began to search in earnest. She had come across the Chrysler in the Funkabo neighborhood, near Göran's apartment. He knew the area well enough to know which streets he could park on for free long-term, so she took this as a sign that he had really left.

During the course of her search, Sara also attempted to contact her father on his cell phone, though not particularly actively, as records would eventually show.

When September 6, the day of Sara's younger sister's, Maria's, eighteenth birthday, came and went without a word from Göran, Sara's concern intensified, she said. It was an occasion Göran would never have missed, no matter how angry or offended he might have felt. The realization that something must have happened finally sank in, Sara said, and it was at this point that she finally called the police.

The conversation lasted for approximately forty minutes. Detective Blomgren took copious notes, then asked permission to search the premises.

"In many cases, oddly enough, missing people have turned up in their own houses," he told them. "The reporting party has been unable to find them because they have hidden themselves away."

There could have been a medical emergency: Göran could have had a heart attack, fallen off his bed, then accidentally rolled underneath it. Perhaps he had gotten himself trapped somewhere on the property. Not the most likely of theories—and if either one were true, Sara and her boyfriend ought to have found him by now. But stranger things have happened, and police work is, to no small extent, all about ruling out possible explanations. Besides, a search of someone's home always helps give a more precise impression of the person in question.

On the ground floor of Ställe Farm, Blomgren found a hallway, a kitchen, and a study, in addition to the living room where their conversation had been taking place. At the other end of the hallway was a larger room, crammed with unused things, furniture, rolled-up carpets, and plastic bags full of recycling. It didn't seem inhabited. Blomgren poked his head in but didn't enter.

On the second floor, there were two bedrooms and an attic storage room that measured approximately 320 square feet. One of the bedrooms had been Sara's before she moved out, and it looked as though Göran might have been using the other. Neither Sara nor Martin gave a clear indication, and in fact, they told him very little about the house or who lived where.

Blomgren continued his search, methodically going through each of the rooms, closets, and storage areas, all to no avail. In his search of the garage, he discovered an expensive Mercedes under a protective cover. He also checked the basement, where there was a laundry room, as well as a room with several pieces of unusual-looking manufacturing equipment, which turned out to be woodworking machines for the family's pipe company.

The outcome of his search: absolutely nothing. The house seemed abandoned.

"There was nowhere a person could hide that I didn't check," the detective reported.

Blomgren continued the search elsewhere on the property, both in the large hall that housed the farm machines, where Göran's Chrysler had been parked since Sara and Martin drove it back from Kalmar, and in the older wooden building that served as a combined barn and stable. Sara kept her two horses in the southern end of the building at night. He took a look in there but was careful not to touch anything or move any straw around.

Ido was also eventually taken out of the car to help with the search, so she ran a lap around the house to try to locate a trail—this too is routine in missing-person cases. If Ido had picked up the scent of anything, the matter could have progressed to a so-called hasty search—further sniffing along roads, sidewalks, or other natural trails in the area.

But it was a hopeless task, given the amount of time that had passed since Göran had disappeared. Of course, his scent, and that of many other people, may have lingered, but what would that prove? Once Ido had finished her lap, Blomgren was certain that no interesting tracks led away from the house or its immediate vicinity.

He continued his search in the apartment Göran owned nearby, but once again found nothing. Blomgren prepared his report on the work done on this first day of the investigation:

> When I concluded my work that evening, it was with a feeling that a number of circumstances had not been brought to my attention.
>
> There was, however, nothing to justify taking further legal action.

The police report on Göran Lundblad's disappearance was assigned the code 9011, for missing person. This is an administrative description that does not actually amount to a crime.

Over a month later, at the end of October, a forwarder machine rumbled through the Norra Förlösa forest. Göran may have been missing, but the forest had no regard for such things. The trees won't wait.

The well-used, rather battered machine wheeled over the uneven undergrowth, full of rocks and tree stumps, with a young woman at the controls. A corridor of green, with neatly ordered trees waiting to be cut, stretched toward the hills and fields beyond, and a crisp autumn sun sparkled overhead.

With Göran missing, Sara now had to do the required forestry work by herself. At around eleven that morning, Detective Blomgren returned to the property, driving down one of the little forest roads until he found her.

Shortly after the interview with Sara and Martin at Stålle Farm in September, Blomgren had, coincidentally, been transferred to the violent-crime unit, a routine transfer to enhance his career skills development. The change would turn out to be rather timely.

The Göran Lundblad case, which Blomgren himself had entered into the system back in September, had since ended up on the desk of a middle manager at violent crime; Blomgren quickly asked to be assigned to the case. He had been there from the start, and since then had been unable to shake the feeling that something wasn't adding up.

As one of the investigators on the case, Blomgren was now free to spend as much time as he liked on it, as long as the rest of his caseload didn't suffer. This was standard procedure for stalled missing-person investigations at the time; they were simply added to a list and dealt with if and when time permitted.

When Sara spotted the detective, she turned off the forestry machine and climbed out to greet him.

"Nothing's happened since you were here before. We haven't heard anything," Sara said. "I can't understand why Dad isn't getting in touch. Even if he is still angry, surely the worst of it should have blown over by now."

No, she told him, no one in her family knew anything either—not her sister nor her stepmother, Irina—and none of Göran's tenants outside Nyköping or anyone else who would normally interact with him had heard a word from him.

In the interview record, Blomgren noted the following:

> When asked about Göran's access to funds, Sara replied that he normally keeps quite a bit of money at home. The sum has, however, never exceeded 60,000 kronor [7,000 American dollars].

On occasion there have been euros, but Sara also said that whatever money Göran might have had at home must surely run out eventually if he is traveling.

There is no money left in his home.

On the other hand, there was money abroad: millions of kronor in a Swiss bank account, as far as Sara knew. There was enough to build a whole new life if need be, she told him. She promised Blomgren that she would contact the Swiss bank in question to inquire about any recent activity.

The two continued to chat a bit longer about the fact that Göran would not be above tax evasion—having done some business under the table—though Sara was quick to point out that Göran had never had any criminal dealings to her knowledge. She had never heard about any contacts of that kind, and her dad had no enemies as far as she knew.

They also talked about how strange it was that Göran—whose entire life revolved around his properties, forest, and land—would leave everything unattended. Even if he were out to punish his daughter, he would surely have been in touch to check on the business, his bread and butter.

During their conversation, Blomgren invited speculation about where Göran might be, and whether he was alive or not. What did she think had happened? And if something terrible had indeed befallen him, what would the course of events have been? And how would the perpetrator have gotten rid of the body?

Sara was clearly unprepared for the direct accusation he leveled at her next:

"It wouldn't be hard to make someone vanish, with a machine like that," Blomgren said, nodding toward the log loader with its giant extendable boom and claw, a machine capable of moving whole tree trunks.

Then he waited to see what would happen. The statement, not entirely appropriate, was not entered into the official report of their interaction that day.

"I wanted to see her reaction, so I said it outside of the interview situation," Blomgren explained later. "And I wanted to make it clear that the police have to ask tough questions to find out what happened to Göran."

Sara had no noticeable reaction, there and then. But the thinly veiled accusation clearly unsettled her. And it festered. If anyone knew whether it were possible to bury a body with a loader or tree harvester, it would certainly be her. That machine was designed to cut down trees, not to dig. You wouldn't use this machine. In order to dig a hole the size of a human body, you would need a front-end loader or excavator. Nevertheless, she felt a finger had been pointed at her and soon told others: "The police think I've buried Dad with an excavator."

It was a rather incredible accusation to throw at a grieving daughter, potentially enough to have Blomgren investigated by internal affairs. But Sara didn't choose that path, and her lack of reaction only served to fan Blomgren's suspicions.

Shortly thereafter, she did, however, call him, feeling upset.

"She was like a child who had been scolded and told me I couldn't say things like that to her, that she didn't like it," Blomgren said.

It sounded as though she had told someone else about the detective's statement and been informed how she should have reacted in the moment. Or perhaps she had mulled it over on her own, pondering what it meant for a police officer to point his finger at her in that way.

"I explained that I appreciated it was unpleasant, and that I knew it was important to treat relatives with respect," Blomgren said. "But we also want to solve this case. Asking unpleasant questions is part of my job."

After the thirty-minute conversation with Sara in the woods, Blomgren also spoke to Martin, who confirmed something he hadn't mentioned in the first interview: that Göran didn't like him. But Martin claimed that he had come to feel more accepted as time had passed. In fact, though he admitted he didn't exactly know Göran as a friend, he insisted that they had a good relationship nowadays.

But of all the people the police interviewed after Göran's disappearance, Martin was the only one to say such a thing. Instead, each and every one of the relatives, tenant farmers, neighbors, property tenants, and people who had worked for Göran stated that Martin was detested, a thorn in Göran's side. And that Göran never missed an opportunity to point that out.

According to the interview records, although Martin was not being formally charged with a crime, Blomgren put the screws to him anyway, pushing and prodding to judge his involvement with the case.

"I'm not the kind of person who could hurt someone. I'm too much of a coward and would rather avoid a fight," Martin replied.

Throughout the twenty-minute interview he maintained that the disappearance was inexplicable, and he promised to get in touch if he thought of anything else.

Detective Blomgren also seized firearms from Ställe Farm during the month of October. Göran had a license for three weapons: two shotguns and a small-bore rifle—a parlor gun. During this visit, Blomgren had a chance to enter the room he had only given a cursory glance to during his first visit: the cluttered room behind the kitchen, which housed the gun cabinet.

It was the size of a standard bedroom, about 160 square feet, and jam-packed with things. Aside from a couple of piles of clothes, there were also several black garbage bags of recycling—bottles and cans—which occupied most of the floor. Blomgren had not brought his dog this time, though a police dog might not have been able to pick out any relevant scents among all that junk anyway. The detective didn't spend a lot of time contemplating the mess. After all, it was the household of an older man who lived alone. Blomgren had seen worse.

In the gun cabinet, he also discovered an illegal firearm, a timeworn automatic pistol, Fabrique Nationale model 1900. The weapon was at least a hundred years old; the model had been discontinued around the turn of the last century. A reasonable explanation for this weapon would be that the pistol was an heirloom, purchased before World War I, when a license was not required to own a firearm in Sweden.

After a forensic examination on October 24, 2012, a ballistics technician concluded that the gun was in poor condition and likely not functioning. The pistol had not been used as a murder weapon, at least not in modern times.

After Blomgren's initial interview with Sara and Martin in September 2012, the Kalmar police pursued the most obvious leads. Their checks reinforced the impression that something was amiss.

Göran's fuel credit card had not been used. His accounts with Swedbank, SEB, and Handelsbanken remained untouched as of October 19, which was particularly ominous, because there had always been, up until he disappeared, a lot of activity on his business accounts—regular payments, withdrawals, and purchasing of money orders. His standing automatic transfers such as, for example, some smaller sums into his children's savings accounts, continued unabated.

There remained the possibility that Göran had left of his own accord. Granted, he did normally drive everywhere, but he could, hypothetically speaking, have left his car in the free-parking zones in Funkabo, where Sara and Martin had found it, and continued on by some other means.

But the taxi companies had no record of him. The main train operator stated that they had not had a Göran Lundblad travel from Kalmar at any point during 2012. The Øresund trains to Denmark couldn't find his name either. A call to the local airport yielded no results. No Göran Lundblad on Kalmar Flyg's flights, or SAS's, as far as they could confirm. These were not ironclad conclusions, of course—you do not need to give your full name to travel by train, coach, or maybe another car. But the police checked everything that could be checked while they waited for any sign of life.

Among the measures taken, another detective with the Kalmar police, Jan Bergqvist, noted this:

> Ongoing contact with Göran's two daughters, Sara Lundblad and Maria Lundblad, as well as Maria's mother, Irina. No information has come to light beyond what is documented in the interview records.

Maria and Irina confirmed in interviews what Sara had already told the police: that when Göran had been missing for a day or two, Sara tried to call her sister, Maria, who was in Stockholm and unreachable. Instead, Sara got hold of her stepmother.

"The first thing Sara said was, 'Dad and I had a fight, and now he's disappeared.' I don't remember the exact words, but something along those lines," Irina said in her interview. "Sara very rarely cries, but this time she cried a lot. So much that she couldn't speak. She was gasping and sobbing."

Irina had tried to calm her down by reminding her that Göran was liable to do as he pleased and had been known to keep himself distanced at times. He might be up checking on his properties in Södermanland, for example. That he was not answering his phone was hardly remarkable for Göran either.

"Wait and see," Irina advised her stepdaughter.

There were more phone calls between the two during the next few days; Sara was consistently distraught. She told Irina, among other things, that she had found his car near Vasallgatan, that she had been up to check the apartment but it smelled fusty, and it was clear no one had been there in a long time.

"I tried to console Sara and come up with reasons why Göran was missing," Irina said. "We speculated that he might have gone somewhere to get away from all the nagging. But he's not the kind to just take off. We lived together for seven years, and in that time, he never went anywhere. But I wanted to comfort Sara and help her."

The outcome of the conversations between the three of them—Sara, Maria, and Irina—was an agreement to wait and see. But when Maria's eighteenth birthday passed without any communication from him, Sara finally contacted the police.

When the results of the investigations into the disappearance of Göran Lundblad were collated that autumn, the police had little to build on. A series of circumstantial facts, gathered through formal interviews as well as more informal conversations, all of which had generated a slowly growing stack of documentation at the police station:

- A missing man who rarely left his home region, who hadn't touched his accounts and hadn't contacted anyone he knows. The pattern adhered closely to a voluntary disappearance, and he had plenty of money to help him get by, but that he would simply leave everything he had lived for since birth seemed unlikely.

- A daughter who delayed reporting him missing for many days, long enough to cover plenty of tracks if she were indeed culpable. Granted, she had discussed the matter with her closest relatives and been advised to wait and see. But it was still an unusually long delay. In addition, her behavior was not in line with what is normally expected from the relative of a missing person. She seemed convinced her father would not be coming back.

- A feud, for lack of a better word, between the missing man and his daughter's boyfriend. And a fight about influence—about money—between the missing man and his daughter.

- Another call to the police in October, this time from the youngest daughter, Maria, the half sister, who suspected that something was amiss.

In a crime novel, this would have been enough to secure the convictions of both Martin Törnblad and Sara Lundblad. But the police live in the real world. A Swedish court would make short shrift of a prosecutor who came in with this kind of concoction, seeking murder convictions. Such prosecutors could in fact themselves be charged with a crime—prosecutorial misconduct.

A central tenet of jurisprudence is corpus delicti, which, directly translated from the Latin, means "the body of the crime."

The essence of it is simple: no body, no murder. Many jurisdictions hold as a legal rule that a defendant's out-of-court confession is not enough evidence to prove guilt beyond reasonable doubt. Nor can a defendant be convicted on the testimony of an accomplice alone. In other words: there has to be tangible proof that a crime has been committed for anyone to be arrested, tried, and sentenced.

If the police have the body, it should be possible to determine whether death occurred naturally or not. But although this sounds self-evident, it is rarely so when it comes to the law. Let's say a body is found with a crushed skull. A collapsed cranium, protruding bone fragments, dead as a doornail. Was the person hit with a rock? Or did he or she fall headfirst from a tree, a ladder, a passing airplane?

With the body at hand, it is also possible to assess whether various kinds of crimes can indeed be proven. To be convicted of murder, a perpetrator must have killed with premeditation and with the intent to cause death.

Was the victim stabbed with a knife or was he shot? How many bullets? Where? In the head, leg, arm? At what distance?

Such assessments provide the basis for the work done by police and prosecutors during a criminal investigation and provide a foundation for the court's assessment of guilt, as well as appropriate sentencing. But when there is no body, everything is pure theory. Without a body to examine, one must resort to hypothetical reasoning.

To convict someone of murder without a body being recovered requires staunch documentation, such as a video recording of the crime. In December 2015, two Gothenburg locals, Hassan Al-Mandlawi and Al-Amin Sultan, were sentenced to life in prison. A video from 2013 showed them being involved in slitting the throats of two captive men in Syria, so the two were convicted of murder and terrorist crimes on circumstantial evidence alone.

There was no physical evidence at all from the scene of the crime presented in court. Nor had the murder victims been positively identified when the trial started. The prosecutor relied heavily on three videos portraying the murders to identify the two defendants. The videos were found on a USB stick belonging to Al-Amin Sultan when he was indicted in another case.

The two men claimed they had not even been at the scene, but the technical evaluation of the films was accepted in full. And the men were convicted, even though they were not directly involved in the subsequent slow severing of the victims' heads from their bodies. Aiding and abetting the gruesome murders was enough for them to get life imprisonment in their home country.

Another way to convict someone of murder without having a body is by acquiring a voice recording in which the suspect explains clearly how they did it and describes other circumstances that can be verified at the scene. Bullet holes in a wall from a certain angle, for example, or where to find the stains from the victim's blood or other bodily fluids in certain places—in the crack between floorboards, under a rug, or perhaps behind wallpaper.

When a body doesn't turn up, a prosecutor must settle for trying the suspect on lesser crimes. In lieu of murder or manslaughter charges, they might focus on proving less serious offenses, such as kidnapping, aggravated assault, or the relatively new criminal offense of severely aggravated assault. In Sweden, kidnapping is punishable by up to lifetime imprisonment.

In the disappearance of Göran Lundblad, at this stage, the case would be a convoluted construction to haul through a court, or, rather, many courts, because an appeal would be all but inevitable. And the appeal, too, would require some form of corpus delicti. Blood spatter, DNA, broken furniture, or other traces of an attack, or, alternatively, overwhelming evidence of some kind of abduction.

Thus, they were back to where they'd started. The body was missing. There were no videos, no recorded confessions, and there was no evidence of foul play.

Something needed to happen or the case would be dead.

4

VOLUNTEERS

November 17 was an overcast day, and the Östra Funkabo school-yard in Kalmar was teeming with volunteers. Dressed in brightly colored yellow and orange high-visibility vests, they were all chatting with each other, some quietly, some more loudly, as if they were about to embark on a school field trip. Some people knew each other already, but others were new to the group and had only come out for this particular search.

In order to join the search, participants were required to be eighteen years old and were preferably to dress in appropriate outdoor clothing and carry something warm to drink. All volunteers had first met in the school building, where they had been briefed, divided into groups, and given maps, vests, and specific instructions:

Walk a yard apart, focus only on your task, ignore other groups.

If you find something that looks interesting, back up twenty to thirty yards and call one of the organizers over.

Finally, more than two months after he had been reported missing, the first large-scale search for millionaire Göran Lundblad was about to begin.

The volunteers had come at the call of Missing People Sweden, a group made up of volunteers who organize grid searches across the countryside in cases of missing people. Those who had appeared today on this gray Saturday afternoon were eager to lend a hand, make themselves feel good, perhaps even get their picture in the paper.

The organization had, during its brief existence, already attracted enormous attention. When Missing People Sweden was founded on the west coast in January 2012, some laughed at the determined men and women in hi-vis vests grid-searching the remote terrain. But the laughs were cut short when the remains of thirty-one-year-old Marina Johansson from Stenungsund were found that same spring. She had, by that point, been missing for two years, feared murdered. But without a body, it had not been possible to have her boyfriend convicted of murder, manslaughter, or even kidnapping, despite a pool of blood in her bed, despite bullet holes in the bedroom wall. No body, no provable crime.

When her remains were discovered by volunteers in the Svartedalen area in April 2012, the body was wrapped in, among other things, a mattress and a white tarpaulin. Following the find, the boyfriend was finally sentenced to sixteen years in prison, and Missing People Sweden was given a medal by the regional police authority.

The discovery was, however, in all honesty, something of a fluke— one of the volunteers was answering the call of nature by a stand of spruce trees when he spotted something white among the branches. On the other hand, if an organized search had not brought people out into the woods that day, the police would have had very little to work with and a murderer would likely have gone unpunished.

That case became Missing People's breakthrough among the general public as well. After the well-publicized incident, hundreds of people joined the organization's Facebook group. Requests for help and searches started trickling in from every corner of the country, and interested people from other counties got in touch to start their own local branches.

Therese Tang, thirty, a mother of three from Oskarshamn, stood in the middle of it all, taking in the scene around her. At five foot eight, she did not stand out in the crowd, but she seemed to be the focal point, the hub around which everything else moved. Her long blonde hair was tucked away under a warm woolen cap, and she wore a padded jacket, hi-vis vest, and winter gloves. The oversize glasses on her nose were a memento from her time modeling for an eyeglasses company. Her ice-blue eyes surveyed her surroundings.

She was the boss, the COO of the new local branch of Missing People that had just been opened in Kalmar. She had put out the call for volunteers a few days ago and was quite pleased with the turnout. But with so many people under her command, she was feeling the pressure. Therese was standing, lips pursed, gathering all her mental energy. It would, she knew, take a lot of focus to make this work.

But in the schoolyard that day, it irked her that the initial search was not being done around Göran's home in Norra Förlösa. She would have preferred to get a better feeling for who he was, his surroundings, relatives, friends, environment.

"Before we started the search, we contacted his relatives, which is routine procedure," Therese said. "Another member of the management team, Tomas Karlsson, contacted the daughter, Sara, initially. I know Tomas thought she was a bit odd. She simply confirmed that her dad was missing but wanted us to talk to her sister Maria instead, the one who had contacted us. He read it as Sara being a bit upset. It was the first time any of us had spoken to a relative, so we didn't really know what it was supposed to be like."

Therese had also spoken to the police, of course, and asked them whether they had gotten any kind of strange vibe during their ongoing investigation. They had told Therese that they had checked with the airlines and things like that, to see if perhaps the missing man had traveled somewhere, but they had gotten no indication that he had left the country. She was puzzled and determined to find out more.

In early November, the police had also published the missing man's name and picture in the media, which had generated quite a few responses. Tenants from Göran's properties outside Nyköping, among others, had gotten in touch with the police, as did neighbors and acquaintances in various places. They had all manner of things to report, but still no one had seen Göran. The police had no concrete leads.

One theory that the police had aired in the media early on was that Göran might have left the country and somehow run into trouble or become ill. But the focus nevertheless remained on his home region, Kalmar County.

Several local media outlets were present in the schoolyard that morning, and a handful of articles had already been written about the search in advance. The police were on site as well, to monitor every step the members of the search teams would take. The temperature was just over forty degrees Fahrenheit, and a mild southerly wind was sweeping up from inland. The volunteers wore hats and gloves to protect against the cold.

They had all been informed that they were looking for the sixty-two-year-old farmer and forest owner, Göran Lundblad. He was not tall, around five foot six; he weighed around 175 pounds and was thus fairly thickset, but muscular, the way a person would be after a long life of working in the fields and forest.

Göran kept his fine, once-blond, now-gray hair combed back. He wore glasses to correct his myopia and was quite wealthy, which at this point had been made known through the media. At the time of his disappearance, he was good for about fifty million kronor (six million dollars), a sum sufficient to pay out an average Swedish salary every month for more than one hundred fifty years. More than enough to make a person financially independent. Cashed out, it would make a fifty-foot-high stack of thousand-krona notes.

Göran was not in perfect health, having been diagnosed with type 2 diabetes, the adult-onset variety, several years earlier. He also suffered from glaucoma and had been taking blood thinners for a few years, out of concern over his heart. There was, at his age and with his health concerns, certainly some risk of him having fallen or even died during a walk through a wooded area near Kalmar.

Around seven to eight thousand people disappear every year in Sweden. The majority are found, either when they run out of money or when they sober up—physically or psychologically—or for other, more or less rational, reasons. Of that number, only a tiny minority are found dead.

The Göran Lundblad case was not looking optimistic. He had been missing for two and a half months. No signs of life. Hadn't answered his phone, or in fact used it at all. It had not been possible to ping its location. He had not crossed any national borders, as far as the police could tell, and he had not yet even touched his well-stocked bank accounts.

The inactivity in his bank accounts was not in itself a confirmation of either life or death. Göran Lundblad was a man who preferred to use cash. He had several safe-deposit boxes in Sweden where he might have stashed wads of cash, but as far as anyone could tell, he had not visited any of them.

Then there was the Swiss account, which had only recently been brought to the attention of the Swedish tax authorities, via a so-called voluntary disclosure, the kind of thing wealthy people do when they need to repatriate money for private reasons, or when they can sense the Tax Agency or the Economic Crime Authority breathing down their necks, now that Switzerland had started cooperating in the hunt for tax refugees. But there was no information about withdrawals from the rich alpine nation either.

Therese Tang and her volunteers had been told that the missing person's Chrysler had been found parked in the Funkabo area, just a third of a mile to the east of them, outside the apartment he maintained as an extra home for when he was in the city. The police had searched the car several times without finding anything. It contained keys to some of Göran's properties, an old hotel bill from a road trip, a handful of parking receipts, and various other sundries that tend to accumulate in cars. No suicide note, no clues.

Finding Göran's car there was hardly mysterious per se. He had owned his apartment in the area for twenty-five years, a studio of 410 square feet on the second floor, with a living room with French doors, a kitchen, a walk-in closet, and a bathroom. But it was strictly an overnight apartment, as he was registered as residing in Norra Förlösa, ten miles further north, where he owned farmland, wooded land, and houses.

Although he had last been seen alive out in the countryside, the car had been found here, so it was natural for Missing People to focus on Funkabo first.

"We had printed out some maps and divided up the area," Therese said, "but it wasn't remotely as well planned as it should have been. For example, we didn't know how long it would take to do a search, that you can only clear about two-thirds of a mile per hour. But a few of us organizers had prepared as well as we could, and lots of people came, so we just had to roll with it."

On a noticeboard in the schoolyard, there was a picture of Göran holding a dog in his arms and looking to the right.

Kenneth Hallberg, one of the volunteers, had brought his dog Akke with him. In an interview with Swedish Radio, he said, "Akke's a trained tracking dog. He usually turns up interesting things in the woods. I never considered not lending a hand here today. After all, we were heading out for a walk anyway."

Eva-Lotta Johansson, who lived in the area, told the local paper *Barometern*, "I saw on Facebook that there was going to be a search, and I felt good about being able to come and help out. It's also exciting to see how they organize one of these searches."

It could almost have been mistaken for a large family outing on this crisp November Saturday, albeit an outing with hi-vis vests and a grave undertone.

At around eleven that morning, the group of about seventy volunteers was ready to set out. Therese blinked a few times and collected herself. She took a deep breath, got everyone's attention, and then started sending the volunteers out in smaller patrols.

The Funkabo neighborhood, estimated to be about eighty acres, has just over 2,700 registered residents. It consists of a handful of clusters of detached houses, but mostly blocks of apartments. The majority of the buildings are from the fifties, when the residential co-operative association Riksbyggen invested across the country, a decade or so before the construction explosion of Sweden's so-called Million Program, where a million apartments with affordable rents were constructed across the land.

In Funkabo, you will find three-story buildings of yellow brick, plenty of parking, and leafy bicycle paths meandering between the buildings. There is a pizzeria at one end, a bicycle shop, and a school with a soccer field. Every small Swedish town has its own version of a neighborhood like this one.

A belt of trees, between 100 and 150 yards wide, flanks one side of the area. Distance and topography were important factors for the volunteers. Göran's body could be more or less concealed right there, among the trees. At the very least, there might be a clue there to help explain what had happened to him.

This was a busy area, with people coming through all the time, so any tracks going to or from a car, bike, or house would likely have been erased by now. Tracking dogs would therefore be of little use. If the missing man had lain dead somewhere among the houses, he would have been found by now. That much was certain. What remained was to look for belongings, such as phones, wallets, papers, or glasses, provided they had not been destroyed by the elements already. The volunteers began their search in the heart of Funkabo and moved out from there within a radius of about a mile and a quarter, paying special attention to bodies of water and wooded areas.

Over the past few months, there would have been countless joggers, young people sneaking a cigarette, and for that matter, even hardened criminals lingering among the trees. But maybe not everywhere. People have been found dead in the strangest places in terrain like this. Like Marina Johansson, in that stand of spruce trees, barely visible. And even if someone had spotted the body of the missing person, they might not have realized what they were looking at, or they might have been too afraid to report it. The body could still be there.

At least Therese and her colleagues must believe as much. They had not yet been informed of the covert police work that had been taking place behind the scenes. Two weeks earlier, Göran's apartment in Funkabo had been cordoned off for a full crime-scene investigation. Forensic search dogs had been brought in to sniff around just two days before the search. And that same morning, the police had been given a warrant to search Göran's permanent home in Norra Förlösa and to open his safe-deposit box. They had also been granted permission to tap the phones of the missing person's daughter Sara and her boyfriend, Martin. But Therese and her volunteers didn't know any of these details.

Notwithstanding the police's recommendations regarding search areas, Therese had already been planning to widen the search to include a path between Norra Förlösa and the nearby neighborhood of Lindsdal in Kalmar. In order to have time to cover it, though, they would need a lot more than the seventy-two volunteers who had joined them that day.

They had been sent equipment from Missing People in Gothenburg the day before—vests, writing boards, and flashlights. Even Therese's mother was there helping out, dividing people into groups and registering them. Therese then instructed each group on how to conduct a search and what to do if they found anything.

"Everyone should line up, arm's length apart. The person in the middle keeps an eye on things and is responsible for everyone walking in a straight line. The people at the end mark the path taken to make sure the areas overlap and nothing is missed."

Therese had been given strict orders by the police that her volunteers must not pick up anything they come across. They were just to mark it on the ground and on a map.

The volunteers spread out across the area and the search went off without a hitch, aside from when Kenneth Hallberg's dog Akke caught the scent of some animal, probably a hare, and dragged his owner off the path and into the woods. Kenneth landed headfirst in the rocky undergrowth and had to be patched up by his fellow volunteers.

The groups even had time to move beyond the immediate Funkabo area. They searched the wooded neighborhood of Tallhagen, at the foot of the Öland Bridge, which leads over to Sweden's second-largest island, Öland. They also searched farther out along the paths to Svinö Island, a recreational area by the Kalmar Sound with designated camping sites, jogging trails, and picnic tables. Despite the peaceful setting, the mood remained somber throughout. At the back of everyone's mind, of course, was the possibility of finding a corpse.

"You can't just look down at the ground when you're doing a grid search," Therese had told the volunteers before they set out. "You have to look everywhere: up and to the sides. For all you know, the person hanged themselves from a tree."

It is not unusual for suicidal people to take to the woods. They want to be by themselves, away from people, alone with their decision. That was perhaps particularly likely in this case, because a forest owner/worker would feel safe and at home among the trees. But if that were the case, shouldn't he have opted to stay near his home—in the area around Norra Förlösa? Therese couldn't shake the suspicion that they were wasting their time in Kalmar. Sure enough, the combing of the woods did not turn up any dead bodies that day.

Therese was mildly disappointed there had been no time to search the path leading north toward Norra Förlösa. She summed up the day to the journalists: "We have found a few cell phones here and there, but otherwise there have been no relevant discoveries. The turnout was great, and everything went smoothly. If we had had another fifty people, we would have been able to cover the whole area. But we did the most crucial parts."

All in all, Missing People volunteers that day found fourteen cell phones, which indicated that they had been thorough. Locating dark electronic gadgets in the undergrowth, fallen leaves, grass, and shrubbery is challenging.

"One of the groups also found a large trunk full of clothes in the woods," Therese reported. "It contained a lot of ladies' lingerie and also a man's shoe. It was not considered relevant to Göran's disappearance, but it certainly was odd."

At the on-ramp to the Öland Bridge, another group found bone fragments, leading to much excitement among the volunteers, but the bones turned out to belong to a deer.

Göran Lundblad did not appear, dead or alive.

The *Östran* newspaper wrote:

> Now Missing People will consider whether to contin-
> ue the search in locations not yet checked. They may
> also choose to conduct searches in Stigtomta outside
> Nyköping [180 miles north], where Göran Lundblad
> owns two farms with several tenants.

> He is said to have visited Stigtomta during the days be-
> fore his disappearance.

It was a successful first search operation for Missing People Kalmar, Therese felt, despite everything. The organization was up and running, people seemed eager to get involved, the police accepted the assistance, and the seventy-odd volunteers did an admirable job during the search.

As she drove the fifty miles back to her home in Oskarshamn, she finally started to relax. She was exhausted, yet there was so much left to learn, so much to sort out. But as of that night, Therese had absolutely no idea what role she would come to play in the nineteen-months-long drama that had only just begun to unfold.

5

GOLD RUSH

In the middle of the nineteenth century, countless gold rushes flared up along the west coast of the American continent and continued until well into the next century. Gold fever drew tens of thousands of people from all over the world to places like Yreka, Shasta, and Coloma in California; Dawson City in Canada's Yukon territory; and Fairbanks and Nome, Alaska.

In Nome, where the Snake River empties into the sea, one of the world's most accessible gold deposits was discovered in September 1898. Lined up at the water's edge, the prospectors panned nuggets right out of the stream.

According to family legend, it was here, in what would one day become America's biggest state, the Lundbladian fortune was begun. One of the many adventurers traveling to Alaska in the first few years of the twentieth century was named Knut Lundblad. He hailed from Balebo in Kalmar County and intended to make a future for himself. Not by following the stream of migrants from Sweden looking to put down roots in the US or Canada, but by saving up a tidy nest egg to bring back home.

For a competent man in possession of good health and his own shovel, pickax, and pan, the chances of making money in the wilderness were good. That is, with a bit of luck—and if the gunpowder in his rifle stayed dry.

Knut Lundblad didn't make his fortune all at once; it took him several trips to the US to scrape together the capital he needed to invest in forest and land in Sweden. But when he stepped off the trans-Atlantic steamer for the last time in his home country, he had enough money to buy his first property, Rogsta Farm in Stigtomta, around sixty miles southwest of Stockholm.

Knut would tell countless stories of bear hunting in the forests of Alaska and the trials and tribulations of gold miners and adventurers. A bear pelt and several other mementos from his journeys held pride of place in the main house at Rogsta. He was the talk of the town. It was said about him that he cast his own gold ingots and hid them.

The new seat of the Lundblad family, Stigtomta, in southern Södermanland, is home to just under two thousand people today. Ancient burial mounds and stone-lined fire pits prove that people have resided here since the Bronze Age. It is a landscape with a long history going back to before the Swedish nations were united under one king and the name "Sweden" had ever been uttered.

The Lundblad farm was located outside Stigtomta proper, with Hallbo Lake and Yngaren Lake to its west and southwest. From Rogsta's first-floor balcony, during the first few decades of the twentieth century, Knut had a view across the water, glimpsing Stigtomta to the south, no more than a couple of miles away but hidden behind trees, and the road to Vrena, Bettna, and Katrineholm to the north.

Knut's son, Gustav Adolf Oscar Lundblad, who went by the name of Jösse, would be pivotal to the family's continuing wealth. He was born in 1922 as one of four children to Knut and his wife, Signe. Having trained as an engineer, Jösse became an inventor and entrepreneur.

He was known among his kin as a restless soul, tough in business, if not outright greedy. His own mother called him a "devil" in business and warned the rest of the family not to cross him.

When he was around twenty, Gustav founded the company Patenta. It was the 1940s, and the Second World War had just come to an end. He had settled down in Segeltorp, a southwestern suburb of Stockholm, and married Maj, a woman with accounting skills who had studied at the Stockholm School of Economics. Among his inventions were a bathroom mirror that could be pulled in and out like an accordion, and a thermostat. But his most eccentric and successful product was dubbed the Dollar Pipe, a kind of tobacco pipe.

It may seem odd to grant a patent on a habit as ancient as smoking. Prehistoric remains of tobacco smoking have been found in a pipe in the US. Christopher Columbus was the one who brought the tobacco plant back to Europe, where the use quickly spread. Clay pipes, corn-cob pipes, meerschaum pipes, and every imaginable type of smoking implement has, thus, been used in Sweden for hundreds of years. But Gustav Lundblad had found a new way to utilize modern materials. Patent number 212646 at the Swedish Patent and Registration Office registers a "device adjoining bowl to shank in tobacco pipe as well as process for the manufacture of bowl with said device, and the tool used therefor."

The patent owner, G. A. Lundblad in Segeltorp, had solved an inherent problem of the world's most popular pipe material, briar. Briar is cut from the root burl of the tree heath plant, *Erica arborea*, which is naturally fire resistant. It is also a hard and compact wood, which makes carving an effective and efficient bowl difficult.

Tar and tobacco residue tend to gather in the bend of the pipe. Anyone who has ever used a pipe cleaner knows how gluey the tar becomes. In addition, finding sufficiently large pieces of briar to make a pipe bowl is not entirely straightforward. The quality of the large pieces varies widely.

Gustav Lundblad wanted to manufacture only the bowl itself out of briar, then attach it to a plastic shank and stem. That way, the smoke would still be generated in the wooden chamber and thus retain the flavor smokers want. But the construction as a whole would be cheaper to manufacture, if nothing else because smaller pieces of dense wood are in more plentiful supply.

He was also granted a patent for the machine used to manufacture his pipes, so he set up his own workshop. The patent is valid in the Nordic countries as well as in the US. When added to the income from his other ventures, Gustav Lundblad's modernized tobacco pipe made him enough money to allow him to invest in a number of properties in Stockholm, around Rogsta, and down in Kalmar County, in the home region of his father, Knut.

The Dollar Pipe is still being produced in a couple of versions today; the materials come from Italy and the Baltic countries. Four manufacturing sessions per year are required to meet demand from the distributor, tobacco giant Swedish Match. Dollar Pipe is a modest cash cow, bringing in no more than a few hundred thousand kronor a year. The pipes are sold for about one hundred kronor (twelve dollars) to Swedish Match, who offer them to the end consumer for somewhere between two and three times that amount.

The Lundblad family owned land in Norra Förlösa as early as the 1950s—the decade of the great modernization. The Second World War was over, and a new Europe was being built. In the years after the war, neutral Sweden experienced an unprecedented rise in the quality of life, largely thanks to industries that, having escaped wartime destruction, were running full speed to supply the reconstruction of the rest of Europe.

At that time, Göran Lundblad was still a little boy; he turned nine years old just before Christmas 1958. During these years, a feud flared up between neighbors in Norra Förlösa, one that would fester and eventually change forever the course of both his life and those of his loved ones.

Beyond a bend in the road in Norra Förlösa, among groves and fields, approximately thirty feet above sea level, you will find Skyttelund Farm. The surrounding land doesn't look like much. Three to five acres of forest, about five acres of farmland—a blanket of soil over densely packed loam.

But this is farm country, land-owning country, going back generations. Every piece of land counts. And this particular piece is at the heart of a dispute that has affected several generations.

When the Swedish National Land Survey surveyed the Förlösa area in the 1950s, a small section was missed, a parcel of land sandwiched between the Lundblads' property and that of their neighbors, the Törnblads. The parcel was not deeded and therefore didn't formally belong to either neighbor. Both laid claim to the land, which was the size of about three or four football fields. "Poorer than average," the Land Survey's archives note about the quality of the soil.

Both landowners refused to back down, but with the help of a local mediator, a deal was eventually struck to split the parcel into two equal parts. At least that was the most widespread story about the origin of the feud between the Lundblad and Törnblad families.

An additional factor adds spice to the narrative: Göran Lundblad's grandfather Knut, the adventurer, at one point purportedly promised to gift part of his forest to an older member of the Törnblad clan, as thanks for services rendered. The Törnblad man cared for the Norra Förlösa land as a kind of forester, and Knut Lundblad wanted to compensate him somehow. But when the time came to convey the land, Gustav Lundblad controlled all the Lundblad properties, and he reneged on his father's promise.

"It's the kind of thing that would stick in the craw, I reckon," said Mats Råberg, a Norra Förlösa farmer who rented his land from the Lundblads. "It's partly about money, partly about being stabbed in the back."

In the Lundblad family, it is said that it was an older aunt of Gustav's who owned the forest in question. After she was moved into a nursing home, her neighbor Karl-Oskar Törnblad would visit, ingratiating himself with coffee, cake, and silver-tongued persuasion. He wanted her to sign the property over to him. But Gustav caught wind of the scheme and managed to stop the transfer.

The words of the foiled Karl-Oskar Törnblad later became something of a mantra for his family: "One day, Ställe Farm will be ours."

At the end of the 1960s, Göran Lundblad was sent away to Ireland by his father. Rumor had it that it was because of Göran's poor performance in school. In fact, he was being ushered into the family business as an apprentice. Gustav kept his son on a short leash, according to his relatives, and neither of Göran's parents seemed particularly caring or loving.

Göran was to stay in Ireland for at least one year to work for his father's pipe manufacturer, Patenta, which had a partner there. In the end, it was five years before he returned; he would later confess that he had not enjoyed his work. It was a tough time, though he did also establish a number of contacts, which he later regretted not having managed to maintain.

Göran returned to Sweden a more experienced, somewhat "hardened" young man with an unmistakable Irish lilt to his English. The years abroad had been long but could be summarized briefly, as Göran was not the kind of person who harped on about his own experiences; rather, he would mention them only if they came up in some other context. He might then share an anecdote and conclude with a chuckle, as if to take the edge off whatever he had just said. He came across as shy and insecure at heart.

Göran lived with his parents, working on the farm and with the pipe manufacturing. He had minimal contact with the rest of the family because of his father. At first, Gustav Lundblad and his siblings got on well. But as Knut and his wife, Signe, grew older, they wanted to divide their assets between their children.

According to the accepted narrative among both family members and acquaintances, Gustav, Göran's father, cheated his siblings out of their inheritance. Sides were taken; Gustav was joined by his childless sister, Stina. And thus, all connection between Göran and his cousins was severed.

There seem to have been few women in Göran's life, but at the tail end of the 1980s, he met a woman named Tiina Nieminen entirely by chance. At the time, she was married to a man who rented an apartment in the building in Mälarhöjden that Göran's parents had owned since the 1950s. The building comprised eight apartments and was located on Tenngjutargränd, on a hill midway between the subway station and the water's edge.

The buildings surrounding the Lundblad property gradually descended the slope toward the shoreline, where one of Lake Mälaren's bays reached into western Stockholm. The view across the water was striking: on the other side was Kärsön Island and the Nockeby Bridge leading to Royal Drottningholm on Lovön Island.

Göran regularly spent the night in Mälarhöjden when in town on business—delivering pipes, for example—but also in order to look after the building.

"We didn't really know each other when we first met in the house in Mälarhöjden and started going out," Tiina Nieminen said.

A concise description of a fairly sensitive situation—committing adultery with the landlord's son. When she divorced her husband at the end of October 1987, she was two months pregnant with Göran's child. On May 13, 1988, she gave birth to a daughter, Sara. That same year, Göran turned thirty-nine. He never married Tiina, and she didn't stay long with her new man and baby.

"Stigtomta was no good, no good at all," she said many years later. "I was miserable. They worked me like a serf, and I never had any money of my own. When I asked to be paid for the work I did, Göran said his mother regularly transferred money to his account. And Göran was tightfisted."

Tiina took part in the family's pipe manufacturing. The pipe wood was delivered from Italy, then stems and shanks had to be cast, shaped, and buffed. Göran's mother oversaw quality control, scrutinizing all individual parts and assembled pipes. Tiina handled the polishing of the pipe bowls. She said, "I was put to work assembling shipping boxes and bagging filters and things like that. No breaks. I felt like a slave. I had no life of my own."

Things quickly went from bad to worse for Tiina in Stigtomta.

"I was so miserable, I started secretly drinking beer. And it got worse from there. I became an alcoholic," she admitted.

A neighbor across the road offered stronger things than beer, and Tiina found herself trapped in the terrible cycle of substance abuse. She never registered residency in Stigtomta, retaining instead her Stockholm address until a few months before giving birth. After Sara's birth, she was soon forced to leave her daughter behind.

"They arranged for me to emigrate," she said. "Göran told me to just sign the papers. I was supposed to go back to Åland, Finland, at least on paper. There was something about him being a single father, that there were financial benefits to doing things that way."

Speaking about her unhappy time in Stigtomta awakened a lot of emotions for Tiina. Her experiences were also indicative of the Lundblad way of life.

"They were terrified I might somehow get my hands on their money. They were constantly talking about money. Göran even told me: 'I suppose you wish Sara would die now, so you could get the money.' He had no idea how I felt. I wasn't allowed to see her after I moved away. Göran told her I was dead."

Tiina describes a tragic relationship, doomed from the outset because she was unable to adapt to the Lundblad way of life, which made her feel like chattel. The Lundblad family refused to accommodate her needs in any way, preferring to continue undisturbed along its charted course: work, grow the fortune, save, invest. She eventually left her baby daughter and her daughter's father in Stigtomta and moved back to Åland, where she remarried in 1991.

With an eighteen-month-old daughter at home on the farm, Göran started looking for a new life partner. There must not have been many forums for such things in and around the farm country of Rogsta and in Stigtomta. The online dating of today certainly didn't exist when Göran was on the prowl in the early 1990s.

Instead, he placed an ad in a Russian magazine. An Uzbek woman, Irina, saw his picture and information there and reached out to him. They married in July 1993. Göran then served as his new wife's "sponsor," which is to say that their marriage made it possible for her and her brother to move to Sweden. Her brother was later hired by Göran's father and developed a good relationship with Göran. Irina also brought a daughter from a previous marriage, and Irina and Göran's daughter, Maria, was born in 1994.

The Lundblad family was at that time still living in Stigtomta, in a kind of multigenerational setup across two farms. In addition to Rogsta, Göran's father, Gustav, had acquired Tängsta, a few hundred yards down the road. Gustav still ruled supreme in Stigtomta. Göran was his serf, dispatched to fields and forests to drive the tractors and forestry vehicles. He also did property maintenance and manufactured pipes, all without being paid.

"My parents just gave me an allowance," he told one of his tenants.

Just like Tiina Nieminen, Irina described a tough life under the thumb of a very demanding patriarch. The picture Irina paints of life in Stigtomta consisted of working, having virtually no privacy, and not spending money. Everything revolved around money—keeping what you had and making more, working hard, minimizing costs. Even at that point, despite the fact that Göran had recently turned forty, his mother was still in charge of all his finances.

Irina described going to the supermarket: she would write a list of the groceries needed and Göran would bring it to his mother, who would give him money. Cash. Always cash. The Lundblad family did not trust banks.

Irina was also expected to care for Göran's older daughter, Sara.

"She was a very reserved girl when we met. She was shy and would run and hide between her father's legs. When she called me Mom for the first time, it was a big occasion for me," Irina said.

As the new millennium approached, Göran and Irina's relationship collapsed. One day, upon coming home after work, Göran found an unknown man standing around the yard.

"Who are you and what are you doing here?" he asked.

"I'm an assessor," the stranger replied. "Your wife has hired me to evaluate these properties."

Irina had gone behind her husband's back to get his money, or at least to find out how much she could make off with in a divorce. Very quickly, it was made apparent that she had outstayed her welcome in Stigtomta. At least, this was the story the Stigtomta locals told.

According to Göran's elderly aunt Stina, Göran told her Irina was taking Swedish classes and had become infatuated with one of her teachers there. This, Stina claims, was a decisive factor in Göran's decision to file for divorce.

The divorce was formalized on September 18, 2001, but the two continued to celebrate high holidays together with their daughters. There was no custody battle over Maria, who initially lived with her mother only. Later, during her school years, she also lived with her father and sister.

In the 2000s, after Göran had moved down to Norra Förlösa and both his parents had passed away, his and Irina's relationship improved. Although Stigtomta was some 180 miles north, a nearly three-and-a-half-hour drive from Norra Förlösa, the Lundblad family retained their farms north of Stigtomta—Rogsta and Tängsta, as well as the houses on the other side of the road, which are best described as laborers' cottages, meant for the people hired to work on the farms in the area.

Rogsta consisted of two main houses and a couple of utility buildings set around a farmyard. On one side, there was a red wooden barn, large enough to house ten or fifteen farming and forestry machines. The second building was used as a stable and storage.

The two main houses sat close together; a car would barely fit between them. They were stone, whitewashed. The sound of traffic was constant in the east. On the other side of the main road was Tängsta, which was not really a farm but rather a regular detached house with an annex.

If they had been grouped more tightly, the Lundblad properties would have constituted a tiny village, and in a way, they were a universe unto themselves. As Gustav grew older, the family scaled back their farming, renting out the land instead. The houses were let as well. Upward of ten people lived in them as tenants during the 2000s, after Göran moved down to Kalmar.

Göran stayed in the main house at Tängsta when he visited. On the first floor, at the northern end of the house, Sara's posters were still on the walls and a toy stove sat on the floor, more than a decade after she had outgrown playing with it. On the ground floor, Göran, who was generally averse to throwing things away, collected both furniture and smaller possessions from the other houses. People who ventured inside the house at Tängsta during the 2000s were shocked to find it so cluttered, filthy, and badly kept. Göran prioritized his rental properties but barely had time to maintain them.

Perceptions of Göran Lundblad varied depending on how people knew him or what type of exchanges they had with him—in a personal capacity (very few) or through business (a few more). Kind, lonely, quiet, sometimes gruff, family-centric, dutiful, tightfisted, submissive, his father's servant, and a lightweight when it came to alcohol.

One characteristic emerges clearly, however: he was secretive. A man who played his cards close to his chest and would never dream of tipping his hand. Some described him as a virtual recluse. Ultimately, it seemed that this was a result of his shyness and insecurity, the way a person can become when they grow up in the shadow of an overbearing and domineering father.

"Gustav was in charge, and Göran never left his side. Gustav watched over everything; it seemed like he mistrusted Göran," said Linda Björkman, who rented a house from the Lundblad family in Stigtomta in the 2000s.

Gustav survived until 2007 and was a very active landlord and entrepreneur even in his old age, despite suffering a heart attack at the end of the 1990s. When he was in his eighties, he climbed the ladder to the barn roof to replace a shingle, only to fall down and almost kill himself. But he survived. He was a man who had difficulty recognizing limits, even the ones imposed by old age.

Gustav's methods had built the family fortune, so Göran did what his father told him to, what his father wanted, and what his father had always done, which was the way it had worked in the Lundblad family since the war.

"Göran seemed kind, to the point of being a bit simple," Linda said. "There was no gravitas to how he comported himself and dealt with people. He didn't seem very independent-minded. He drove this old clunker and didn't seem to feel a need to boast. And he never talked about money."

Some claimed that his tenants in Stigtomta exploited him. They were able to keep their rents low by pleading with Göran, or promising to work in lieu of rent, without ever following through, and the landlord was too kindhearted to forcibly collect debts.

One reason for that perceived kindness may have been that the Stigtomta properties were in relatively poor condition. Over the decades, the Lundblad family consistently chose the cheapest solutions to everything, from boilers and plumbing to the quality of windows and paint. If a landlord can't provide a certain standard, it makes sense to offer a discount to dissuade tenants from complaining or leaving. That may not have been something Gustav, who was a "devil" when it came to business, would have done. But he was in a nursing home by the mid-2000s, and his son, Göran, was a different breed of horse.

Göran did seem to have inherited Gustav's stinginess, in relation to both properties and forestry. When he decided to renovate one of the kitchens at Rogsta, he ripped the floor out, heaved everything out the window, drove the rubbish to the landfill, and put a new floor in, doing most of the work himself, with the help of only one of his other tenants.

The few times he couldn't do everything himself, he hired people, but only the cheapest labor available, primarily Polish citizens, whom he paid under the table, in cash. No visible bank transfers, no taxes, no employee benefits.

Not even Göran's closest relatives—cousins, aunts, and uncles—knew him very well, partly because of the feud over the division of the family properties. Aunt Stina, ninety-five years old at the time of his disappearance, was the person who'd had the most contact with him. Göran took care of her finances and saw to practical tasks after she moved into a nursing home in Nyköping, acting as something akin to an unofficial guardian when he was able to spare the time.

"He always worked a lot, always had a lot of things to get done," said Stina. "When he came to visit, he was always really on his way somewhere else. Usually he had been up to Stigtomta to sort something out there and was on his way back down to Kalmar. It was stressful for him."

Göran did have some minor business dealings with his cousin Håkan Lundblad—they owned a couple of properties together in Kalmar County for a while, but they divided everything up around 2010. They did, however, meet up in 2011 and have a long conversation.

They were trying to reconnect, according to another cousin, Ingela Gullstrand. Göran seemed lonely and had no one to talk to. But when the police spoke to Håkan in the autumn of 2012, he hadn't heard from Göran in six months. Nor had Ingela seen Göran in ten years or so. She said Göran didn't really have a social life at all, neither in Stigtomta nor Kalmar.

"Göran didn't have a lot of friends, none he talked about, anyway. Just one acquaintance in Stockholm," she said.

That acquaintance, Rodney Ahlstrand, was probably the closest Göran had to a friend. The two had gotten to know each other twice. The first time was in the early 1970s when Göran dated Rodney's sister, whom he'd met in agrarian college. After that relationship ended, Rodney and Göran would not meet again until the late 1980s.

Rodney was, at that time, looking for land to grow oats to make sheaves, the kind you put out to feed the birds around Christmas. He had been put back in touch with the Lundblad family and ended up renting about five acres from them. This time, he got to know Göran a bit better.

"Göran and his dad owned a building in Stockholm and delivered pipes in the 1990s," Rodney said. "When they were in town, Göran would come visit me in Södertälje. He and I would party a bit when we got together; we laughed and had a good time. We saw each other when it worked out, and he had business to see to in Stockholm."

Rodney said he normally spoke to Göran about once every other month. For the most part, Göran turned up without much notice. That seemed to have been his modus operandi: to leave off planning in case something went awry logistically. At the same time, Göran was not entirely without social skills.

"He would often stop by for a coffee or dinner with me and my partner," said Daniel Erixon, one of Göran's tenants in the 2000s. "But we were never invited to his place. That's just how he was."

Rodney described Göran as having been very strictly raised. "His father, Gustav, ruled that home. Göran wasn't allowed to pick his own friends, and I assume it was the same with girlfriends. His parents probably had the final say," said Rodney. "I was surprised when he got himself a girlfriend from abroad. But he must have had his parents' blessing."

Rodney agreed with the general impression of Göran as withdrawn, a person who wouldn't talk about his affairs until they were concluded, and a man who had become very lonely in the time before his disappearance.

"He seemed to be troubled that he didn't have a woman in his life," Rodney lamented. "He never said anything specific, but it was clear he didn't want to live alone."

Göran was caring toward his family, even when he didn't need to be. When Irina's oldest daughter completed her degree in Linköping, he helped her out by buying an apartment in Norrköping and subletting it to her, despite the fact that she wasn't his biological daughter and not really his responsibility. His own children were also given allowances, as well as monthly contributions to their savings accounts.

Maria had a special bond with her father while living with him at Ställe Farm to finish comprehensive school. They had a shared affliction—insomnia.

"He had terrible sleeping habits. I'm sure it was related to stress," Maria said. "I had trouble sleeping, too, and used to go down to the ground floor when I couldn't sleep to see if he was up as well. If he was in bed, I would sit in the kitchen and talk to him. If the TV was on, I would join him in the living room and we would chat in there."

They would sit there for a few hours in the middle of the night, the teenage girl and her dad, both with too much on their minds—adulthood, school, work, the forest, the family. Chatting about everything and nothing, watching TV.

"Sometimes he fell asleep on the couch," Maria said.

Even after she moved back to Norrköping for high school, they spoke on the phone several times a week, the calls sometimes lasting for hours.

As the details about multimillionaire Göran Lundblad collected, the picture that emerged was one of a lonely person who was too busy to enjoy his life. When he disappeared in late summer 2012, his domineering father, Gustav, had not been in the ground for even five years. After his father's passing, Göran, by then almost sixty years old, was finally allowed to make his own decisions for the first time, and to do whatever he wished with his entire fortune and all the family assets.

In some ways, he was the epitome of the dutiful baby boomer, even though he was born at the early part of that generation: the mind-set was that you had to work hard and save your pennies. He was, after all, only one generation away from nineteenth-century Småland, a place of starvation and despair. In those days, hoarding money was the only way to survive if something went terribly wrong. And in the Lundblad family especially, it was imperative that you be able to stand on your own two feet.

Outside Göran's closest circle, the rest of his contacts were of a more fleeting kind, mostly tenants or people with whom he did business.

Family connections were scant. In that loneliness, he relied on his first-born, Sara, the way his father had once relied on him. Sara was the one who was supposed to take over after he was gone, tend to the inheritance, take care of the family legacy.

His shock must have been substantial when Sara, when the time came, refused to do his bidding and bow to family tradition. Instead, in his mind, she betrayed him utterly by going out with the neighbors' boy—the oldest son of the family who had tried to steal the Lundblad family land those many years ago.

6

THE SECURITY GUARD

The first time Therese Tang heard about missing multimillionaire Göran Lundblad was in the autumn of 2012, right after starting the local branch of Missing People. It happened almost by chance.

"I had liked the organization's Facebook page, and someone from there spotted my name and recognized me, so they got in touch," she said.

Several circumstances conspired to place her at the heart of the Göran Lundblad mystery. One of them was the fact that the organization, Missing People Sweden, existed at all, that it was founded that same spring on the west coast, and that its founders were keen to spread the organization to other parts of the country.

Another is that there was a case in her area almost immediately. Once Maria Lundblad finally felt suspicious enough to contact the police in October, believing that the Kalmar investigation was being neglected, the case popped up on Missing People's radar.

A third circumstance was more intangible. As it happened, an event in her own life from a couple of years earlier had profoundly unsettled Therese, and as a result, she had started to care deeply about cases of this kind.

"I was friends with a woman I used to work with," Therese explained. "One day, she found out her husband's sister Linda had disappeared. The woman was from my town, so it resonated with me for that reason."

Therese's husband and mother-in-law hailed from Asia, and her friend and the missing woman also shared those roots. All of them had ties to Oskarshamn, where there is a strong sense of community among the Asian residents. They help each other out when needed and consider themselves parts of the same family.

Linda Chen's disappearance became one of the most talked-about Swedish court cases of the new millennium. One Saturday evening in August 2009, Linda, dressed all in white, left her fiancé, Mats Alm, in their apartment to go outside. It was one week before their wedding.

After that, she seemed to vanish from the face of the earth. The next day, Sunday, the police received a call from a worried Mats, who told them Linda had never come home.

The police seemed only mildly interested at first. Perhaps it was a case of cold feet? But her family and friends didn't believe that, so they joined forces. Therese's husband and her friend used their annual leave to travel up and help Mats Alm look for his missing fiancée, Linda. They handed out fliers with her picture to anyone who might have seen something and drove around the area in ever-widening circles, asking people if they had seen Linda. It was an unsystematic search, which obviously could have been conducted in a more professional, organized, and effective manner, but what was to be done? There was no one to turn to for official help, and Mats told the volunteers that the police were dragging their heels, even though her friends and family were sure that something terrible must have happened. There was just something odd about her disappearance.

"My friend called me after being up there for just a short while, saying that Mats was acting weird," Therese said. "He had a manic need for control and was incredibly pedantic. If they set down a cup without a coaster, for example, he would get upset and cause a scene. They had a bad feeling about it. I tried to suggest that anyone would act weird if their partner went missing. 'Sure, but something's wrong,' she replied."

Back in Oskarshamn, Therese followed the search and tried to help figure out what might have happened as best she could.

"When they talked to the police, I was on the phone, explaining certain words and concepts and such. It was incredibly frustrating to try to help from so far away. She [Linda's sister-in-law to be] asked me for help as well: 'Since your blog has so many readers, can't you send something out?'"

Therese, who at the time had a hugely popular wedding blog, posted a call for help and information, along with a link to a newspaper article about the disappearance. Enough people shared her post that even more people started looking for Linda, but she remained missing.

Linda's relatives made some progress in their search after a few days, when they came across a potentially promising witness. He said he was out riding his bike when he saw a man usher a woman matching Linda's description into a dark car with tinted windows. The police stepped up their investigation at that point and reclassified the case as a kidnapping.

Linda's partner, Mats, went on TV to talk about the case, crying openly during prime time. But although he denied everything, he continued to behave strangely, according to Linda's relatives. He went out drinking with his friends the day before the wedding was meant to take place.

"What I remember most clearly is probably when they were out with Mats, driving around outside Falun, looking," said Therese. "They stopped by a patch of forest they have driven past several times before. Linda's brother asked if they should get out and search it, but Mats said he'd already been there. So they drove on. And it turned out that's where she was. Of course he had already been there."

More than a month after the disappearance, Linda's dead body was found behind a rock near a parking spot in a patch of forest. The discovery happened under mysterious circumstances. First Mats went missing—he failed to turn up to a scheduled police interview—only to later appear in the middle of the woods, acting confused and with burns on his clothes and body.

He claimed he had been kidnapped by two "Chinese men"— drugged with white pills and abducted. A series of circumstances contradicted him—the most glaring one being when pictures of him turned up that had been taken in Stockholm during the time he claimed to have been held captive.

"He was clearly lying about being kidnapped by Chinese people," Therese said. "The Chinese men supposedly dumped him in the woods near Linda and set him on fire, but he woke up and managed to get away."

Mats's story contained any number of other odd elements: for example, that he supposedly had information from a fortune-teller or medium about where his partner could be found.

Once the body had been found, Mats was finally arrested, charged with the murder of Linda Chen, and was put on trial. But the case built by police and prosecutors collapsed. Linda's body was in a bad state—there were, among other things, bears in the area. The investigators suspected strangulation, but vital parts of the bones and soft tissue of the neck were missing, so the forensic doctors were unable to even establish a cause of death.

Theoretically, her death could have been an accident. At least that was the view of the court, which did not consider Mats's guilt proven beyond a reasonable doubt. He was, however, convicted for crimes against the peace of the grave, meaning for handling a dead body. Instead of serving a lifetime for murder, he was sentenced to a mere eighteen months in prison.

Therese was furious at society's apathy in the face of what seemed so crystal clear to most people with any insight into the case: a murderer had just gotten off scot-free. Innocent in the strictest sense of legal procedure, but guilty beyond all reason.

"It could have ended very differently if she had been found sooner," Therese said. "Then she could have had justice. That was when my interest in missing people began. I wanted to be able to help where there was a real need. The police do great work, but they don't have the resources to solve everything, especially not to search for a deceased person."

Consequently, when Therese was contacted by Missing People at the end of the summer of 2012, it was as though a missing puzzle piece had finally fallen into place.

"Are you really interested?" they had asked.

"'Absolutely,' I replied. 'Fantastic,' they said. 'You're in a region where we need people. What are your qualifications?' 'I don't really have any,' I replied, but I told them about the Linda Chen case. And that was that."

By the autumn of 2012, Therese could look back on a more eventful life than most, even though she was only thirty. Over the course of her relatively short life, she had been a fashion designer and had had many gigs as a fashion stylist, all a result of a short but successful modeling career. After that part of her career life was over, she went on to add many more skills to her résumé.

Therese grew up in Mönsterås, in Kalmar County, with divorced parents and a couple of siblings. She spent most of her time with her mother, but her father bought a house fifty yards away to stay as involved as he could.

"I tried a couple of different high school programs," Therese said. "First I started a tourism program in Högsby. It was brand new, and they took all the students on a two-week trip to Spain. That was obviously a really good time, but the education was terrible. Half the class dropped out after the first term."

Instead, she arranged an internship at a stud farm in Rävemåla. Several of the animals were world-class national-team horses. Her plan was to transfer to the equine high school program at Ingelstorp Agricultural College outside Kalmar. She had owned a horse back in Mönsterås for years and felt at home in the stable. Safe.

"It was among the horses I found peace and quiet and was left alone," she explained. "That was where I could just be. If I'd had a bad day, I would ride my moped out to the stable and just sit there and cry. It was my haven as a teenager."

But she soon realized that, while horses made a fine hobby, they were less conducive to making a decent living, so she abandoned those plans and dropped out of school.

"While I was trying to figure out what to do with my life, I worked at a nursing home. And then I got pregnant."

Her boyfriend, Magnus, worked in agriculture, and at the time, Therese was taking temp jobs as a care assistant. They lived in a house her sister had inherited. It was hardly the ideal situation for starting a family.

"We had been together for quite a while and were serious for two people our age. I was eighteen weeks pregnant when I found out, so having an abortion would not have been entirely straightforward. At the same time, I was terrified of telling my mom. I mean, I was eighteen, a child myself. We had been to the ultrasound appointment and seen the baby move in there. After that, I took pictures and sent them to his parents, my sister, my dad, and finally my mother. 'Here's a picture of your grandchild,' I wrote."

Then Therese unplugged her phone.

"Mom was on my answering machine as soon as she got the letter: 'Call me back, damn it.' And: 'Therese, I know you're there. Pick up now or I'm coming over.' But just an hour or so later, she relented. She called in tears: 'I'm going to be a grandmother.'"

Waiting out her family's fury proved a smart move.

After the death of one of Magnus's relatives, he and Therese were given a farm a couple of miles inland, in the middle of nowhere. They planned to farm and raise beef cattle. But before the farming plans had a chance to bear fruit, the new family broke.

"Our daughter Emilia was barely eight months old when I found out that Magnus was cheating on me with my best friend. I had known for some time that something was wrong. He was distant, and I suspected something was going on."

Therese took her firstborn and left both the farm and her partner. In May 2002, at just twenty years old, she moved back in with her mother. It would be several years before she and her daughter's father were able to resume regular relations.

Therese worked as a care assistant in Oskarshamn to pay the bills and establish a new routine, a new role. Not a farmer's wife, but a single mother with shared custody. Then, during a night out in Oskarshamn in 2003, something unexpected happened.

"I was on my way out for a night on the town when a guy approached me and said, 'You're good-looking.' What does one say to that? I just replied, 'Okay, thanks,' and was about to walk away, but he was determined, handed me a business card, told me he was a photographer, and asked me to call him the following Monday."

The man turned out to be exactly what he said he was; he worked for a serious modeling agency. She had her picture taken and quickly built up a portfolio. It was one of those on-the-street discoveries you only ever see in films.

This was not, as Therese immediately realized, the beginning of an international modeling career. But still, it was completely different from what she'd thought her future would hold.

"I ended up booking quite a lot of jobs over the years, for various catalogs, Swedish magazines, even farming magazines. And I did fashion shows for hairdressers and stylists. I probably stood out among the other models. I wasn't skinny or anorexic; I had curves and shapes.

It was interesting to experience that world. I had a chance to see the different sides of the industry that people have preconceived notions about—people snorting cocaine, models with serious eating disorders, all that bullshit. But mostly just good things."

Extra money, a glimpse of glamour and of what the wider world looked like outside of her small town. She averaged one job a month for most of the 2000s, not enough to live off for a single mother, but an exciting break from everyday life. She was able to travel, see new sights, have interesting gigs, and meet new people.

When a restaurant in Oskarshamn was looking for waiting staff in May 2013, Therese applied and was hired straight away.

"That was where I met Richard. It was his mother's place; he worked there too. He was good-looking and so kind—an enormous security for me in life. He was my knight in shining armor. We became very close because the restaurant was so busy. I worked more than sixty hours a week."

Over the next few years, Therese was given more responsibility at the restaurant. She did the work of a restaurant manager, being in charge of both staff and ordering. She worked those long hours, from five in the morning to late at night, while also finding the time to become a mother again. Twice.

"Havannah arrived in 2006. There are not a lot of people by that name in Sweden; it was pretty unique."

Therese's daughter had an early brush with death. At only two weeks old, she had a violent reaction while breastfeeding. Her breathing just stopped, and she was taken to the hospital in an ambulance. It was to be the first of many visits.

"The doctors didn't know what had gone wrong, but they thought she might have had residual amniotic fluid blocking her airway. They didn't consider allergies until she was six months old. When they tested her, they knew right away that's what the problem was."

Therese had no notion of this as she continued breastfeeding her newborn.

"I wanted to make sure she ate, but the whole time I was forcing down more of what she was reacting to. It was horrific. All her skin was peeling off during the first four months; there were wounds and scabs all over her body."

At six months, Therese's daughter suffered a pseudoseizure. It was something many parents would be familiar with: a child hurts themselves, is frightened or disappointed by something, or is admonished by a parent, and they launch into a fit. The world falls apart, and the child screams until they are blue in the face, perhaps even fainting or convulsing.

But this was something else. Something worse.

"Havannah had these attacks when she was six and seven months old and had just started crawling and moving about on her own. But she wouldn't scream or anything when she hurt herself; she would just pass out in my arms and stop breathing. It was an unusual presentation; there was only one other registered case in Sweden. She would kind of just shut down—inhale until she passed out."

For Therese and her husband, parenthood became a balancing act on the edge of disaster.

"I remember when Richard turned thirty. She was three years old then and had an episode. I did CPR on her for almost seven minutes. It was horrible watching the life drain out of her. We lived with this enormous fear. How could we even risk leaving her in day care? It felt like I was the only one who could fix her when something went wrong. It made me really overprotective. I'm always trying to anticipate the worst—keep everything under control all the time."

Two years later, in 2008, Emilia and Havannah got a new sibling—a boy named Dexter. They again had hoped to find a different name, something memorable. One night, they were watching the TV show *Dexter*, and the name struck them both. Although she and her husband did not necessarily want to honor a convicted violent offender, their son's name was indeed taken from Dexter Morgan from the eponymous TV series—a fictional serial killer who leads a double life, as a blood-spatter analyst mapping out crimes and crime scenes during office hours and killing evildoers in his spare time.

The same year the Linda Chen drama unfolded, another disaster struck the Tang family. Emilia's stepmother, Anna-Karin, was found dead on the kitchen floor in her home.

"She had a daughter with another man, but social services had already picked her up," Therese explained.

Therese got involved, even though it was not her own child. After going several rounds against social services, the child was at least allowed to celebrate Christmas with the Tangs.

"I had five hundred kronor (sixty dollars) in my wallet and we had no Christmas presents for her, so we went to the nearest superstore and got as many little things as that money would buy us just so there would be a lot of presents. We cried and laughed and felt very close. It was intense, and really hard. She's part of our family as far as I'm concerned, even though she's not my biological child. I have fought social services a lot for her. Right is right."

"What happened with Anna-Karin was a milepost in my life," Therese said. "I think it made me realize how important family is, that you have to cherish your life because you never know what tomorrow will bring. Live in the now and be happy about what you do have, not about what you could have. I started reevaluating what I was doing. I obviously wasn't getting any younger; I was about to turn thirty. That's when you start earning less in the modeling world and, eventually, you get replaced. What could I do to stay in that business for as long as possible?"

Therese decided to start training to be a hairdresser and makeup artist, styling models, doing their hair and makeup, instead of modeling herself. In that context, she was noticed by a designer from Milan.

"He invited me down to help with various outfits. This guy worked with both industrial design and fashion. He was A-list, so it was really cool to be part of his projects."

During 2010 and 2011, Therese traveled back and forth between Sweden and Milan for various jobs, such as the product launch of a big Italian makeup brand.

"It was the first time I had done this professionally. It opened up a whole new world for me—an alluring one. Travel, hotels, successful people."

But back in Oskarshamn, her family beckoned—three children, a husband, and a newly built house. The question was growing ever more insistent: What is more important in life? Relationships, family, work? What is true success?

Or put a different way: What is true happiness for a person who feels like half of her is missing when she falls asleep alone in a hotel room with her children six hundred miles away?

"I spent a lot of time on planes and buses during those years. It gives you time to think. I've always found it hard to be away from the children. Working's one thing; it keeps your mind busy. But then, when you're alone . . . It made me restless, and I wasn't enjoying myself."

In late summer 2011, she decided to quit. Models, styling hair and makeup and clothes: it was a decent side gig, but not the stuff to build everyday life on.

"I didn't want to lose my family. So I had to stop and consider: What jobs are available to me in Oskarshamn now, immediately?"

Kalmar County is dominated by manufacturing industries, which can mean monotonous work on an assembly line for many locals. The more qualified work requires more education and experience. One of the county's biggest employers was the Scania truck factory in Oskarshamn, established as early as 1946 as a supplier and later bought by the automotive giant. But for a female high school dropout of almost thirty, it would be difficult to find work there.

There certainly was no niche for someone with Therese's muddled résumé of restaurant work, styling, and modeling among Kalmar's smaller employers either. But on the nearby Simpevarp peninsula, there was a nuclear power station with its three reactors.

"One of Richard's friends got me in there for an outage job. You can make forty-five thousand dollars a year after taxes. Long shifts and fairly heavy work, but the pay's good. They gave me a job as a decontamination technician. It was very different from anything I'd done before. It was weird getting the question: 'Are you planning to have more children in the near future?' I told them no, so they gave me the job."

Instead of doing makeup in Milan, she was now a heavy-duty cleaner in a potentially radioactive environment at a nuclear power plant.

"One of the units was called the submarine. It was a kind of cooling element that extended something like eight hundred feet down into the ground. You needed a headlamp to get down there, because there's no lighting. You were climbing up and down narrow rungs in a wet, slippery environment. We wore orange overalls with an additional suit over the top, a face mask to filter the air, and doubled-up gloves and shoe covers. If anything were to break, we could have been exposed to life-threatening substances."

The elements in the submarine, essentially huge tanklike objects where heated steam is condensed back into liquid form when the power station is running, weigh somewhere in the range of nine tons.

"I'm small enough that I was able to get in under them. The idea was to clean and then vacuum out all the water. Try to imagine what it was like pulling yourself along under these huge tanks, flat on your back. It was a tight fit, just two inches between my nose and the metal. That's where we worked, with only the extremely faint lighting from someone shining a flashlight down one of the few gaps."

One day, a water pipe burst right next to Therese.

"The panic. I couldn't get up, couldn't run. Couldn't even crawl. And there was nothing to grab to pull myself out. The opening for getting out was ten or fifteen yards away. The only way to get there was to slide there on my back, heave my body in that direction, and push forward. Meanwhile, the water was rising all around me. The two guys on my crew, standing up at the top, kept calling out: *stay calm, stay calm*. I was *not* staying calm. The water was up to my cheek and still rising. I'm not someone who's easily spooked, but that really rattled me. I didn't go down there after that."

Somehow, the experience didn't deter Therese from continuing to work at the power station. In April 2012, the plant's security provider was hiring security officers and welcomed female applicants.

"I had no idea what it entailed, but I figured it would be fun to do the training, to learn something new. It seemed an interesting job, with all kinds of psychological drills and fire drills. And we were taught about how people react under pressure—to always be prepared. It suited me."

In the spring of 2012, Therese walked through the well-manned security checkpoint—"like an airport but so much bigger"—in a new capacity. She was now certified and approved by the Swedish Security Service.

From the finer salons of Milan to the concrete floors of Simpevarp, where you were called for a medical screening if your dosimeter went off, where you wore a uniform and carried a nightstick that you had to be prepared to use. And where a perfect workday was one where *nothing* happens.

One day in April, she and the other recruits, numbering about twenty, were brought in for orientation. They were given study materials, uniforms, personal dosimeters, and a tour of their vast new workplace.

In the building housing reactor 3 alone, there were approximately fifteen hundred rooms, thirty-five hundred doors, and winding corridors, stairs, and passages. The building extended one hundred feet down into the ground and rose over three hundred feet above it. The reactor itself was two hundred feet tall and the size of a soccer field.

Almost all the rooms were windowless. After turning a few corners in the corridors and walking down a flight of stairs and through a door, most of the recruits had already lost their bearings. It took them forever to learn their way around.

One of the more experienced security officers present at the orientation was Anders Lindfors.

"I was going up on the roofs to test the alarms after meeting the new recruits," he said. "Two of them said immediately that they wanted to come with me and learn by watching. One of them was Therese. After only a few weeks on the job, she started talking about Missing People. They were all over the news at the time. She wanted me on board, because I know my way around and have spent a lot of time navigating the wilderness. It didn't take me long to realize that she was special. Interested and eager to get involved. And she doesn't let things go. Once she's made her mind up, she never gives up."

7

GOOD ENOUGH

At the end of the 2000s, Sara Lundblad was a young person with a clear path in life. She was the heir of the Lundbladian multimillion-krona empire of forest, land, and properties. But she had to work for it. If her father, Göran, was his father's serf all his adult life, then Sara was now his.

She completed the economic track of the social sciences high school program and then worked alongside her father in the forest for a year to learn the business. She was taught forest management, planting, felling, and the subsequent handling of the timber.

Her father wrote this in a reference around that time:

> She has become increasingly interested in the business and is now part owner and therefore wants a solid education. Her duties and work as a trainee on the farm can be verified by many people, such as the Swedish Forest Agency as well as various buyers within the forestry business, neighbors, and lumber merchants.

After high school, she studied for a year in Värnamo in the so-called foundational forestry program—an advanced vocational program. The move across the county border, about 125 miles from home, was another step on the road toward becoming a tree farmer. The students there learned concrete things like how to best operate a chainsaw and a brush cutter and how to drive a logging machine over roadless terrain. They also studied theory: how forest management can maximize site productivity and how to deal with the administrative side of a business.

In the autumn of 2009, Sara embarked on a two-year forest technician program at Gammelkroppa School of Forestry in Filipstad. She was now even farther from home, but the program would lead to a license to practice, with an optional third year to follow if she chose. The local paper reported in an article that the 2009 school year marked a revival for the one-hundred-year-old school; that fall, they had twenty-five students—compared to eighteen the previous year—accepted after an initial aptitude test.

Among the people interviewed was Sara Lundblad. She told the paper that she had learned how to drive a forwarder on her family's farm in the Kalmar area, but that she was attending Gammelkroppa to learn a proper profession.

"I'm going to leave the forwarder in the garage unless someone else wants to drive it. That's just how it is," she said.

A determined young person with a plan, who wanted to earn a bachelor of forestry degree and then work on the family farm.

A photograph in the industry magazine *Skogsaktuellt* from September 2, 2009, shows a young, golden-haired woman in profile. Sara was hugging a compendium of books and pamphlets, paying rapt attention to her teacher, who was holding up various plants: water plantain, tufted loosestrife, and calla lily.

During her time in Värnamo, she visited her father and sister almost every other weekend and during the holidays, and she talked to her dad on the phone almost every day. But while studying in Filipstad, her home visits became less frequent. It was an almost 250-mile drive back to Norra Förlösa through the forests of Värmland.

A degree in forestry comes in handy when dealing with other people in the family business. But things came up, and Sara didn't even finish the first two years of the program. She dropped out after the 2010 autumn term.

She wasn't doing as well in her classes as she'd hoped, and after her grades fell, she decided she no longer liked it at the college. And then there was the boyfriend at home in Förlösa, who had become a serious long-distance love affair.

When the relationship with Martin Törnblad, three years her junior, began in 2009, Sara was twenty-one years old. Like her father, she was fairly short—around five foot three—and slight. Even so, she was able to carry out the heavy manual labor required in the forest and the long hours in the pipe workshop. She would work eleven, twelve hours a day, if necessary.

Most days, Sara was functionally dressed in a simple top and pants. A summer picture shows her next to a picnic blanket in a clearing. Slanted sunlight illuminates the scene; she is on the ground, turning toward the camera, wearing jeans and a baggy top. A basket next to her, coffee in a thermos, and a big bottle of Coca-Cola.

One or two of the countless people who would offer their opinions after Göran's disappearance described Sara as badly dressed and unconcerned about her appearance. Others talked about her as a "young, attractive but reserved" woman. Her hair was mousy; she bleached it on occasion, as some summer pictures show a blonde. Her face was heart-shaped, without identifying marks. She had gray-blue eyes and a cautious manner, as though she didn't quite trust anyone. In that respect, she was fairly similar to her father.

"Sara is a kindhearted person. Shy. She is a person who is difficult to read," her stepmother, Irina, said. "A careful person who it's hard to get close to. She doesn't let a lot of people in."

Sara was sometimes described as awkward, unfamiliar with the world, or ignorant about how things work outside of her home and the forest. She stuck close to her father, Göran. He was her mentor, in control of everything. In charge.

"I never interacted much with Sara," said tenant farmer Mats Råberg. "She always walked one step behind Göran and didn't say much."

Cecilia Eriksson was one of the police officers who participated in the search for Göran in the autumn of 2012. "My impression was that Sara was fairly lonely. She had met her boyfriend because he lived on a farm nearby."

Others described her as slow-spoken, but mostly because she didn't blather on, preferring to think before she spoke. They said she was smart, that she chose her words carefully. She rarely smiled, but she did not lack a sense of humor. At the end of the day, she had been raised to be a businesswoman. An heir.

The impressions of Sara Lundblad varied widely, as impressions tend to when people extrapolate from superficial interactions with someone. Very few people ever got close to her.

Doris Nydahl, one of the Stigtomta tenants, eventually became one of Sara's confidants. She had this to say: "Sara grew up very sheltered. I don't know how many boyfriends she's had, but it can't be many. I reckon she met Martin from next door and that she may not have had much to compare him with."

Martin Törnblad was eighteen and attending Ingelstorp Agricultural College west of Kalmar when he and Sara started going out. He was still a teenager, but of legal age. He had two younger brothers, Mikael and Oscar. They were farmer's sons, children, but by this time, at least Martin was used to doing the work of an adult. His days started at 4:00

a.m. or earlier, milking the cows. After that, he kept busy with general farming chores, such as feeding, mucking out, and maintenance.

Martin was a child of divorce as well, or became one soon after he started dating Sara. His mother chose to leave the farm for several reasons. The last straw was when her husband, Åke Törnblad, asked to borrow fifteen million kronor (1.8 million dollars) for an investment.

"He asked me to cosign the loan and I didn't want to," Martin's mother said. "It was too much for me, so I decided to move out and start my own life. I wanted to get away from the animals, the cleaning, the cooking, the child-minding and from basically being a domestic servant. I had my own life to get on with."

Wicked tongues claimed that the Törnblad family was living beyond its means, being greedy and suffering from delusions of grandeur. Borrowing themselves into bankruptcy. According to the local gossip, their cows were going hungry and the farm was mortgaged to the hilt.

"I have nothing against him personally, but he's not humble when it comes to business," said Mikael Schildmeijer, a business contact.

Åke himself believed he was running his company to the best of his ability and wanted to develop the business further and maximize its productivity. He also wanted his sons by his side.

Martin, his eldest, was tall and lanky with short, brown hair, a long face, and marked dark eyebrows. He knew how to talk, inexhaustibly and with seeming authority. He talked a big game, but rarely delivered; at least, that seemed to be the most common impression among most of the people he had a relationship with.

Just like his father, the teenage Martin was described as hot under the collar, easily annoyed, and liable to get worked up over nothing. He was often perceived as bragging and being immature.

"He's not exactly a modest person. He wants to be in charge," said Rune Jansson, one of the Stigtomta tenants, who saw quite a bit of Martin over the years after he became the boyfriend of heir apparent Sara.

An employee on the Törnblad farm echoed the sentiment that Martin thought highly of himself: "He talks a lot. Always opening his trap. He says a lot of peculiar stuff, but you can't take it too seriously—after all, he's just talking, right?"

Doris Nydahl in Stigtomta also took a dim view of Martin. "He's arrogant sometimes in a way I can't say I care for," she said. "I can't explain why I feel that way, but it could be that he's actually shy."

Ann-Kristin Simonsson in Melby, who would soon become more deeply involved with the family than she ever could have predicted, insisted that Martin was a good boy at heart. "But something's not right. He often lies about how fantastic his family is, that he has the biggest harvest, and that they are buying big, new machines."

At the same time, Martin did know his stuff. He was raised among all types of agricultural equipment, diggers, and bulldozers. But he tended to drive his car too fast around the village, which irked the other residents.

"He would floor it. Turn his hazard lights on so everyone would know who was coming," said Ann-Kristin.

How the heir of Ställe Farm and the three-years-younger braggart at the Törnblad farm ended up together is the subject of quite a bit of gossip.

The first time they met was on the school bus in the mid-2000s after the Lundblads settled in Norra Förlösa. But it took another year or so for anything to come of it. Then, at some point during 2009, Martin invited Sara over to his house. They watched a film and talked.

"It was when I was doing the foundational forestry program," Sara would later describe. "We'd see each other maybe once a month or once every other month for a year and a half."

That summer, the Törnblads were building a large barn. It was to feature, among other things, a milking carousel, for automated milking of the family's cows.

"I went over to the Törnblads' when they were building their new barn," Sara said. "Martin and I were friends then. And a month or so later, we went to Denmark together."

The investment in the barn led to financial difficulties for the Törnblad family. The milking carousel didn't work right; instead of raising efficiency, it inflicted a loss of hundreds of thousands of dollars. But throughout this difficult time, Martin and Sara's relationship only grew stronger.

Sara commuted between her home and her school program in Värnamo and then, less frequently, to and from school in Filipstad. Martin stayed in Norra Förlösa with his own dreams and his daily toil at the dairy farm, every day, up and about at four in the morning.

It is easy to imagine Sara, sitting lonely by the phone in her dorm room in Värmland, without the support of her until-then ever-present father. Talking to the boy next door, increasingly captivated, or at least interested enough to see where the relationship would go.

They developed a recurring code phrase, one that popped up much later when the police began tapping their phones. The phrase "you and me." An incantation of forbidden love.

He would say, "you and me." She would answer almost reflexively, "you and me," only to then pick up the conversation where it had broken off, talking of the farm, the livestock, the milk, the forest, the neighbors, business.

From the first, people had opinions about how serious Martin was about Sara.

According to her stepmother's, Irina's, brother, Martin bragged to all and sundry at his school about having bagged the daughter of the lord of the manor. About how he had tons of other girls, but that he was using this particular one to achieve his main goal in life—to become rich. It supposedly upset his classmates to the point where they contacted Göran to warn him. His contempt for his intended son-in-law grew and grew.

Finances were, indeed, strained at the Törnblad farm. Martin was never paid at all; he worked for room and board, and a small allowance. For even the most even-minded people, seeing how good everyone else has it has a way of tipping the balances.

In this way, Martin's childish boastfulness and outlandish claims can be understood. He so badly wanted to have more, to succeed, to get ahead. Now he, the pauper, had gotten together with the millionaire's daughter. The future looked bright, if only he could seize the moment.

But surely it is also possible to fall in love with a girl only three years older, one with whom he shared so many things in common? Perhaps possible to truly be in love and also think that eventually merging the two farms is a good idea? Of course, it wouldn't hurt if the girl was rich. Or at least would soon become rich.

"You can have anyone you want," Sara was told, in no uncertain terms, by her father. "Martin's not good enough for you. He's only after your money."

One can't help but draw the parallel to Stigtomta and Sara's mother, who wasn't good enough for the Lundblads either. Tiina had developed a drinking problem because she was so utterly miserable at the farm and was put on a boat back to Finland.

Göran's words about Martin not being good enough and Sara being able to "have anyone she wants" were a constant mantra. Even in conversation with casual acquaintances, he uttered these words again and again.

From the time that Göran found out about Sara's relationship with Martin, in 2009, until his disappearance three years later, father and daughter clashed regularly over it.

Their fights were filled with spite. Göran dismissed the Törnblad family in general, given their financial situation and behavior, and complained frequently about the underlying gripe concerning the contentious parcel of land by Skyttelund. He often specifically demanded that Sara break off her relationship with Martin. When Sara refused to obey, he took heart in thinking she would lose interest once the novelty of the affair wore off.

A vain hope. If Göran had known how long the couple had known each other before getting together and what they had been discussing, he might have acted differently. But he was unrelentingly dismissive, as if he couldn't bear to take the relationship seriously.

"It's hard to say what Göran was like as a person," said Pernilla Söberg, a Stigtomta tenant. "He didn't exactly trust people, but he was still open. Not easy to read, and sometimes you had to feel him out. When Göran was troubled, he withdrew. He would speak to people only in private about what worried him. Göran told me Martin and Martin's father were after his land. That Martin had wrapped Sara around his little finger in order to get his hands on the land and money. Göran was both worried about what was going to happen and angry about the situation, saying that Martin was after nothing but money."

Eva Sterner, also in Stigtomta, had this to say: "Göran was livid with the Törnblads, and he took it hard when Sara and Martin got together. It was the worst thing that could've happened. He said he couldn't sleep at night. He was anxious and stressed."

Sara's younger sister, Maria, lived at Ställe Farm while finishing elementary school, but she moved in with her mother in Norrköping in 2010 to attend high school. As far as she was concerned, her older sister and father seemed to be butting heads constantly. Granted, she was not there to witness the rest of Sara and Göran's life together, which likely revolved around practical matters for the most part. But all Maria heard about was the quarreling over Sara's relationship with Martin, and that Sara wanted more independence, to find her own path in life.

"He also said they fought about the fact that Sara wanted some land to look after all by herself," Maria said.

Göran was not entirely averse to that idea. That is, after all, how it happened for him—his father, Gustav, transferred his property to him in stages. But Göran was worried about subdividing the family land, about the family fortune being squandered.

As Irina put it: "It was all about money. Göran was prepared to give Sara everything she wanted, if she would only break it off with Martin. He told her there was not an ounce of good in Martin. He would have bought her a farm. They went to look at three or four different ones. One of them cost thirty million kronor (nearly 3.6 million dollars). But none of them was good enough for Sara; there was always something wrong. And then there was the condition that she break up with Martin; she wasn't prepared to do that."

The price of thirty million could be anything from a misunderstanding to a more or less conscious exaggeration. It doesn't sound at all like Göran to have agreed to cough up that kind of money, which would have required leveraging more than half the family's assets, to buy a new farm. But several people in Göran's life confirmed that he was, in essence, trying to bribe Sara to dump Martin.

"Dad kept saying the Törnblads were using Sara for her money. That she was going to get knocked up and then she'd be stuck for life," Maria said.

8

THE HEIR

On a summer day in the early days of the 2000s, the lord of Tängsta and Rogsta farms in Stigtomta, aging patriarch Gustav Lundblad, was through mulling things over. He was no longer young; in fact, he was to turn eighty-one in a few months. His wife, Majvor, would be eighty in August. Granted, they had a number of years left to live, but they were feeling their age. It was time to see to the future, to ensure that the family's properties and capital remain undivided.

The Comstedt law firm in Nyköping was tasked with formulating a mutual will:

> If I, Majvor Lundblad, die before my husband, I want the following conditions to be met: All my property shall fall to my husband without restriction or qualification and after both our deaths, all my remaining property shall fall to my grandchild Sara Lundblad.
>
> This shall be considered compensation for Sara's mother likely dying without property of any kind to bequeath.

As far as Gustav and Majvor were concerned, Sara's mother, Tiina, was permanently out of the picture. The family consisted of their son,

Göran, who lived with them in Stigtomta, and his daughters, with Sara being the chosen one, the one who would ride next to her father on the tractor whenever Majvor wasn't looking after her.

Majvor's signature on the document is shaky; it seemed to have taken her some time to write. Perhaps she was ill, her health already in a poor state at that point. She passed away the following year.

Over the course of the next few years, Gustav transferred many of his assets to Sara. He, who according to family legend was called a devil by his own mother, did everything in his power to ensure the family property would remain undivided in the future. Gustav gave his son, Göran, the lion's share of the fortune, but also passed him over by transferring properties of a total value of almost eleven million kronor (1.3 million dollars) to his granddaughter as a gift in 2006, the year she came of age.

Gustav did include several precautions in his gift to Sara—any future partner would, for example, be blocked from cheating her out of her money.

> If the donee is in or at any point enters into a legally
> binding relationship, the property shall not be included
> in a division of assets between the donee and her partner
> nor be subject to restrictions on the right of usufruct or
> transfer.

Gustav also stood to reap practical benefits from transferring his ownership to Sara, including his half of the pipe company Patenta. He was, at that point, increasingly finding the daily routines challenging, and not just the forestry work. Even looking after himself—visits to the toilet, for example—had become more difficult. Being assisted by his son and granddaughter was too embarrassing, so he managed to secure a place at a nursing home. The fee structure there was income-dependent;

residents with a lot of property paid more for room, board, and care. Poorer residents lived for free.

As usual, it was all about money. Without the income from the pipe factory, his fee for the nursing home would drop substantially.

No more than a year or so after Sara's eighteenth birthday, in the summer of 2007, Gustav Lundblad died, leaving his only son in charge of everything, along with his two daughters.

But all the arrangements made to keep the estranged mothers out of the picture and the fortune and business undivided were put in jeopardy when Sara started going out with the wrong boy.

For this reason, it looked like a deliberate strategy when the gift from Gustav to Sara happened to be transferred on to Göran in its entirety in February 2011, just after Sara decided to drop out of her degree program in Filipstad. It seemed to be a carefully thought-out maneuver aimed at neutralizing the unwanted son-in-law. Göran drafted deeds of transfer for all Sara's properties and made her sign them.

Her stepmother was, for her part, sure that he had tricked his daughter, but only in order to protect her. "He said Martin was only going out with her because of her money and that he would cut and run as soon as he found out she didn't own anything. Göran wanted to show her that he was only interested in her for her money," Irina said.

The story of how the wily father hoodwinked his disobedient daughter was told by the Stigtomta tenants as well.

"He promised Sara that she and Martin would be allowed to live together in the apartment in Kalmar if she signed everything over to him," said Eva Sterner. "She did, but then they weren't allowed to live together anyway."

Sara told a different story, of tax planning, or stinginess, depending on how you looked at it. "I had an annual income of about forty thousand kronor (about five thousand dollars) but paid sixty thousand kronor in taxes (about seven thousand, five hundred dollars), which is to say I made a loss of twenty thousand (about two thousand, five hundred dollars) a year. According to the Federation of Swedish Farmers, the simplest solution was to transfer everything to Dad," she explained. "Dad also wanted to make it possible for me to get financial aid for studying, which was out of the question while the properties were in my name, he told me."

Later that year, in October 2011, Göran changed his will. He dropped Sara as the heir apparent and instead decreed that everything be divided equally between her and her sister Maria.

Point four of the will was a familiar safeguard in Swedish law:

> All property inherited through this will or by descent by any person shall be that person's separate property.
>
> The same stipulation shall also be applied to any property replacing the property as well as any income arising from the property.
>
> In cases where the Cohabitation Act is applicable, the stipulations set out above regarding separate property shall be binding.

No boyfriends would ever be able to get their grubby mitts on the Lundblads' money or land.

Even so, Göran seemed concerned that Maria's mother might still be able to get at the money. And he didn't entirely mistrust Sara; she was, after all, the one who worked in the forest and had shown that she was both able and willing to take over the business. In point five of the will, Göran appointed Sara as Maria's financial guardian until she turned twenty-five if Göran were to die before then. Maria's mother, Irina, would be kept out of it.

Göran also put several different measures in place to paint his oldest daughter into a financial corner.

"I had named Sara as my sole heir, but Göran wanted me to change my will so he would inherit instead," said Göran's aunt Stina.

She, who took Gustav's side in the family feud, had about a million kronor (about 120 thousand dollars) to pass down. Göran regularly assisted her with her paperwork and various communications with the authorities and so on, but this time he made an extra visit, just to discuss the will.

"It was urgent, Göran felt. I signed the new will," said Stina. "The reason was that Sara couldn't be trusted, he said. She was doing shady deals, and he didn't trust her."

Whether you see it as Göran conning his daughter out of all her money, or as him consolidating the family's—including Stina's—capital for business reasons, one thing was clear: neither Sara nor her father openly admitted that by signing the deeds, Sara had been made virtually destitute.

It would be a long time before Sara's boyfriend, Martin, found out that the daughter of the big landowner was flat broke. She saw no reason to tell him; on the contrary, she was raised to keep mum about her family's business interests. Martin for his part shouldn't care either way, since he was in love.

Theirs was a relationship under siege. Both Sara and Martin were just starting their adult lives. They had no more clearly formulated plans than to keep working for their respective families' companies. Both dreamed of merging them somehow into a bigger, more functional business with forestry, land, and cattle, with its headquarters in Norra Förlösa, ten miles from Kalmar.

Ställe Farm, which is registered as Norra Förlösa 124, is a peaceful spot. The main house sits on a small hillock. There is no well-kept lawn or kitchen garden or flower beds; the occupants had no time for things like that. A handful of pines are scattered around the house, as if in remembrance of the forest that once covered the area.

When arriving at Ställe Farm for the first time, a visitor could be excused for thinking the door to the basement is the main entrance. The split-level house is built on a slope with the basement entrance facing west, from which a staircase, barely shoulder-width, leads up to the ground floor, which comprises a kitchen, living room, study, hallway, and one bedroom. Another set of stairs leads up to the first floor with its two additional bedrooms.

North of the main house, on the surrounding land, by the foot of the hill, is a dilapidated wooden barn, uninsulated—nothing more than plank walls and a roof, functional and simple. It was intended as a temporary parking lot for the machines, to keep the worst of the rust off, though there are a few smaller adjoining rooms inside as well. Across from the barn, on the other side of the farmyard, is a newer machine shed, with metal walls and roll-up doors. Sturdy padlocks on the doors protect the expensive vehicles, equipment, and cars inside. A gravel path winds up to the farm from the intersection that, according to the map, is Norra Förlösa proper.

The Lundblad property is located a mile or so west of the E22 highway, in what urbanites would call the dark heart of Småland.

Rural communities, forests, farms. The densest forests start slightly farther west still, stretching virtually uninterrupted from there all the way across the county border to Kronoberg and the Växjö diocese, from which the expression "dark heart of Småland" originates, a reference to the social conservatism and high church Lutheranism of the capital of Kronoberg County.

Considering the tangled web of history between the residents of Norra Förlösa and the nagging, long-standing conflict over five acres of land, it is an apt expression in this context too.

In Norra Förlösa, people keep an eye on each other. If you were to exit Ställe Farm through the main entrance and walk around the corner, you would be looking at Mats Råberg's farm. There are several neighbors in between, but Mats's farm is slightly raised above the others on a small hill. He has farmed land rented from Göran Lundblad for decades.

Åke Törnblad's meat and dairy farm can be seen farther to the west. That, too, is on a hill. To the right, in the northwest, is a field with a strip of forest at its northern end. Behind it, more fields stretch out like an asymmetric patchwork quilt to the north.

If Sara were to start her red pickup as she usually would and set off toward town, it would be noted in the village. The same is true of Göran and his gray Chrysler, the car he took wherever he was going, even if it was just a few hundred yards.

Social control in its purest form. And it applied to everyone.

If Mats Råberg were to look out his window, he would see any movements over at Ställe Farm. If there were strangers there, for example, which is not inconceivable even in such a remote location, he would notice. There were plenty of stories about robbers and burglars going after isolated farmers, so people tended to pay close attention to newcomers in these parts.

Mats has an unobstructed view of the Törnblad farm as well. The Törnblads can, in turn, easily keep track of the comings and goings at the two other farms. Everyone knows who lives here and is familiar with the movements of their neighbors, though it is debatable how much store to put in the information they give. What is fact and what is fiction? Extrapolated assumptions, based on various movements, sounds, and lights, about the happenings in and around Norra Förlösa can hardly be taken as conclusive, can they?

The Lundblad family harvester could often be heard roaring through the forest. It was a tractor-like, articulated vehicle, with robust wheels capable of traversing the uneven forest floor. At the front was a boom, like on an excavator, which the driver controlled from the cab.

The machine was designed for felling trees. The head of the boom is placed around a tree, which is cut through by the built-in blade—a bit like a remote-controlled chainsaw. The tree is then de-limbed as sharp metal rollers feed it past the de-limbing knives. The finished logs are left on the ground as the harvester moves on to the next tree.

A thirty-foot tree ready for felling weighs around three thousand pounds, give or take. It's obvious that the harvester is a powerful machine, though simply constructed. In the wrong hands, it would turn into a terrible tool that could be used to demolish a building, blow by blow, if anyone were crazy enough to try it.

The harvester can snap a tree in half, or, for that matter, crush a person. A death of that kind could easily be registered as a logging accident. Because who would be able to prove otherwise? Would there be any witnesses? Modern, small-scale forestry is more often than not solitary work, though you could bring an employee along to assist you. Maybe a relative—a son or a daughter.

Five people die in forestry accidents every year in Sweden, most in conjunction with tree-felling. But Göran had survived all these years. He was the one who operated the harvester in the family's forests. His daughter Sara followed behind in the boom logger, the forwarder, gathering up the logs and transporting them to the landing area. Anyone who has ever driven through Småland will have seen piles of such logs stacked by the side of the road. The timber is then picked up by agreement with a suitable sawmill, pulp factory, or other similar industry.

It is, of course, also possible to use your legs to get around the forest and to fell trees manually, with protective gear and a chainsaw. But this is only for light thinning, to keep the forest healthy and let the best trees grow unimpeded. If you want to make money from the venture, traipsing about on foot and felling by hand would take too much time and effort. The Lundblad family had the required equipment. Granted, the vehicles were by no means new, and the forwarder was uncomfortable to operate. Both were also fairly small. But they fit in Ställe Farm's garage, and when luck was on their side, father and daughter could make it through several workdays without having to repair them.

Göran owned around two hundred fifty acres of forest around Norra Förlösa. Down the road in Balebo, he owned a slightly larger tract, plus another one hundred fifty acres up in Stigtomta. Certainly enough to put food on any entrepreneur's table.

The duties were varied, but the days regimented. Some entries from Sara's notebook detailed the weekly schedule:

Tuesday

10:00 a.m.–2:00 p.m. Repair forwarder, service, plan, drive
2:00 p.m.–4:00 p.m. Walk the forest, check on potential areas for felling, thinning, clearing, etc.
4:00 p.m.–6:00 p.m. Check and plan potential building repairs, what needs to be done
7:00 p.m.–9:00 p.m. Patenta, assemble pipes

Wednesday

8:00 a.m.–2:00 p.m. Drive forwarder/harvester in scheduled area
2:00 p.m.–3:00 p.m. Lunch
3:00 p.m.–6:00 p.m. Continue felling

Such was everyday life for father and daughter in Norra Förlösa. They worked closely together, him leading and her following. He drove the harvester, she drove the forwarder. And then there were the ever-present pipes that needed to be turned, plasticized, assembled, packed, and shipped.

Ultimately, they were close, father and daughter. So said everyone who knew them well. Not twin souls, exactly, but she did grow up with him as her only parent and spent countless days riding around the Stigtomta fields with him, working with him in the forest for hundreds of hours. They were close.

On a good day, when there was less to tend to, they sometimes bunked off to head over to Öland and just cruise around in the car. They might have had dinner out and talked about uncontroversial things, the kind of topics that didn't stir up conflict. Things other than Martin Törnblad.

"Sara didn't really want to choose between Göran and Martin, because they both meant too much to her," Irina said.

Father and daughter would talk about almost anything, just not about boyfriends or anything that happened in puberty, according to Sara. She had learned a lot from her father, but she did not feel he had a right to control her. Instead, she wanted more responsibility, to know more about the company and the properties, and to learn how to keep the books.

They started to quarrel with increasing frequency during Sara's teenage years in the early 2000s. "Dad told me at one point when we were fighting that he was going to cut me off, but I never believed him," Sara said. "We were in Stigtomta, fighting about my relationship with Martin. Dad didn't want Martin to be able to get his hands on anything."

The fights revolved around forestry management, where to fell, plant, work. Sara, due to her time in forestry college, thought Göran was too conservative—that he should consider new ideas, think big, and invest in new machines to make the work easier.

But above all, it was the Martin problem that poisoned relations at Ställe Farm. On one occasion in 2010, when Sara was twenty-two years old and Maria still lived there, Sara called Martin in tears. She wanted to run away, she told him. She packed her bags, and he turned up at Ställe

Farm in his car at the appointed time. Where they planned to go—to Martin's or just out on the road—is unclear.

Sara was out of the house, bags in hand, and on her way to the car before Göran reacted. He caught up with her before she could get in the waiting vehicle, grabbed her by the arm, and pulled her back inside by force.

"Can't we at least talk about it?" was all Martin could get out before Göran slammed the car door shut and angrily waved him aside.

That was the first and only time in the Göran Lundblad case file that anyone mentioned violent behavior between father and daughter. Otherwise, their interactions never went beyond angry words and hurt feelings.

"Göran said Sara changed dramatically when she started going out with that urchin," said neighbor Karl-Erik Sidentjärn. "That was Göran's word—*urchin*. He said there was no talking to her anymore and that she would come and go as she pleased."

For example, in 2011, Sara went to Italy with her father and sister Maria for a combined business trip and holiday. An old business associate had passed away; the Lundblads were going to meet with the new one. Good relationships were crucial for upholding old agreements about the delivery of pipe bowls. But instead of accompanying her father to the meeting and participating in the discussion, Sara stayed outside with her phone pressed to her ear, talking to Martin back in Sweden.

"She would do that constantly while they were in Italy, Göran told me," said Irina's brother. "He felt she was ruining the entire trip; he was furious."

Martin's actions merely stoked the conflict, both indirectly through his conversations with Sara and more directly. As early as 2010, he talked openly about wanting to acquire the land Göran was leasing to his neighbor Mats.

It was a sign as good as any that he was hoping to gain something from his nascent relationship with Sara. Leaseholds were a sensitive topic in farming communities, and it comes as no surprise that his words were soon reported back to the affected parties. The swirl of rumors only fueled everyone's suspicion of Martin and his dark intentions.

Around the beginning of 2012, Martin made a formal proposal to Göran to acquire that land, promising that the Törnblads would pay him more—at least two thousand kronor (240 dollars) per acre, twice as much as Mats was paying.

That was the final straw for Göran.

"He told me he grabbed Martin by the scruff of his neck and the seat of his pants and physically threw him out," said Karl-Erik Sidentjärn. "He didn't care that Martin could have been hurt. The Törnblads were going to take over that lease over his dead body."

Göran might have been exaggerating the physical altercation, but the message was clear—Mats and no one else would rent Göran's land, at whatever price point Göran deemed appropriate.

Alas, other than circumscribing Sara financially by appropriating all her properties and making himself the sole benefactor of Aunt Stina's will, Göran was, at the end of the day, powerless to do anything about their relationship.

He tried bribery. He offered Sara, who loved riding, a new horse worth one hundred thousand kronor (twelve thousand dollars), according to Göran. She already had one horse; now she had two. Both animals were stabled in the older of the Ställe Farm barns.

Göran and Sara also discussed buying Sara that farm they had gone to look at, but only on the condition that she broke off her relationship with the Törnblad family. With Martin. She refused.

Over time, however, something that could best be described as a balance of terror was established between father and daughter. Sara moved out, for all intents and purposes, and spent as much time as she could with her boyfriend at the Törnblad farm.

She didn't participate in the work there, but she shared a room with Martin on the ground floor, next to the kitchen, where her key to Ställe Farm hung on a hook. She often stayed in bed while Martin and the others rose with the sun to tend to the animals.

Sara usually got up around nine to have breakfast, drive over to Ställe Farm to let her horses out, and then go to her father's house. By that time, Göran had normally already left for the forest, but he would leave Sara a note with instructions. He might ask that she go over the paperwork in the study, or get in the forwarder and catch up with him to pick up the logs he had felled.

In the evening, her work done, Sara would drive back over to the Törnblads' to spend the night.

When the summer of 2012 arrived, several people noted that Göran seemed to have finally given up the fight for his daughter's heart. It was not that he suddenly accepted his intended son-in-law or that he had stopped arguing with her about him, but he seemed somehow resigned to the fact that his constant complaining was not going to change anything.

"I'm never going to babysit," he told Sara. "You'll have to sort that out for yourselves. And if you're getting married, you have to make sure there's a prenup."

As always, property first. The family fortune was paramount.

"Martin was not welcome into the family," said Eva Sterner. "Göran never budged on that. But then, near the end, he did say that he didn't give a shit about them."

Sara's younger sister, Maria, made similar observations: "He seemed more indifferent to their relationship as the years went by, though he would never have agreed to let Martin move into Ställe Farm."

At the same time, it looked as if Sara's professional future was back on track. In the autumn of 2012, she was accepted into the Forestry and Wood program at Linnaeus University, which had campuses in both Kalmar and Växjö.

It would be a perfect degree for Sara, since she had to balance her work in her family's forests with her studies. The program was online-based with only a handful of physical classes—labs—each term. After three years of education in close partnership with industry organizations, students had to produce a dissertation and would receive a BA. A graduate from this program would be an academically educated forest owner who could take over a profitable family business.

Nine hundred sixty miles south of the farms and fields of Norra Förlösa lies the Swiss city of Zurich, in the canton of the same name, part of the Swiss Confederation since 1351.

The city was founded a couple hundred years BCE as a customs station at the point where Lake Zurich turns into the Limmat River. For a long time, the Roman occupiers made money taxing the goods being transported along this waterway in northern Switzerland.

A few hundred yards west of the river and the Munster Bridge, lie the headquarters of one of the world's most prominent financial institutions, Credit Suisse. The bank, because it is as such that the Swiss financial services company is best known, is housed in a four-story stone palace at Paradeplatz 8, occupying one whole side of the square that serves as a hub for trams and local traffic.

It is one of the most expensive addresses in the traditionally secretive banking nation.

On a sunny summer's day in 2012, the Lundblad family arrived at Paradeplatz. Göran and his daughters Sara and Maria walked through the stone archway into the lobby, where Göran issued brief instructions in German. The three were then shown to an elevator that took them up to the waiting room, before the next bank employee led them deeper into the building, to the office of their personal advisor. The entire encounter was a model of Swiss efficiency, politeness, and discretion. For decades, Credit Suisse has been known for handling rich people's affairs impeccably. They have also never felt compelled to reveal anything unnecessarily about any of their clients.

Göran's father had opened the account many years ago, back when the political dominance of the Swedish Social Democratic Party had been unthreatened for decades, back when there was still a wealth tax.

For a long time, Swiss money had been synonymous with secret money. Bank secrecy was absolute, especially for anyone in possession of a numbered account, which withholds its owner's identity from all but a handful of bank employees. All you had to do was siphon some funds off your books through creative accounting in Sweden, and you could take a bag full of cash to Switzerland.

But things had changed. By 2012, when the Lundblads traveled to Zurich in Göran's gray Chrysler, three years had passed since Switzerland's biggest bank, UBS, had lost its court battle against the United States about providing the identities of rich Americans guilty of hiding large fortunes in its vaults. Several other banks had since come under similar international pressure. Step by step, Switzerland had opened up, handing over information to other countries, especially in cases where there was suspicion of criminal activity.

Several EU countries were also putting pressure on the Swiss banking industry in an effort to repatriate smuggled money and tax it. Göran had sensed which way the wind was blowing, so he had decided it was time to make a voluntary disclosure. He had contacted the tax authorities and informed them that he had several million kronor in a foreign account.

To be precise, Göran had capital to the tune of just over six million kronor (more than seven hundred thousand dollars) with Credit Suisse, his account statements show. The money was distributed across various investments—bonds and shares in several European countries.

The primary reason for the bank visit in the summer of 2012 was to get an overview of the investments. At the same time, Göran wanted to familiarize his daughters with the family's financial affairs. It seemed indicative that younger sister Maria had been brought along as well. She would be turning eighteen in a few months.

Göran was, at the time, in the process of writing a new will, which he had mentioned to both his daughters. His intention now was to divide the family assets equally between them when he died, they had been told.

Göran had already taken other steps to consolidate his fortune. Plainly put: he planned to repatriate as much of his capital as possible and collect it in one place. It was time to simplify his affairs.

The apartment building in Mälarhöjden, where Göran had first met Sara's mother, had already been transferred to a limited company by deed of gift, which is a maneuver designed to avoid paying capital gains tax. The profit, totaling several million kronor, was put into the limited company that administers the Stigtomta properties.

It would appear that the Swiss money was being brought home as well. As early as April 2012, 237,400 Swiss francs were paid into Göran Lundblad's Swedish private account. Based on the exchange rate at that time, it was the equivalent of two million Swedish kronor, two hundred thousand euros, or two hundred fifty thousand dollars.

And for the first time in a long time, Göran did something unexpected, something his father would likely have frowned upon. In June of that year, he bought a dazzlingly white sporty Mercedes convertible with bright-red leather seats from a dealership in Kalmar. Paid in full in cash.

Price tag: 1,304,600 kronor, or over 160,000 dollars. Top speed: 150 miles per hour.

Tenant farmer Mats Råberg commented to Göran at the time that it was an expensive gift to give oneself. "He replied: 'Who the heck am I saving my money for?'" said Mats. "He was a little angry with Sara, to put it mildly."

When Göran and his two daughters sat down at the desk a few floors up in the building on Paradeplatz 8, it was with some relief that Sara realized their advisor spoke Swedish. It would make it much easier to understand how the investment portfolio was put together and to comprehend the different investment alternatives the advisor presented.

Perhaps Göran should lower the risk by reducing the amount allocated to shares. Maybe he should buy gold or sell off some of his investments to have liquid means available if the need should arise back in Sweden?

One solution could be to sell off everything and fully repatriate the money. The wealth tax was, after all, abolished in 2007. But after discussing it for a while, Göran decided to keep the portfolio as it was. It had been performing well, generating returns of several hundred thousand kronor a year. And the investments were low-risk, in real estate companies, among other things.

Late one evening, there were electronic basslines thumping out of the Rogsta Farm kitchen. Göran Lundblad was dancing. Someone in the group was filming with an unsteady hand—the grainy cell-phone videos show that the withdrawn, almost timid man with the reserved manner could, in fact, cut loose.

Sometimes, when he visited his friend Rodney in Södertälje when he had business in the Stockholm area, the two of them would go for a pint or two and, on occasion, Göran could turn boastful and lavish. Not with money—he would never buy rounds for people or be generally wasteful—but in his manner of speaking and acting. He would curse in

English with an Irish accent, talking about how rich he was and what he could do with all that money if he wanted to.

The same thing happened occasionally when he attended parties thrown by his tenants in Stigtomta.

"He was a lightweight," said tenant Mats Söberg. "Drinking made him stupid sometimes. All his inhibitions went out the window. At one party we threw, he got wasted and took us all to task. He thought we were worthless and told us he didn't like any of us. The next day he was racked with guilt."

Göran rarely lowered his guard. It only occurred when he felt completely safe and content, which was rare given all the things he had to worry about. The forest and fields. Maintenance on the Stigtomta properties. The pipe manufacturing. All the money, the taxes, the Swiss bank accounts. The problems with Sara.

But on that summer night in his childhood village, at Rogsta, where his family's roots went back a hundred years, Göran Lundblad danced, dressed in suit pants and a white shirt, a big smile on his face. One hand pumped back and forth through the air. His hips swayed as he laughed along with the other people in the kitchen. After a lot of food and drink had been consumed, his troubles seemed to melt away.

Later, after the music stopped, his feelings bubbled up and he spoke of the problems at home, of his concern that Martin was only after his money. That Martin was using his daughter, and that Sara was refusing to understand.

"He expressed anger at Sara, saying she had found herself a pile of shit. It was unusual for him to express himself that way," said Linda Björkman, a tenant in Stigtomta when the relationship between Martin and Sara began.

Nevertheless, in August 2012, it did seem that Göran Lundblad had finally listened to his daughter, at least as far as the forestry equipment was concerned. He ordered a backhoe loader that was to be kept in Stigtomta and used for work there. It was an investment of over a quarter million kronor (thirty thousand dollars).

Later that month, Göran and Sara were in Stigtomta to work on the properties, but they also had time to attend a summer crayfish party thrown by one of their tenants on August 18.

"Göran was happy and in high spirits, as usual," said Henry Nydahl.

He held on to those high spirits even when he received a notification regarding Norra Förlösa from his security provider, Securitas. Someone had tried to break in, but the intruder must have taken off before the security officer arrived.

The alarm did sometimes go off for no discernible reason, but among those at the party, the question arose of how many people knew that Göran was rich and preferred to deal only in cash. What might a burglar be willing to do to get their hands on that kind of money?

As August drew to a close, Göran kept working in Stigtomta along with, among others, Sara, and they continued to quarrel. Sara's stepmother's, Irina's, brother witnessed one clash and reacted to the tone of it.

"Sara was so angry, her eyes flashed. It was true hate," he said.

Her father was no less agitated.

"You take care of all of it, then. You'll see how fucking easy it is!" he roared.

A day or two later, Sara made her own way back to Norra Förlösa; Göran stayed another day or two, then he traveled down to his local bank in Kalmar on August 29 to pay a bill of almost two hundred seventy thousand kronor (thirty-two thousand dollars) for the backhoe loader.

That expensive yellow vehicle, with a big bucket in the front and a backhoe in the back, is of particular interest because the delivery was scheduled for mid-September, a date Göran specifically approved in his agreement with the supplier so that he could be there to accept the delivery in person.

The conflict between father and daughter was reignited once he arrived back home, Sara said. But it was never to be resolved. That night, Sara left her father on the couch in front of the TV at Ställe Farm and walked out. She slammed the front door and headed over to the Törnblad farm. It would be the last time she ever saw him.

Around nine that same evening, Göran talked to his younger daughter, Maria, on the phone. She was stressed, as she was in the middle of booking train tickets. She was headed to a concert the next day; Lady Gaga was playing the Stockholm Globe Arena as part of her Born This Way Ball tour.

Even so, they talked for thirty minutes. Nothing memorable or dramatic, just a conversation about everyday things, work, something about the future, the same way they used to talk when Maria was still living at the farm and would sit in the kitchen when neither one of them could sleep. Perhaps they touched upon her upcoming birthday. Maria can't recall her father mentioning a fight with Sara. They hung up at exactly 9:44 p.m.

This was Göran Lundblad's last known conversation.

When he put his phone down for the night, he didn't know there was a hole in the ground ready and waiting for him, not far from Ställe Farm. It was freshly dug, at that point probably no older than six hours.

9

BLOOD

When a shotgun bullet penetrates a body, the pellets spread through the musculature along different trajectories. The effect of the cumulative force from tens of pellets is like a powerful blow from a fist. Smaller animals, such as deer, hares, or foxes, are knocked over.

A human normally can withstand the impact better, especially if hit in the arm or leg rather than at center mass, the torso. One would stand an even better chance if the gun were fired from a greater distance.

If, instead, the shotgun is fired at close range and aimed at more sensitive parts of the body, the effect is devastating.

The shotgun blast that kills Göran early in the morning of August 30, 2012, hits him from a distance of about five feet. It is likely fired from a long-barrel hunting shotgun. The shot, each pellet with a diameter of between one and two millimeters, is aimed directly at his head.

Göran is lying on his left shoulder when the gun is fired, his head turned toward his right shoulder, as though he had been roused by some kind of noise and had turned to look. The shot enters his skull from the right side of his chin, traveling in the direction of his brain.

The pressure from the impact is stopped by the skull, which fractures in several places along the left side of his face. The cranium loses its structural integrity, but human skin is tougher than you would think. The skin covering Göran's skull remains intact. Consequently, the force of the impact has nowhere to go in the closed space of the skull. The path of least resistance is through the eye sockets.

One of Göran's eyeballs is forced out of his head, pushing the eyelid to one side and making it look as if the eye had swollen to three times its normal size. It is a sight that would haunt anyone for the rest of their days.

Death is instantaneous, though Göran has time enough to draw one last breath. Both soot and blood are pulled into the lungs. The control center of the living organism, the brain, is knocked out forever.

The rest of Göran's body shuts down with only a few seconds' delay. His heart beats a couple more times before stopping. But Göran continues to bleed thanks to the pressure of the circulatory system. Approximately two to four pints of blood seep out of his body.

When a bullet or bird shot rams into the center of the nervous system, right into the core of the brain, the effect is instantaneous. It also gives rise to reflex movements—muscle contractions and jerking. The twitching body expels urine and feces. A sharp smell spreads through the room where Göran Lundblad spends his last living moments.

That death is so quick is also a mitigating circumstance. The victim's experiences before death—suffering, pain, fear—are often the subject of debate during trials. Is the prosecutor able to substantiate a claim that the murdered person experienced strong fear during their final seconds? Is it possible to prove that the murderer caused "unnecessary suffering," by, for example, torturing the victim before the murder, physically or psychologically? Or by keeping the victim locked up for some time before the killing took place?

In such cases, a court is more likely to hand down the harshest punishment Swedish law allows—lifetime imprisonment. And the more serious the crime, the greater the sum awarded to the victim's loved ones. Depending, of course, on what part they played in events.

The shotgun is fired at such close range that the plastic cartridge wad ends up in Göran Lundblad's head and a few fragments lodge in the corner of his mouth. His skin is sprayed with gunpowder residue. Göran's mouth is likely open when he is shot, as though he is about to say something or call out. Whether it is in surprise, anger, or terror, it is impossible to say.

The shot hits his cheek just below the right corner of his mouth, breaking off several teeth, which end up inside his brain.

The impact sends microscopic droplets of blood flying. They quickly dry in the air and land on the floor. Spatter of this kind can spray across an entire room. It is easy to find if you know what you are looking for and have the right equipment—special solutions and goggles as well as ultraviolet lamps.

The blood spatter that makes it to the ceiling is visible only under a magnifying glass. In a perfect world, from the murderer's perspective, the room should be covered in plastic beforehand, to minimize the risk of being discovered. But it all depends on how much time you have to clean up afterward and how long it will be before anyone comes snooping around.

Blood also spatters across the wallpaper. The room is filled with traces a cadaver dog would pick up in seconds if it came anywhere near. Dogs can smell individual molecules if need be. But it is always hard to know where to start searching in a house of this size. That is, if anyone even thinks at all to look for signs of foul play.

To make things even harder, the house itself has a bloody history. A tenant farmer had blown his brains out with a shotgun there in the early seventies. Barrel in the mouth, thumb around the trigger, and then: bang! Several neighbors had to help clean it up.

A shot to the head and the subsequent exsanguination of several pints of blood from a human body is a messy business, especially if the corpse lies undiscovered for some time.

The man who killed himself in the seventies was a depressed drunkard, abandoned by loved ones who had had enough. Coincidentally, his name had also been Göran. The house had been cleaned and scrubbed and the wallpaper changed several times since then, and yet cadaver dogs can pick up the scent of death decades after the fact. Consequently, any corpse smell on the ground floor could be explained, if necessary.

What happens after the shot that kills Göran Lundblad is fired at Ställe Farm involves at least two people. One fetches a tarpaulin to heave the dead body onto. A standard green tarpaulin you can buy at any gas station or home improvement store, the kind people use to cover their boats in winter or to protect stacks of firewood from the rain.

The murderers bundle up the body using equally unremarkable blue nylon rope, like a tow line, slightly thicker than a thumb. They thread the rope through the tarp grommets and then wrap it tightly around the corpse. Half-inch grooves cut into the body, which will have time to go through rigor mortis and soften again before the package is eventually opened.

It requires both strength and planning to move a dead body through Ställe Farm's many rooms, especially one that is wrapped in a tarp slick with blood. A dead body will continue to ooze blood during transportation.

The body would have been about 175 pounds to lift and carry down through the basement to the waiting car. One person would not be able to do it without great difficulty and certainly not without leaving drag marks of blood and bodily fluids. Even a strong farmer or forest worker could hardly do it on their own.

The murderers drag and haul the wrapped body down the stairs and turn left into the garage, where they pause for a bit before heaving it into the flatbed of a pickup truck. During that pause, blood leaks out onto the floor. Not a big deal; the floor can always be hosed down, or you could pour gasoline over it to erase any traces of blood. Then it will all disappear down the drain. But you always run the risk of blood ending up somewhere you can't see it.

The murderer with the long-barrel shotgun must have been intimately familiar with both Göran Lundblad's habits and the layout of his house, or must have had the help of someone who was. The murderer must have known that they would have to tread carefully in the hallway to avoid creaky floorboards. They would also need to know exactly where the victim would be on this particular morning: the room through the door on the right after the short corridor if coming from the front door, but only if he hadn't fallen asleep on the couch in front of the TV the night before.

The shooter must have also known that the intended victim would still be in bed around seven o'clock in the morning. Göran was a fitful sleeper and had been for a while. In fact, he hadn't slept well since about three years earlier, to be precise, ever since he'd found out Sara and Martin had become a couple.

Given how poorly Göran slept and how often he rose early, the murderers would seem to be lucky their plan works as well as it does.

Because this is clearly not a spur-of-the-moment attack, conceived in a flash of abruptly flaring anger. Because beyond the forest, on the other side of Skyttelund Farm, in a triangular field with poor drainage, that hole has already been dug. It is only a hole, for now. It needs a body to make it a grave.

The hole is approximately eight and a half feet wide, about the width of the bucket of a wheel loader, which is a common piece of equipment in these parts. It would take only two or three scoops for the machine to dig fairly deeply into the ground—the hole is almost six and a half feet deep—through topsoil and hardpan.

To a lot of people, suddenly digging a big hole in the middle of a field would seem odd. A wheel loader is loud. You can hear it driving both there and back through the forest. Also, there would be big piles of soil and loam around the hole. Those kinds of things should draw attention.

But not here. In this area, there are a lot of farmers, and during the summer months all kinds of heavy machines are running at all hours of the day. A farmer who can't find the time to maintain his road or move his dung hill during the day, because the calves need tending to or the forest needs thinning, has to go out at night if the task needs doing. And digging in your own fields is common—to enlarge them by removing rocks and tree stumps or to grade them to improve the drainage.

The choice of location is significant. Buried drainage pipes criss-cross the field to improve growing conditions. They run the length of the field. Whoever dug the grave knew exactly where it was safe to dig without breaking anything.

A person's routines and habits can be identified by spending some time in the area, simply observing their movements. In Norra Förlösa, everyone notices everyone. Who drives what, to where, when, and how. But who, other than a local resident, would be able to map out Göran Lundblad's life? A stranger spying on the village in preparation for a raid would have been discovered immediately. Stopped, challenged, at least seen.

Ställe Farm's front door is locked at night and whenever the house is empty. The murderer and any colluders must therefore have used a key to get in.

Over at the Törnblad farm, the day would have started several hours before the shotgun blast that ended Göran Lundblad's life. Had they heard anything over there? Doubtful. At the Törnblad dairy farm, the cows make a constant racket, and the early-morning milking makes a lot of noise as well. Besides, with doors and windows closed, the sound of the shot would likely not have traveled far.

The body is loaded onto Ställe Farm's red pickup. The sides of the flatbed are almost a foot high, concealing what is inside it, so there is barely any point in covering the bloody load. The wrapped body keeps leaking into the flatbed while it is transported. The stain will have time to set considerably before anyone takes an interest in it.

The truck rumbles along between the fields of Norra Förlösa. The easiest route to the field with the hole runs west through the village and up onto a road that cuts through the Törnblad farm. It is possible to go around in the opposite direction as well, but that would mean having to drag the body farther through difficult terrain. Better, then, to load the body into a wheel loader in the farmyard, hide it in the bucket. That also makes it easier to transport it across the field.

Out in the field, the view to the north is unobstructed for about half a mile. Theoretically, anyone from a bird-watcher with rubber boots and binoculars to a local farmer could be moving about the area, which would speak against transporting and burying the body in broad daylight.

On the other hand, driving around winding forest roads in the middle of the night with a dead body could easily draw even more attention, especially here in Norra Förlösa, where everyone notices everyone else at all times. Better, then, to pretend you are doing regular work in the fields during the day.

In late August, the flies are more active than ever. But no fly eggs are laid on Göran Lundblad's remains before he is put in the ground, which suggests that the body, wrapped in the green tarpaulin, is dumped into the hole on the morning of the murder. The corpse falls about 170 to 180 centimeters before hitting bottom. The height of a man, around six feet down. The timing of the burial will play a deciding part in determining how guilt will be assessed in this case. But that is a long way off yet.

When the grave is filled in, the topsoil is mixed with the clay of the hardpan. Considering the volumes that need to be shifted, this too is likely done using a wheel loader, which would also make it easier to tidy up afterward. But when the black nutrient-rich topsoil is mixed with the less fertile, lighter clay, it leaves striations in the field that can only be erased with persistent plowing.

By around lunchtime on August 30, 2012, Göran Lundblad has vanished off the face of the earth. Buried under hundreds of pounds of soil. Gone.

For the first time in days, there is heavy rain. Almost an inch of rain falls on Norra Förlösa that day. The downpour helps mix the soil in the field, obliterating the tracks.

PART TWO

CORPUS DELICTI

10

REASONABLE SUSPICION

The Kalmar Police Station is located at 4 Galggatan, Gallows Street, on the western edge of the city. An appropriate address, one might say, as this was the local execution site until well into the nineteenth century.

According to local legend, Kalmar residents would sneak out here at night to cut the fingers off evildoers because the blood of the executed was thought to possess magic healing powers.

It was not because of the street's history, however, that the police headquarters, which also house the prosecutorial authority's offices, were relocated here at the end of the 2000s, but rather because factory closures had made the property available. The building, with its patrol vehicles and offices, was practically located near a thoroughfare for easy access to every part of the county.

The gory local history was not at the forefront of Detective Chief Inspector Ulf Martinsson's mind when he went through a stack of memos and reports in his office in the autumn of 2012. It wasn't until late October that the stalled case was passed up to Martinsson from his uniformed colleagues. His supervisor, Ann Åsenius, had asked him to go over and assess a missing-person case: the disappearance of one Göran Lundblad.

This was not usually the kind of case violent crime would concern themselves with, but this case turned out to have many layers, as Martinsson soon discovered. He read through the memos from his colleague Jonas Blomgren.

"Uniform had taken the case as far as they could, with some interviews and checks, but they didn't have the means to process anyone, not without access to more resources," said Martinsson. "More means were needed to get to the bottom of the matter, that much was obvious. I was heading a team of detectives at violent crime, and I agreed that something was off. There was nothing to indicate that Lundblad had been attacked and robbed, that there could have been unknown assailants who had found out he was rich and so on—no indication at all."

He noted the lack of bank-account activity or records of travel, as well as the existence of several ongoing projects and planned meetings that the missing man had simply abandoned.

"The report said his daughter Sara had told officers they had quarreled and been at odds. And there was quite a bit of information about the conflict between the Lundblads and their neighbors the Törnblads. But nothing concrete."

Other pieces of the puzzle affected his early assessment as well, chief among them the younger daughter's, Maria's, call to the Södermanland police earlier in October, during which she had pointed the finger at Sara.

Or a phone call that autumn from an Eva Sterner, Göran Lundblad's tenant in Stigtomta. Among other things, Eva had pointed out to the Kalmar police that Göran had vanished without confirming a contract with a new tenant farmer up there. That was not how things were done in the country. Tenant farming was serious business, especially for Göran Lundblad.

Martinsson noticed several small, simple pieces of information, which, considered individually, seemed meaningless enough, but when taken together, gave the unshakable impression that something was awry.

"Reading through everything we had, it just didn't tally with Göran Lundblad's way of life that he would abandon all his business interests and obligations, from Stigtomta down to Förlösa," Martinsson said.

On that autumn day, his supervisor, Ann Åsenius, stopped by his office. The time had come to make a decision: either they put the case on the back burner and wait for Göran Lundblad to turn up one way or the other, dead or alive, or they reassign their staff and do everything in their power to solve the case.

"We didn't have a formal meeting about Göran Lundblad," Martinsson said. "It was like any other workday. Ann sat in the visitor's chair and I sat at my desk, and we went over the case. She also had the strong impression that something was amiss. That more needed to be done."

Such are the ostensibly simple workings of a criminal investigation. The basic everyday decisions made by the police can mean the difference between prison and freedom for a suspect, or, in extreme cases, the difference between life and death.

The police, of course, aren't free to do whatever they please, not even detective chief inspectors or more senior management. Martinsson and Åsenius must always adhere strictly to the laws, as well as ordinances on how to interpret the law and apply it to daily police work.

That day, the conversation between the two detectives on Galggatan in Kalmar was graver than it may have first appeared. On one hand, they could order steps to be taken that would make life hell for just about anyone who knew Göran. Background checks, interviews or interrogations, covert surveillance, interviews with neighbors, friends, employers. Activities that ruin reputations and invade personal spheres. Or they could close the folder and walk away.

If they chose the first option, even a completely innocent person could have their social framework destroyed when police procedure kicks in. That being said, anyone abusing their position of authority that way, without very good cause, would be charged with misconduct and lose their job. There needed to be a solid reason to justify reaching for the more extreme tools. Martinsson and Åsenius couldn't be sure what else might be found out about multimillionaire Göran Lundblad if they were to commit all available resources to the investigation.

If they did so, they risked all other criminal investigations being neglected, other unrelated victims being affected, perpetrators remaining free, and the rule of law being undermined as other crimes are not responded to as swiftly. Yet, they could not shake the sense that there was the call for justice for a man who had disappeared under strange circumstances. What if the two detectives were dealing with a murder case, where one or more perpetrators could be convicted?

Or it could all turn out to be nothing, after a number of able police officers had wasted meaningless man-hours on a case that was never going to go anywhere.

It takes nerves of steel to assess a case file under such circumstances.

Anyone who thinks the police can throw together an investigation team comprising interviewers, technicians, detectives, and administrators in an afternoon and launch a murder investigation based on a missing-person report, just to be on the safe side, has spent too much time watching TV.

What in fact takes place is a constant balancing of cases, where no one knows, or can know, at the outset which one is more important, which one has a higher "success factor."

Around one and a half million crimes are reported in Sweden every year, a number that includes everything, even bicycle theft. If the statistics are whittled down to violent crime only, the number drops to around one hundred ten thousand a year. In Kalmar: around two thousand. These big numbers are difficult to comprehend, given that the police employ around twenty-eight thousand people nationally. Of those, fewer than twenty thousand are trained officers, and the rest are civilians.

If we home in on the most serious crime, lethal violence, which would include both murder and manslaughter, something like eighty to one hundred cases are typically reported in Sweden every year, an average that goes back a number of decades. Almost all are solved.

There are strict guidelines for these kinds of investigations; specifically, there is a handbook that is known as the Murder Bible. The name was coined as early as 1970, when the document was first drafted by the then-active National Murder Commission. Back then, it was a thirty-five-page handbook with a checklist of initial measures—roadblocks, background checks, the use of K9 units—as well as flowcharts on how to set up an investigation with a lead investigator, a communications center, and several teams of investigators.

The Murder Bible has subsequently been revised as technology has developed and methods have been refined. For example, in 1970, DNA techniques as we know them today didn't exist. Meticulous crime-scene investigations have become increasingly important to discover the smallest flake of skin from a suspect.

To untangle convoluted personal relationships or keep track of several thousand instances of evidence, interviews, and steps taken, computers have taken over what used to be done with pens, papers, and binders.

In its modern form, the Murder Bible is ninety-seven pages long, with detailed instructions on which roles need to be filled—lead investigator and assistant, crime-scene coordinator, head of the interview unit, head forensic technician, various caseworkers, tips receivers, and administrators. An investigation team needs to have at minimum twenty-five people on it to be considered fully effective.

As all readers of crime novels know, the first few days, not to say hours, after a murder are crucial. The more time passes, the smaller the chance of the guilty person being found, if experience is to be believed. It is all the more important, then, to quickly secure evidence according to the Murder Bible checklist, which includes everything from seizing CCTV recordings before the camera records newer material onto the old film, and interviewing witnesses as thoroughly as possible before their memories are affected, to identifying all conceivable evidence before it is destroyed by the elements.

Of course, it is also about trying to apprehend the perpetrator while he or she is still in the area, which requires roadblocks, door knocking, and searches of vehicles, properties, and people. These techniques are primarily effective in relatively fresh crimes, but the regulations contained in the Murder Bible are to be followed regardless of the age of the crime.

A dead mobster, shot to pieces in his car, or a person stabbed to death in the street—in these cases, things are straightforward. Cordon off the streets, stop everyone in the vicinity, and take statements whether they want to give them or not. Extract data from phone companies about which cell phones have been active in the area, then map every phone within a couple of miles' radius.

But the code at the top of Martinsson's papers didn't indicate a violent crime. It was simply an administrative code—0911, missing person—which barely gave him the authority to do anything.

All he and his supervisor really had to go on was an unsettled feeling based on previous experience—whether that be called prejudice or empirical knowledge. Hunches need to be combined with cold, hard facts in order to constitute what is termed *reasonable suspicion* about a crime having been committed. Only then can the police formally launch an investigation.

Reasonable suspicion is a vague concept in jurisprudence, not an exact science. This is what the law, chapter 23, section 1, of the Swedish Code of Judicial Procedure says:

> A preliminary investigation shall be initiated as soon as possible when there is cause to believe that an offense subject to public prosecution has been committed, either through a crime being reported by someone or for other reasons.

Pretty straightforward if a member of the public comes forward to point out a criminal, or when the crime is obvious because a dead body has been discovered.

But what are the "other reasons"?

Granted, Göran Lundblad had been missing for too long for it to be voluntary. Given what was known—no bank-account activity, no signs of life—common sense would argue that there was reasonable suspicion. But there was no body. And the common sense of a police detective isn't enough to have someone convicted in a court of law.

For its part, Sweden's Parliamentary Ombudsman defines reasonable suspicion as the police requiring "concrete, objectively provable circumstances" with "a level of certitude" that would indicate that a person has committed a crime.

Without getting bogged down in just how certain "a level of certitude" is, the police would typically achieve reasonable suspicion with the help of, for example, contradictions in what an interviewee says on different occasions.

Like when Sara Lundblad was inconsistent about when she last saw her father—was it August 29 or 30? The length of time she took to report her father missing also raised questions. What did she get up to in the meantime? Was she getting rid of evidence?

Moreover, several witnesses insisted that it was unlike Göran Lundblad to not honor agreements and that he had never left without warning before. And once again, more decisively: the fact that Maria Lundblad had called the police to report that her sister may have harmed her father.

"My god, that's incredibly bizarre," Martinsson said. "Why would this young girl contact the police to say she suspects her sister? That's a fairly serious charge if she has nothing to back it up."

In an effort to get to the bottom of the matter, the police planned to interview a large number of people in several locations across the country about their interactions with Göran. At the same time, they still had to consider the possibility that what they were dealing with was a voluntary disappearance, so they needed to take a harder look at potential travel plans and contact other countries' border authorities.

"It's important not to get stuck and start speculating about this and that and the next thing," Martinsson said. "You'll never get anywhere that way. Instead, what you do is set a course and check each thing off as you go—flights, relatives, business interests, and so on. Then we'll see."

Put differently: formulate the hypothesis that Göran Lundblad was killed, then test it systematically.

After much discussion in the office on Galggatan in Kalmar, Martinsson's supervisor concluded that what they were looking at was a murder case and gave the go-ahead for further action.

"Ann Åsenius is an experienced detective herself and had the same feeling I did," Martinsson said. "We agreed I should start moving on this with a number of colleagues from Kalmar. But we also agreed that we should head up to Stigtomta and take statements from the people there and bring in both technicians and forensic dogs."

Martinsson contacted the detectives on his investigation team and asked them to prioritize the case. They needed to start calling around to schedule interviews, contact all relevant authorities to map out the life of the missing man, and request documents.

At 4:23 p.m. on November 1, 2012, he logged the formal decision to initiate a police-led preliminary investigation of the crime of manslaughter, a crime that carries a minimum sentence of six years.

"I chose to label it as manslaughter since the perpetrator was unknown. But with the launching of the preliminary investigation, the toolbox was opened."

Based on that decision, the police gained the right to enter Ställe Farm and the farms at Rogsta and Tängsta, to use forensic dogs on Lundblad lands, and to search cars and interview people.

Some doors remained closed a while longer. In order to use phone tapping, bugging, or geolocating, one or several suspects must be identified and a prosecutor must be brought in. In order to get to that point, the police need to be able to present more substantial hunches, compiled in a persuasive way. When this happens, a prosecutor can sign a decision to take more coercive measures.

In early November 2012, the police apparatus rumbled to life in earnest. Before long, it began picking up ominous signals.

One of the first steps the police took in this new phase of the investigation was to request from network operators all available data connected to several phone numbers. The request included Göran's known cell phone and landline, as well as the cell phones of Sara and Martin.

This is not the same as phone tapping, but rather a request for long lists of how these phones had been used since the disappearance, how the phones themselves had moved, and what other numbers they had been in contact with.

When the lists arrived, an unexpected pattern quickly emerged. Sara Lundblad had, for example, not exactly exerted herself trying to locate her father via his phone. During the first seventy-four days after his disappearance, she called his cell phone a total of eleven times.

None of the calls lasted longer than four seconds—maybe enough to get his voicemail, but certainly not long enough to leave a message. She sent no texts. (As a point of comparison, Göran's friend Rodney in Stockholm would call Göran's phone more than two hundred times after he found out about the disappearance.)

Alternative means of communication could be disregarded—Göran knew nothing about computers, let alone things like Facebook. He did not even own a smartphone.

In fact, Sara hadn't used her phone much at all, even in those first few days. On August 31, the day she realized her father was missing, she made precisely three calls to her father, none of which lasted longer than three seconds. Shouldn't an anxious daughter try a bit harder?

Another circumstance also called Sara's story into question. The last known call from Göran is from the night of August 29, when he talked to his younger daughter, Maria, for half an hour. Between that time, around 9:30 p.m. on August 29, and the afternoon of September 1, when Sara called Maria and her stepmother, Irina, in tears, Sara's phone barely moved. It remained in Norra Förlösa the whole time, connecting only with three local towers.

There is nothing to suggest that Sara went into Kalmar during these days, or to Vasallgatan, where she claimed to have found her father's Chrysler. She had definitely not been driving all over the county, checking every conceivable location, as she had claimed.

But perhaps Sara had left her phone at home when she went looking for her father. That may seem implausible to most people, as one would think a phone would be the one thing you would want to bring when you're out looking for someone who has gone missing—to receive calls, to call for help, or to contact emergency services. Yet another suspicious circumstance was added to the slowly growing police log.

After the decision to initiate a preliminary investigation was made in November 2012, the circle of interviewees was expanded. This is a process that can become complex, and elaborate planning is needed to ensure there are no leaks. The next person interviewed, and the next one after that, could have advance information about both questions and answers and therefore adjust their narratives—consciously or unconsciously.

When dealing with regular citizens in particular, rather than professional criminals, there is a greater risk of memory alteration. The interviewee is often eager to be helpful and therefore adds irrelevant details to the answer they believe is expected.

But even when the results of the interviews in the Göran Lundblad case were stripped down as much as possible, they were unambiguous.

"They painted a picture of a slightly odd man, a bit of a recluse, who was nevertheless very caring toward his children," said Martinsson. "And the people we interviewed spoke well of him. He was old-school, a dutiful person. When we searched his house, there was no indication he was wealthy. His home looked almost impoverished."

Through tenants and previous interviews, the police were given new names to follow up with, such as Göran's friend and sometime-business-associate Rodney in Stockholm. His reaction upon being contacted was one of shock. Until the police contacted him that day, he'd had no idea about the disappearance.

"Why haven't his daughters contacted me?" he asked. "We're best friends, me and Göran." But he had no clue as to where Göran might have gone, other than that his friend often talked about Scotland.

The Stigtomta tenants were equally bewildered when contacted. Tenant Mats Söberg told the police that Göran had looked a bit physically run-down the last time they'd seen each other, at the end of August, but that he would never take off without finishing his ongoing renovation projects.

"His disappearance just doesn't seem natural, it's not like Göran," he said. "Not like the Göran I've known for the past four years."

Once the news was out, Mats Söberg's neighbor Henry Nydahl contacted the police of his own accord and pointed out how much Göran had to live for.

"He was happy about the new car he had bought, and he had just purchased a tractor for his farm," Nydahl said.

He then added this: "Göran told me that if Sara continued to date Martin, he would disinherit her."

They now had a clear financial motive, which would become more prominent as the investigation progressed.

Rune Jansson, another Stigtomta resident, stressed, like so many others, that Göran really didn't like Sara's boyfriend, Martin. "He often talked about removing her from his will because Martin was a bad influence on her. He was sure Martin was only after his money," he said.

In other interviews, a similar claim about Göran planning to drop Sara from his will, in favor of her sister, Maria, were common. And that Göran was planning to sign his new will in connection with Maria's eighteenth birthday on September 6, 2012.

On their own, each claim about how Sara was going to be cut off amounts to little more than hearsay, secondhand information, easy to disregard. The interviewee might have misunderstood or misinterpreted something. But the plausibility of the claim naturally increased as more people said the same thing; hearsay can be highly significant in the course of an investigation, even if such information carries low probative value in a court of law when left unsupported.

A conceivable motive was emerging: Sara Lundblad had killed her father—with or without assistance—to prevent him from disinheriting her.

Göran's ex-wife, Irina, presented another possible scenario in an interview recorded on November 7: that Göran had gotten into a fight with his despised future son-in-law, Martin.

Göran had told Irina that "as long as I live, that chump won't be getting his hands on my property." Martin wasn't even allowed to stay overnight at Stigtomta.

Irina speculated about Göran finding Sara and Martin in his apartment in Kalmar and things coming to a head. That Göran might have told Martin he was in for a beating, that Martin defended himself and Göran fell, was struck, or something along those lines.

The interviewer asked where she had gotten this scenario from—had someone told her about it? If so, there might be a key witness. But no, it was all Irina's own conjecture and speculation, partly because she had been told about Maria's suspicions and partly because Martin and Sara had started renovating the apartment on Vasallgatan so soon after Göran's disappearance, probably to cover something up, she believed.

The same scenario figured among the police's hypotheses.

"It wasn't necessarily a premeditated crime," Martinsson said. "Göran disapproved of their love, they had words, a quarrel that ends with him being pushed, taking a bad fall, and breaking his neck. And then they're terrified and take various steps. Causing death by negligence, not manslaughter."

Toward the end of 2012, Martin and Sara moved into Ställe Farm, making her childhood home their shared abode. They started removing things from the house as early as November. Göran was a man who found getting rid of things difficult, even when they were old and run-down. His daughter did not share that difficulty.

It raised a lot of eyebrows in the area when the couple was seen carting Göran's possessions off. Some were burned in the forest, which is standard in these parts, environmentally friendly or not. Some of it was brought to a recycling station.

Martin and Sara had become a couple for real, not married but cohabitating in their own house. Göran would never have approved if he had known, the neighbors exclaimed, as news of their annexation of Ställe Farm spread.

What the neighbors couldn't have known was that in early November, Martin and Sara had built a new dining room. It had happened around the same time as the police reclassified Göran's disappearance as potential manslaughter, and no more than a week before the police would arrive to search the house with specially trained forensic dogs that could pick up the scent of most bodily fluids, including blood. From that perspective, the renovation seemed suspiciously well-timed.

Sara and Martin dragged the weapons cabinet out of the cluttered room next to the kitchen and then they redid the room—not dramatically, more of a spiffing up.

Together, they removed the wallpaper, especially in the corner by the window, where a wallpaper steamer was used. But it turned out to be too much of an effort to peel the wallpaper off the wall, which was made of porous wallboard that absorbed fluids like a sponge.

After a lot of hassle with the steamer in that corner, they switched tactics to just washing the old wallpaper with an all-purpose cleaner. Then they sanded down the worst bumps and slapped on the new rolls of wallpaper, light with gray stripes. Very similar to the old pattern.

They also ripped up the old vinyl floor and put in an almost identical new one, faux wood, meant to look like a hardwood floor, but cheaper and easier to keep clean.

Martin and Sara finished the renovation quickly, in just a few days. The job was far from professionally executed. The wallpaper was not cut at the moldings, for example—little flaps of wallpaper were left sticking out.

Later on, they bought a new dining room set—an edge-glued, oiled oak table. The chairs were oak as well, with black seat cushions. Now, in their new shared home, they had a dining room next to the kitchen, in the very room where Göran used to sleep. His bed had been moved, his wardrobe emptied. Not much remained of him now, after only a few months.

Martin and Sara slept on the first floor, in one of the old children's rooms.

Mere days after the renovation of Ställe Farm had been completed, and right around the time Therese and her Missing People volunteers were gearing up for the search for Göran in Kalmar, a handful of police officers gathered outside Ställe Farm on November 17. Sara met them there, let them in, and showed them around the house, the study in particular. Jonas Blomgren was back to seize computers for a forensic search.

Granted, two months had passed since Göran had gone missing, and if Sara really was behind her father's disappearance, she should have had ample time to erase anything incriminating. But maybe not fully—some residual data can usually be found, depending on the technical skills of the suspect.

No one had yet formally identified Sara or any other individual as a suspect, despite hypotheses, musings, and hunches. The confiscation of the computers was just another item to check off the Murder Bible's list.

Police officer Cecilia Eriksson noted that Sara was guarded and seemed remarkably unperturbed by her father's disappearance, even though it should have been clear to her by then that he was dead.

"Her voice was very calm and collected," Eriksson said. "It was hard to judge whether her manner was caused by grief, shock, emotionlessness, or something else. She gave the impression of being 'tough,' as though she wanted to prove that she was equal to the situation and didn't need any help."

Eriksson and Sara had to carry on their brief conversation in the yard in the November cold, because once the computers had been carried out, two dog handlers and their cadaver dogs entered Ställe Farm, one at a time. Both dogs indicated in front of the washing machine in the basement. One of them was also interested in a rug on the first floor. The dogs don't know exactly what to look for, but they're primarily trained to search for three things: corpses, blood, and semen.

An indication could mean anything from a bleeding murder victim having lain in front of the washing machine to some other bodily fluid having ended up there, when bedsheets were laundered, for example.

But an indication is an indication. And this was a manslaughter investigation, after all, so forensic investigators were called in.

"I was told the room where the dog indicated was so bright, they had to black it out to be able to look for blood spatter," Eriksson said.

But in the end, the examination of the indicated location revealed nothing to suggest a crime had been committed in the house.

During their search of the house, both cadaver dogs passed through the Ställe Farm dining room, the one that had been serving as a kind of junk room when Blomgren had done the initial visit in September, with no reaction. During this visit, police at the scene were still unaware that this had once been Göran's bedroom, nor did they know that it had been renovated very recently.

"If photographs had been taken during the first visit, we would have had a point of comparison. It would have been clear things had been changed," said Martinsson. "That routine would have been useful in this case and in all similar cases. But as it was, we had no point of reference."

Under the basement stairs, a sticky wallpaper steamer sat in a cardboard box that had once contained pipe-making materials. During the house search, it went completely unexamined.

In parallel with the search of the house, one of the county's own dog handlers had been given high-resolution maps of the Lundblad lands around Ställe Farm. His assignment was to head out there whenever he had some time to spare and search the terrain little by little for clues. Someone might have discarded an item or dropped something important. There might be a hidden grave, possibly even a dead body.

The land around Ställe Farm, roughly one-third to two-thirds of a mile from the house, was divided into six segments labeled A through F and classified as everything from fields to forest, but also "horse pasture with rough terrain; difficult to search."

The border of the northernmost segment, A, was drawn along a road that passed close by Skyttelund Farm, just where the fields began to stretch out northward. Beyond that line, no canine searches were conducted.

A pity, as it turned out. Granted, the tracker dogs were having a hard time, with November temperatures and quite a bit of rain during those days, but dogs' noses are wondrous things. With the right wind and other auspicious circumstances, they can even pick up the scent of a dug hole.

Although the canine search was a bit of a long shot for the police, especially since so much time had passed since Göran disappeared, it was well worth a try. If nothing else, it was yet another box to check off to rule out other possibilities.

"Lots of thoughts and ideas are thrown out there during an investigation," Martinsson said. "And it's not always possible to tell what's right and what's wrong at first. You have to prioritize the steps you can take and work through them one at a time."

But sorting through and stacking up possible steps in a murder inquiry takes time, no matter what order you undertake them. Time is always scarce when possible leads start to trickle away. Or where they run the risk of being buried.

11

THE MONEY TRAIL

Either something momentous happened during the renovation in November, triggering a collapse, or Sara had stored up enough anxiety and doubts about the repeated police searches to make things unbearable. She, who had held together so well over the past few months that she had come across as cold, hard, dead inside, maybe even calculating by the people around her, had an unexpected nervous breakdown.

On the afternoon of November 7, she sought psychiatric help. Her first police contact, Jonas Blomgren, had advised her to see a therapist if things started feeling too difficult. He had pointed out that when someone goes missing, it can be very traumatic for that person's loved ones, especially considering that there is very little they can do but wait. Wait and wait, for the police, or for the authorities, or for the missing person to be in touch. While they wait, people do have to go on living their lives—eating, sleeping, working, spending time with the people who are still around. If things became too difficult, seeking help was the right thing to do, he encouraged her.

After Sara's breakdown, she did decide to talk things through with a psychologist. They partly talked about the stress of not knowing her father's whereabouts and partly about her work situation. The properties, the companies, the accounts that had to be kept—it was all just too much for her. Martin had even asked her to handle his own family farm's paperwork.

"Reaction to severe stress," the on-call doctor wrote in her records, noting also the code F439—without further specification.

Sleeping was difficult, Sara told the doctor. She was beset with too many thoughts. The doctor prescribed her the sedatives and antianxiety medications Atarax and Theralen, mild drugs, marked "nonaddictive" in Sweden's national drug registry. They were medications that were to help calm her racing mind at bedtime, the doctor told her, perhaps make it easier to fall asleep and to have the energy to get through the overwhelming list of things she needed to accomplish every day.

And there was a huge number of things Sara had to see to that autumn. For example, two large orders for pipes had to be filled by Christmas, which required working the machines in the basement at night. She couldn't miss the deadline on the order, because they needed the money desperately. There had been no significant payouts to Sara. None at all, in fact, aside from the standing order of seven hundred fifty kronor (ninety dollars) monthly from Göran's account and whatever she could make from the pipe production.

There were other ways of making money—the forestry business, for example—but formally speaking, Sara had no access to her father's assets in autumn 2012. For any money to be forthcoming, the missing man had to be declared deceased. That could take up to ten years and would require a great deal of paperwork and multiple court appearances to persuasively argue that the missing person really was dead. Only then would the process of executing the will begin. In the meantime, society protected the missing person's rights and took care of whatever needed taking care of.

On October 26, 2012, the Kalmar County Chief Guardian Committee had decided that a guardian needed to be appointed to safeguard Göran's rights. A neighbor, Ann-Kristin Simonsson, was chosen.

She had some experience in the role, having assisted elderly locals with their paperwork and liaisons with authorities in the past.

It was also assumed that she knew something about forestry and property ownership. In addition to being nodding acquaintances with Göran and familiar with the Lundblad family, she had also long leased her own land to Åke Törnblad.

Göran's guardian lived a couple of miles south of Norra Förlösa, in Melby. Her assigned tasks included mapping out Göran Lundblad's assets, companies, and commitments, and doing an inventory of properties, vehicles, machines, buildings, business accounts, stocks and shares, bank accounts, and any safe-deposit boxes—anything she could find. She was to write it all down and submit it to the Chief Guardian Committee.

She also was asked to see to the day-to-day business and look after the missing person's interests to the best of her ability, such as paying bills and collecting rent and other incomes. But Ann-Kristin was having a hard time of it. Sara and Martin did not seem to grasp that they had no say anymore. None whatsoever.

In addition to renovating the main house at Ställe Farm and moving into it, Sara had also given the Törnblad family permission to make use of the machine shed at Ställe Farm. There had already been mutterings among the locals about Sara and Martin being a couple and moving into Göran's house; when Martin and his father, Åke, parked several of their machines in the Lundblad machine shed, the neighbors reacted strongly.

Tenant farmer Mats Råberg rented space at Ställe Farm's facilities himself, and when he noticed the Törnblad machines in the shed, he reported this to Göran's guardian. Such privileges were normally the kind of thing you pay rent for, after all.

"It was obviously well known that Göran would not have approved," said Ann-Kristin. "And Sara didn't have a mandate to make decisions about that anymore."

Ann-Kristin called Åke Törnblad to lay down the law, telling him that she and no one else had been appointed to handle Göran Lundblad's affairs and safeguard his interests.

"He replied he thought it best left up to Sara, since she owned half," said Ann-Kristin.

At that point, Åke, and likely his son Martin as well, were plainly unaware that Sara was flat broke and that she had signed assets worth eleven million kronor (1.3 million dollars) over to her father a year earlier.

The guardian's phone call with Åke quickly turned unpleasant. "He also said Mats Råberg had refused to sign a termination of his lease. That came as a surprise; Göran would never have allowed a termination, and the lease contract ran until March," said Ann-Kristin. Why was anyone even discussing a lease termination, when that would plainly be against both Göran's and Mats's wishes?

In the background, Ann-Kristin could hear Martin losing his temper. He had been listening in on her call with Åke, and now he started shouting and swearing.

"He said he had to talk to me. I refused to meet with him and told him I only discussed my work with Sara. I was simply Göran's representative. And then I ended the call."

A few minutes later, a car turned into her yard. It was Martin, who brought his car to a screeching halt, climbed out, and strode toward the house angrily. He entered without knocking and sat down at her kitchen table.

"He was incredibly worked up," Ann-Kristin said. "He told me that Mats had been in Göran's house around the time he disappeared, going through his papers. He also claimed that he and Sara had called Irina when Göran went missing, and that she had told them to stay calm, that Göran could be like that sometimes."

Exactly what Martin was trying to achieve with his outburst was difficult for Ann-Kristin to judge, but it was clear that he was very upset about Sara not being able to make decisions about her own farm. The visit was a distressing and intimidating experience for Ann-Kristin. Why was Martin talking about the disappearance at all, about Mats, about Irina, with her? She was merely the guardian who had been discussing business affairs with his father, which had nothing to do with Martin or Sara's guilt or innocence.

Several circumstances had colluded to begin to put pressure on Martin and the people around him at this point in time. The police had become frequent visitors in the area. They popped up with little notice, looking around the house, having their dogs sniff around everywhere, and asking a lot of questions.

The police visit with forensic dogs might well have unnerved Martin. Furthermore, Martin was of course aware that the disappearance had just been reclassified as a potential manslaughter. The newspapers had been reporting that Göran might have been the victim of a violent crime. The day before Martin's brief visit to Ann-Kristin's home, Missing People and their volunteers had performed their well-publicized search, scouring several areas in Kalmar, near the apartment on Vasallgatan, an area the police had already cordoned off.

And then there were the finances. That Sara was both broke and unable to make decisions about the farm were grievous setbacks for anyone planning on merging the two farms. His own father was knee-deep in debt and struggling to make his farm profitable.

In Martin's tirade at Ann-Kristin's, he had defended himself without even having been accused; she had simply been trying to explain her guardian duties to the unwelcome visitor. The two were at odds when Martin finally left. Ann-Kristin made a note of the visit in her report to the Chief Guardian Committee and informed Jonas Blomgren about it that very same day.

Martin's actions at Göran's guardian's house did nothing to improve his and Sara's standing in the eyes of the police. Declaring yourself innocent of everything without prompting tends to indicate the opposite.

Director of the Chief Guardian Committee Ann Wribe summed the matter up in a memo:

> Ann-Kristin Simonsson very soon discovered that it was difficult to impose structure in the matter and to work with the relatives. Shortly thereafter, slander and rumors about her started spreading.

At this point, neither the guardian nor the Chief Guardian in charge of the case knew that Sara had been, for quite some time, transferring funds to Åke Törnblad. As early as the spring of 2012, months before Göran's disappearance, Sara had used her own savings to transfer one hundred thousand kronor (twelve thousand dollars) to Åke, without collateral and without an IOU. Åke had received the money into his company account.

"Martin asked me for the money, and I transferred it from my account," Sara said. "I didn't know what the money was being used for. I didn't ask. Dad didn't like it, but I did it anyway. He thought I should demand some kind of collateral."

It was in conjunction with her father finding out about this money transfer that Göran had asked his aunt Stina to remove Sara from her will.

On August 31, just one day after Göran's disappearance, Sara transferred a further sixty thousand kronor (seven thousand dollars) as something akin to a personal loan to help Åke pay that month's bills, which suggested that the Törnblads were in direr financial straits than ever before during her relationship with Martin.

A few days before she finally contacted the police to report her father missing, she closed a savings fund that her father had opened, a value of one hundred eighty thousand kronor (twenty-two thousand dollars). On September 10, the same day she made her missing-person report, that money, plus an additional seventy thousand kronor (eight thousand dollars), was transferred to Åke Törnblad. In a little over six months, she had transferred close to half a million kronor (sixty thousand dollars) to her boyfriend's father.

"I did it because I thought there was a future for me and Martin," Sara said to explain the multiple loans.

On September 28, 2012, Bäckebo Sawmill paid Sara Lundblad one and a half million kronor (one hundred eighty thousand dollars).

"She contacted us about a week before, demanding payment for the felling," said Ulrika Fransén Friman at Bäckebo Sawmill. "She both called and visited Bäckebo in person. We felt unsure about paying her the money; we had always dealt with Göran before. It felt odd to pay Sara without speaking to Göran first."

It was only when the sawmill administrators asked to speak to her father that Sara informed them that he was missing and that she had reported it to the police.

At that point, Sara signed an order, and the money was paid out, mostly so the sawmill would be in the clear should Göran turn up at a later date. It was the simplest possible solution for the sawmill's administrators, since there was in fact a contract in their possession where Sara was listed as part owner of the business. The contract was dated 2010, the year before Göran assumed ownership of Sara's property, but that was, of course, unknown to the sawmill.

When the money from Bäckebo came in, on October 3, she transferred the largest sum to date to Åke Törnblad: seven hundred thousand kronor (eighty-four thousand dollars). Later that winter, she sent another three hundred thousand kronor (thirty-six thousand dollars).

It would be difficult not to be suspicious of such a rapid series of transfers after Göran's disappearance, as though everyone involved was completely unconcerned about how he might react when he came back. If he came back.

In addition to the loans, Sara also purchased various pieces of equipment for the Törnblads, including a corrugated roller and a manure spreader, all together worth around four hundred thousand kronor (forty-eight thousand dollars). All resources available to her were, in other words, pumped into her future father-in-law's business. Her accounts were utterly depleted in less than a year. And yet, the Törnblad farm still made a loss of over a million kronor (one hundred twenty thousand dollars) in 2012.

Åke Törnblad's accountant, Sara Widerström, described how she reacted to the large sums of borrowed money: "I had informed Åke that a promissory note had to be drafted, primarily for Sara's sake, since it was her claim. Åke told me that he would bring it up with Sara. I haven't seen any promissory notes," she said.

There were further circumstances of interest with regards to Göran's money. On September 5, Sara visited Swedbank in Kalmar. She had brought the key to her father's safe-deposit box. The bank's internal system showed that she entered the vault at 1:25 p.m. on the day in question.

According to the log, the safe-deposit box was open for exactly one minute and fifteen seconds, not enough to do inventory of a large number of items, but enough to grab something you already knew was there.

Exactly what Sara brought with her—a purse, a plastic bag, or something else—will never be established, nor can we know exactly what she took from the bank. The CCTV footage was only saved for thirty days, which had long since passed by the time the police reclassified the disappearance as a manslaughter and gained the right to request such a thing.

Just over ten minutes later—a bank employee noted the time as 1:36 p.m.—Sara signed a form to gain access to Patenta's safe-deposit box at another bank, Handelsbanken, fifty yards farther down the street in Kalmar.

When asked later by the police, Sara would claim that she had been alone when she visited the banks. Martin, however, would claim in other contexts to have gone with her.

"I had never seen so much money before," he would tell people. Phone logs also showed that Martin had called his father, Åke, in conjunction with the bank visits. What they talked about on those calls remains unknown.

It was yet another circumstance that could be added to the others regarding the motives for making Göran Lundblad disappear, one way or another. The only thing that was certain was that after the visits, there were still vast amounts of valuables in the safe-deposit box at Handelsbanken: around two hundred thousand kronor (twenty-four thousand dollars) in dollars and euros, two gold bullions worth around thirty thousand kronor (three thousand, six hundred dollars) apiece, two pocket watches, two wristwatches, a gold necklace, cuff links, and a gold ring. But there was no Swedish cash left.

Considering that Göran was inclined to keep large sums of cash on hand, it seems likely that Sara emptied both safe-deposit boxes in Kalmar of the Swedish money they had contained. But this cannot be proven. Sara herself claimed that there was only "jewelry" in the well-guarded boxes.

Either way, at this point, the police were quite clear that if anyone stood to gain from the multimillionaire's disappearance, it was his neighbor Åke Törnblad, a man of whom Göran never thought very highly.

Another nugget of investigatory gold soon rolled in. As the police began looking into Göran's business dealings, more red flags popped up almost immediately. There wasn't a lot to say about the properties, as Göran had been listed as the sole owner, for over a year, of the forest, the land, and all the buildings.

The companies, on the other hand, were a different story. As it turned out, Sara owned half of pipe manufacturer Patenta. She was also alternate director of the company Göran and Sara Lundblad Management AB. She owned half of the stock in the company, which had been founded for tax reasons after the sale of a property in Stockholm.

According to the most recent obtainable annual report, which ran until mid-2012, the company had assets totaling almost two and a half million kronor (three hundred thousand dollars), tied up in stock and bonds. The annual report had been submitted to the Swedish Companies Registration Office and approved at the company's annual meeting, exactly as it should have been. It was signed by both Sara and Göran.

The date of those signatures: September 6, 2012. Precisely one week after Göran's disappearance.

The police's surprise when the document opened on their screens on the morning of November 13 is easy to imagine. Were they to understand that Göran came back, signed a paper, and then disappeared again? Or had everything been signed in advance and set aside for a later date? How odd.

Toward the end of the third week of November, the investigation results that had been compiled were well above what was required for probable cause—tangible, objectively well-supported circumstances clearly pointing in a certain direction. At this point, prosecutor Gunilla Öhlin formally took over the preliminary investigation.

Early in the morning of November 17, 2012, two and a half months after Göran's disappearance and the same day Missing People's volunteers set out on their grid search for Göran Lundblad in Funkabo,

Martin and Sara were formally registered as murder suspects. Öhlin requested and was granted permission to wiretap the two main characters under investigation.

No one outside the core team of investigators who had access to the case log had any idea of this turn of events. The suspects were to be given as little warning as possible that interviews were being scheduled to take place within the next few days. The two suspects would be interviewed simultaneously, so they wouldn't have a chance to compare stories.

At this point in the investigation, the interviewers had several awkward questions to ask—especially about the counterfeit annual report and the substantial sums that had been transferred to Martin's father. Even if the interviews yielded no concrete results, there was some hope they might unsettle the suspects and cause them to start discussing sensitive matters over the phone.

Tapped phone call between Martin Törnblad and Sara Lundblad. Sara is in the Ställe Farm yard with her phone to her ear. Two K9 teams have just searched the house and the dogs have indicated in a couple of places.

Martin: Are the police inside?

Sara: Yes.

M: They're inside with the dogs?

S: No. The dogs are outside now. Now there's just a lot of police in the house.

M: All right. The dogs are outside.

S: Mm.

M: All right, then.

S: Well, now they're coming out again.

M: Oh well. (Giggle)

S: Now they're . . . Yep. Yes. Now they're all out.

Was this a murderer beset with the curiosity of the guilty talking to his coconspirator? Or a naturally curious boyfriend wondering what is going on and how long he and Sara will have to put up with constant intrusions?

The recorded call was not particularly focused or concentrated. Neither one of them asked the other suspicious questions or gave incriminating answers. The main impression was that Martin seemed to want to know what the police were up to and what they might have found in the house. In other recorded phone calls with Sara, he asked whether the dogs had been searching the forest as well.

When he talked to other people—with his brother or his cousin—Martin swore solemnly that the companies were in a poor state, that there was barely enough money to keep them afloat. He stuck almost exclusively to workaday topics of conversation for a farmer. He also continued to complain about Göran's appointed guardian—Ann-Kristin was still refusing to do what he and Sara wanted and cancel tenant farmer Mats Råberg's lease, and Martin was furious.

In one phone call, Sara and Martin had been discussing the tenancy they wanted to take over and all the paperwork Sara was forced to do together with the guardian, when Martin flared up:

Martin: Do you want me to tell you that I'm going to go blow my brains out or do you want me to just do it and shut up?

Sara: No, you're impossible.

M: I don't know.

S: Aaahh, just stop it.

M: I suppose that's the only way to get some respect in this fucking world.

S: I don't think you should say stuff like that, Martin.

Sara dismissed his purported suicide plans as some kind of joke, which made it clear that Martin routinely expressed himself this way—he could flare up quickly and become quite dramatic.

When the topic of Ann-Kristin, the guardian, came up again, he thundered: "I'm going to shoot the fucking bitch!" He also promised to drive up to Mats's house and break the windows of his tractors with a shovel. The threats seemed petty, bordering on the ridiculous, coming from an adult, but at the same time, his need to vent his growing frustration was obvious. He said, "It makes me so fucking furious that we never get anywhere."

At regular intervals, that familiar phrase popped up again and again: "you and me." In the recorded conversations, Martin was always the first to say it, then Sara responded. Like a secret code.

"Later on, we realized they had counted on having their phones tapped," Martinsson said. "They had come up with a plan, which relied on their feelings for each other. They each had something to hold over the other. I do imagine, though, that it must have been difficult for two people to build a relationship and a future on the basis of having killed one person's father."

There it was, a very concise summary of what the detectives at the police headquarters on Galggatan in Kalmar had gradually become convinced of: the daughter and her boyfriend had killed Göran and had done away with his body in some mysterious way. What remained, of course, was to prove it.

The recorded phone conversations unfortunately didn't reveal where they had buried him. Sara and Martin were too tight, not just because of love, but also due to the pressure. The pressure was coming at them from all sides—the police, neighbors, tenants and tenant farmers, the guardian—pushing them closer and closer together.

On Thursday morning, November 22, the Kalmar police launched a coordinated effort. It had to be low-key, not involving violence and handcuffs. Although Martin and Sara must have known that they were under suspicion, given the gossip about them and the sudden intensification of police interest, they were probably unaware of the extent of the case being built against them.

But what had come to light so far was certainly not concrete enough to prove the existence of a violent crime. So the police had to ask nicely—they requested an interview with both Martin and Sara as "others," as if they were just any other potential witness who might have seen something.

Around ten that morning, both were asked to come in at the same time to tell the whole story once more, but in front of separate interview teams.

When Sara was confronted with the fact that everyone who knew Göran felt that the disappearance was very unlike him, she was dismissive, claiming she and his closest family knew him better than anyone. She reiterated her theory, now with more confidence, that he had probably taken off to force her to take on more responsibility. She had little time for questions about the old feud with the Törnblads; her father, she insisted, had already given her relationship with Martin his blessing.

Over the course of the interview, police could find no chinks in her armor. She confirmed the course of events exactly as she'd given them in the first report: she and her father had quarreled, she'd left, then Göran had disappeared; she had held off on reporting it mostly because her stepmother, Irina, had felt it was best.

But when the interviewers showed her the signed annual report of the family's management company, she failed to keep her cool. Her face flushed violently.

From the interview record:

> Sara flushes and says she signed the document before Göran disappeared. Göran wanted her to sign.
>
> The interviewer informs Sara that the two signatures look very alike.
>
> Sara claps her hands to her mouth and says she wrote both signatures. She knew she had to send in the report and didn't know what to do with Göran missing. Sara is aware that she has done something wrong.

During the police interview, Sara admitted to forgery, blaming the legal requirement to submit annual reports to the Swedish Companies Registration Office, which is what the Federation of Swedish Farmers, who helped with the financial side of things, had told her.

That much was true—the legal obligation does exist. But the deadline is generous. The report would have had to be submitted only by January of the following year, 2013. Sara could have, in other words, waited several months longer for her father to come back to sign it himself. Instead, she forged his signature and dated it several days before even contacting the police, as if she were certain he wouldn't be coming back.

After questioning them both for a couple of hours, the police searched Ställe Farm yet again. This time, they seized Göran's Chrysler to examine it meticulously with special lights in search of fibers and biological traces. They also looked for blood—perhaps Göran's body had been transported in his own car? The inside of the car was sprayed with a special solution called Bluestar. But nothing was found.

The police also seized Göran's toothbrush and comb from Ställe Farm to construct a DNA profile. Theoretically, traces of DNA matching the profile could turn up in other investigations. And if blood or anything else was discovered by investigators, they'd need something to compare it to.

After two weeks, the forensic technicians released the car, and it was driven back to Ställe Farm. It was December, and Martinsson's investigation team had formed a firm impression: Göran Lundblad was dead, and Martin and Sara were more deeply implicated than they cared to admit.

If the two of them had not been so close, it may have been possible to turn them against each other. But as it was, the investigation was stalling. Not even the phone tapping had yielded any useful results.

The Göran Lundblad case finally screeched to a complete halt at exactly 9:37 a.m. on December 14, 2012, when emergency services received a phone call about an unrelated house fire. Hundreds of such calls are made in Sweden every year, but this one turned out to be different. The fire had started in a garage in the small village of Flakeböle in Borgholm Municipality, fifty miles north of the Öland Bridge.

The flames had spread to the main house before emergency services could get there. But the signs of what happened inside remained after the fire had been put out. In what was left of the garage, firefighters came across two charred bodies, the corpses of Gustaf and Annika Nordander. They had not died in the fire.

Upon further investigation, the police concluded that Gustaf Nordander had been beaten to death with a blunt object, and Annika Nordander had been shot at close range with a shotgun. Their dog was dead, too, also beaten to death. The couple's safe had been opened with an angle grinder. The autopsy would later establish that Gustaf Nordander had still been alive, having suffered severe head injuries, when the fire started.

It was a spectacularly gruesome lethal robbery and subsequent arson, and in this case, there were two bodies and copious amounts of other technical evidence to investigate. The police were forced to redistribute their resources.

On December 19, the phone tapping in the Göran Lundblad case was discontinued with no significant results to show. The searchlight had been turned away from Norra Förlösa, despite the fact that other conflicts there were about to reach their boiling point.

12

LOST AND FOUND

After the first search of her Missing People Sweden career, Therese Tang had let the image of Göran Lundblad slip away to the back of her mind. No big deal, she was a project person anyway. Göran's disappearance and the ensuing search party was as good a reason as any to focus on building a highly effective branch of MPS. It was a process she was happy to immerse herself in, given the lingering effects of the Linda Chen affair on her psyche.

Make a name for herself in the process? Maybe. Make a difference? Far more important.

But Therese knew she needed to keep the different strands of her life from getting tangled up into a bundle. Rather, she had learned to compartmentalize them. Leave one strand lying there as she picked up the next and gave it her full attention. Then she would move on again.

Such a mind-set was needed to keep all the aspects of her life up and running. The family part of it for one, with her somewhat rocky relationship with her husband. She still loved him and had a lot to thank him for, for giving her stability in life all those years ago. He had given her a solid, warm home to return to between her missions in modeling, styling, and designing, and for that she would always be grateful.

He still worked long hours at the restaurant, with Therese helping as much as she could. As of 2012, she was no longer putting in several hundred hours a month, as in the early days, but it still required her attention, as any family business would.

And the kids, of course, with Havannah's seizures a constant threat looming over their daily life, keeping Therese constantly on guard. But Emilia and Dexter also needed her attention and love—let alone help with homework, school, and activities. Therese wanted to be as good a parent as her own mother and father had been.

"They divorced when I was three years old, yes, but they kept living close to each other and prioritizing their children," Therese said. "I always had them near when I was growing up. There were three of us kids. I was my mother's second and my father's only child. He was a great father to all of us."

The family had their share of problems and tragedies. The father of Therese's half sister, Linda, for example, committed suicide in his own garage when Linda was in her teens. She was left with his house and a deep hole in her heart.

Therese also had personal problems early on. "My first school years were very bad, with me getting beaten up a lot. The other kids cut my hair sometimes.

"In fifth grade it was too much, so I was moved to another school and things turned completely. I went from being looked on as a nerd to being one of the most popular girls in my class."

But the experience of being bullied stayed with her and perhaps made her even more set in her own ways.

"I have my opinions and I say what I think, even if it doesn't suit everyone," she said. "So be it. I'd prefer to be on my own. Even today it bugs me that they moved *me*—the one being bullied—rather than the ones doing the bullying."

Therese had always been good at staying busy, even when she was younger. She got her horse when she was a teenager, but she also did gymnastics and played handball, and at fourteen she entered the Air Cadets, a sort of voluntary group to prepare teenagers for the military.

"That went on for several years. Two weekends a month, we went to the barracks. It was very exciting—I got to fly gliders at the age of fifteen. It probably helped me with my self-discipline as well."

And self-discipline was just what Therese needed to juggle all the aspects of her life at the end of 2012. She was working nearly full time as a security guard at the nuclear plant, which at least wasn't too far from home, but as a job was sometimes rather tedious. It was mostly just going through the motions—the daily, never-changing routine of making sure all the alarms worked and all the sensors were clean and in good working order so that possible trespassers would get caught.

But nothing much ever happened there. She was merely marking off her checklist. Every day. And then doing the same thing again the next day. Perhaps it was no surprise that MPS became a release valve for her pent-up energy—an escape from the daily grind, a way to find the excitement she needed to feel alive.

Together with her colleague and mentor from work, Anders Lindfors, she formed a board for MPS in Kalmar, with herself at the helm as COO. She and Anders traveled together to Gothenburg for courses at the MPS headquarters; they also networked with other groups across the country and held rallies in their home region to get more people interested. Locally, more and more people volunteered as the hype around MPS spread. And they began to have just enough local success to keep the momentum going.

Several months after the first MPS search for Göran Lundblad, in the summer of 2013, a man in his sixties took his car out for gas and simply vanished. Therese and Anders had gone out looking for him in various places around the county after their initial meeting with his loved ones. They searched an associated address on Öland, the missing man's office, and several addresses in Kalmar.

They had kept at it for several days, a long way from their own homes—though finding accommodation had proven easy, given the good reputation of the organization. Therese could usually just call ahead and introduce herself as Missing People, and hotel owners would give them rooms for free, as a form of sponsorship.

It was only when they finally had a chance to speak with one of the relatives alone that they found out the missing man had tried to kill himself in the past and had a history of alcohol abuse and failed business ventures. They were even given the approximate location of the previous attempt. To Therese, it seemed as though the other relatives neglected to mention these things out of respect for his memory.

"Families know much more than they let on, we realized," Anders said. "If the police show up, they might tell them something like 25 percent of what they know. If it's us, with no uniforms and a different approach, they might share something closer to 50 to 75 percent at first."

Unfortunately, this time the missing man had indeed succeeded in taking his own life. He was found dead in his car by a farmer. If more information had been forthcoming sooner, might things have ended differently? How could they have gotten more information, and sooner? And the question Therese couldn't stop thinking about: How could Missing People Sweden become a stronger, more successful organization?

Over time, they were learning the answer to that question. They needed to become better at relating to the relatives' situation in order to build trust. They also needed to learn to assume the worst—that the missing person could even have been murdered by his or her loved ones.

During 2013, MPS in Kalmar had a total of six missing-person cases. All were solved, although sadly, all but one had been found dead.

"We formed a good connection with the police during this period," Therese said. "It was mostly coincidental: the same police commander just happened to be on call several times in a row when we were called in, so we met up out on the searches and he came to trust us when he saw us work. He saw we were quite effective when we got enough people together to do a proper search."

By 2013, the American-developed technique, Managing Search Operations (MSO), had been applied for about fourteen years in Swedish police tactics but was still not widely used. And it was seldom applied with a bunch of volunteers at hand. The knowledge and training were there—probability theory, lost-person behavior studies, clue awareness, search detection probabilities, and research, all of it—but it wasn't used systematically. That all changed as MPS expanded its organization.

"They obviously wanted to know that our methodology worked together with their tactical deployment of the method," Therese said. "We sat with the police several times, talking through how we worked and how they wanted us to work. We quickly developed a good working relationship with them, to where they started handing us lots of information at an early stage. And we showed we were worth trusting. They called us in much more quickly than they did with MPS in other parts of the country. I think this was because we were very clear, early on, that we didn't want to play cops or do their job for them, but we wanted to complement the police effort. We were humble and said we just wanted to help."

As it turned out, their help would be much needed in the Lundblad case. Because life in Norra Förlösa had its own dynamic, and the events unfolding there were becoming more and more troubling.

13

ALONE TOGETHER

On an early spring day in 2013, a handful of people gathered in the Chief Guardian Committee's offices on Smålandsgatan in central Kalmar. One person was already upset. Another was about to cry.

The missing man, Göran Lundblad, was being represented by caseworkers Ann Wribe and Olof Andersson, who were accompanied by the incoming guardian, Larz Bimby, a resident of Öland with fifteen years of experience working as a guardian.

Larz was now in charge of the Lundblad estate, because, back in December 2012, the Lundblad sisters had asked for a new guardian to be appointed. The reason given was that Ann-Kristin Simonsson was "spreading rumors around the village," gossiping about Göran's affairs and assets. In addition, they complained, she was too rigid when it came to the finances. Sara felt she didn't have enough to live off, even though she was putting in the same amount of work—in the forest, with the pipes, and with the maintenance of the Stigtomta properties—as always.

Ann-Kristin had no objection to being relieved of the task; on the contrary, she wanted it out of her hands as soon as it could be arranged.

The relationship between Ann-Kristin and Sara was made even more difficult because of the Mats Råberg situation. The tenant farmer's long-standing one-year lease contract to use just over 115 acres of the

Lundblads' fields, a contract that had been in his family for forty years, had become a contentious issue.

According to the 2012 contract, he paid less than one thousand kronor per acre annually. This amounted to an unfair discount, according to Åke Törnblad, who paid double that—approximately two thousand kronor per acre—for the land he rented from none other than Göran's guardian, Ann-Kristin.

As early as the spring of 2012, it had become clear that the Törnblads wanted to take over at least part of the rented land. A former employee at the Törnblad farm could recall at least one occasion that spring when the Törnblads had discussed building a barn for their yearlings. Martin wanted to build it down in the fields, the fields Göran leased to Mats. Another employee said, "Surely that's not your land," to which Martin had replied ominously, "It will be soon."

On December 14, 2012, Mats received a letter by registered mail, a termination of his lease contract. It was especially odd, Mats thought, because the termination was dated July 8 and carried Göran's signature.

The termination came as a complete surprise to the tenant farmer, according to the document he drafted to contest it:

> The undersigned has . . . never before seen this termination or been informed of it verbally by Göran. During the period July–August '12, Göran and I met on a number of occasions and a termination was never discussed. I have until the arrival of the termination letter assumed the tenancy would continue.

Mats had also planted on just over one-third of his rented land the previous autumn, an investment that would go down the drain if the contract were to be broken. Besides, he claimed, the termination was formally invalid: according to the tenancy contract, a termination would have to be undertaken at least eight months before the last day of the contracted tenancy.

Oddly enough, the termination letter is dated July 8, which is eerily close to exactly eight months before the current contract's end date, March 14, 2013, and yet, it hadn't arrived until mid-December.

Sara, for her part, claimed that she had found the termination letter in a binder several months after Göran's disappearance, that she assumed it was her father's copy of the document, and that Mats had not signed and returned the other copy. Consequently, she had sent it, by registered mail, for his signature.

"And Martin was hassling me about it as well," she said.

She never explained why she didn't contact the tenant farmer first, by, for example, walking the three hundred yards to Mats's farm to talk it over with him in person.

Practically speaking, there wasn't a lot to discuss. As autumn turned into the winter of 2012/2013, Ann-Kristin was still Göran's sole representative. She drafted a new one-year contract with Mats, which was signed on January 7, 2013. Shortly thereafter, she resigned her post as guardian.

Now, to the meeting to acquaint the new guardian, Larz, with the details of the Lundblad case, Sara had brought her partner's father, Åke, who had in fact applied to take over as Göran's guardian. His application had been rejected.

"When we did the usual background checks, things didn't look too good for Åke with the Enforcement Agency," Ann Wribe said.

For anyone with a firm grasp of the situation in Norra Förlösa at this time, several other plausible reasons to not let him be Göran's guardian might have sprung to mind. Village gossip and more or less well-founded claims about there being bad blood among the farmers on account of a disputed piece of land would have been impossible to ignore. But the fact that Åke Törnblad had already been given around 1.3 million kronor (160 thousand dollars) by the missing man's daughter, without documentation of the loans or collateral, was something else entirely.

The institution of guardian is defined by law; its objective is to help anyone who can't fend for themselves with anything to do with their estate or their financial matters. Plainly speaking—the guardian takes over everything, almost as a stand-in parent, or at least a manager of all practical affairs. The caseworkers and the new guardian explained to the family how it was supposed to work. The question remained whether Åke and Sara really understood what they were being told.

At one point, Åke raised his voice and started talking about Göran's will. Only a few months had passed since he'd found out that Sara was broke. But he apparently had detailed knowledge about what the will from autumn 2011 said: that any inheritance would be split between sisters Sara and Maria, but that Sara would be formally in charge until Maria's twenty-fifth birthday.

"She has lost her father," an irate Åke exclaimed several times.

Not that he could really know that. The police were still treating the disappearance as potential manslaughter. But the body was missing, and there were no outstanding clues to investigate. As long as there was no evidence to the contrary, Göran was still alive in the eyes of the law.

"I reflected on his word choice and replied that Göran's death had not been proven," said Ann Wribe. "Which is why a guardian had been appointed, and that was final. It had nothing to do with wills."

The tenancy agreement, the purportedly terminated but recently renewed contract with Mats Råberg, was also brought up for discussion yet again.

Sara repeatedly claimed that the guardian and the Chief Guardian Committee were mistreating her. She cried several times but was also noticeably angry.

"She said she wanted things to be like they were before, when Göran was alive," said Ann.

Any hopes she might have had to that end were dashed utterly when Larz Bimby took over.

"I made it clear to both Sara and Maria from the get-go that I would be in charge of and manage Göran's assets," he said. "I said explicitly that I wanted things as neat as a pin, and I drafted guidelines for Sara."

By the time they had the initial meeting at the Chief Guardian Committee's offices, he already had a firm grasp of Göran's finances. He knew that over a million kronor had been deposited into Sara's account—the lumber payment from Bäckebo Sawmill. What he didn't know, however, was that she had already transferred that money to Åke.

Shortly after the spring meeting at the Chief Guardian Committee's offices, a few days into April 2013, Larz drove out to Ställe Farm to inventory the machine shed because there had been reports of unauthorized vehicles being kept there. Either they needed to be removed or their owner would have to start paying rent.

"Sara didn't want to give me the keys to the padlock, so I called a locksmith to let me in," Larz said. "At that point, Åke came running over from his farm and started yelling and shouting. When things had calmed down, it came out that Sara had called Åke and riled him up."

Larz was accompanied on his visit by Ann Wribe from the Chief Guardian Committee. This is how she described the event, according to interview records:

> When Larz and Ann were outside the machine shed Åke arrived with Sara, Martin, and his younger brother Mikael Törnblad. After a while, Åke approached Ann in an intimidating manner, raising his hands close to Ann's head like a cat scratching.

> While making this gesture and using threatening body language, Åke screamed at Ann, "I want to scare you." Ann found the situation very unpleasant and was frightened.

Larz changed the locks on the machine shed and ordered Åke to either remove his property or start paying rent, or he would sell his equipment.

During an inspection of the Stigtomta properties, Larz also noted that the buildings were in a poor state of repair. And to his surprise, he noted several cases of nonexistent tenancy agreements.

Göran's relationships with the tenants often rested on oral contracts, Larz found, sometimes several years old, where rent was not always paid in cash. Instead, the tenants could work in lieu of payment by renovating or taking care of the upkeep. Larz felt the setup was impossible for a guardian, whose office was hundreds of miles away, to keep on top of, so he set to work regulating all agreements with formal contracts, complete with signatures, terms, end dates, and termination clauses.

Now Sara was no longer the only one who wanted things to "be like they were before, when Göran was alive." Doris and Henry Nydahl, new Stigtomta tenants, immediately locked horns with Larz. In the summer of 2013, they wrote in a letter:

> We consider Larz Bimby to be an unpleasant person who will not tolerate disagreement, and we feel that he is trying to be a bully and that he demonstrates enormous ignorance and a sarcastic manner.

Tenant Eva Sterner, on the other hand, felt grateful that Larz was finally sorting things out—renovations were being completed and promises kept.

Regardless of how Larz Bimby was perceived by Göran's tenants—effective and rational or insensitive and pushy—his fundamental view was that Göran should enjoy market-based returns on all his assets. Sara should, for example, pay rent for staying at Ställe Farm, keeping her horses in his stable, and using the car.

She was welcome to pay herself a salary from Patenta, Larz announced, but no other money would be forthcoming, given that she did not in fact own anything else that could pay dividends.

Larz, who had felt disrespected every time he had asked for transparency, keys, information, papers—the kinds of things he needed to do his job—had decided to take a hard line with Sara.

A letter he wrote Sara on April 10 delineates his frustration with her clearly:

> You never showed up to a meeting with the accountant, nor did you cancel.
>
> You have shown in a number of ways that you are unwilling to cooperate, even though I have stated several times that I want to work with you. You have also said that going forward, "you will have to speak to my advisor."
>
> Your advisor, who has a foreign accent and goes by the name of Ove Andersson, refuses to give his address and has only provided a phone number, which is not in service.
>
> Sara, you're not taking this seriously.

"Ove Andersson" was, in fact, a half-American man named Owen, and was Maria Lundblad's boyfriend who lived in Nyköping. Sara had asked him to act as a liaison, which Larz, clearly, refused to accept.

During the first half of 2013, Larz instead threatened Sara with debt collectors and the closing of pipe manufacturer Patenta. He was of the impression that someone other than Sara was pulling the strings. He and Sara would have a meeting, discuss matters, agree on a solution, and plan how to proceed, only to have everything thrown overboard a couple of hours later when she would send him an email retracting previous promises and demanding other arrangements. As though she had come home, told someone else about the meeting, and been persuaded, or ordered, to change her mind.

"I had the feeling that Åke controlled his son Martin, who in turn controlled Sara," said Larz.

Åke had on one occasion asked Larz how long it would go on like this before Sara would be allowed to take over the farm, forest, and so on after Göran. Larz had replied that he would not be surprised if it was ten to fifteen years before Sara would be able to take over Göran's assets. That had made Åke heave a deep sigh.

In August 2013, Larz Bimby summed up his efforts as Göran Lundblad's representative in a report to the county court. Sara and Maria Lundblad had, at that point, already begun a long fight, with the assistance of a lawyer, to have Larz removed as guardian.

The end of Larz's time as the Lundblad guardian coincides with the beginning of a different relationship. That same month, a black stroller of a fairly ordinary model rolled eastward along the road through Norra Förlösa, with a baby boy, no more than a few days old, asleep inside. He had been given his own room in his parents' yellow house that sat on a hill farther down the road.

Sara and Martin were walking home with their newborn son, Vince, in the stroller. Gravel crunched under the wheels. It was late August 2013, just under a year since Göran had vanished without a trace. There were many hypotheses about what might have happened to him, but most contained one commonality—the man was dead and buried.

The past year had scarred the couple with the stroller. They were entangled in a number of things that seemed impossible to unravel. Yet the harder they tried to sort things out, the more knotted they seemed to become.

Time had not been kind to their relationships with the other locals in Norra Förlösa. And the police were still hounding them. Not very actively, granted—it had been a long time since they'd had to deal with nosy officers, forensic dogs, and technicians—but they could both still feel the eyes on them.

Money was another big problem. They were broke. Martin had virtually nothing to his name; he still worked for room and board on his father's farm, which was encumbered with debts and cash flow problems. Sara's resources had long since been depleted after she had pumped over a million kronor into the Törnblad family business.

The great Lundbladian fortune—fifty million kronor—was a mirage on the horizon. Since Göran had still not been declared dead, his will had not come into effect. At the moment, all they had was a lot of work to do: the pipe-making, the forestry maintenance, and the upkeep of the Stigtomta properties. And now the baby. It seemed endless.

The stress and anger over their situation was never far from their minds as they wandered through the landscape of their childhood, saturated with memories and pictures. Martin had never lived anywhere else. This was his entire world. They turned down the gravel path toward Ställe Farm, that spacious but run-down 1940s house on the hill.

Their son, Vince, had not been born into the most harmonious of situations. After being together for several years, and living together for some time, everything had changed, and not for the better.

For Sara, the birth of her son was also the start of something new. It was not just that there was a new little creature to care for; his birth had also triggered a fundamental change in her life. Her focus had suddenly shifted away from her own career plans and toward her wish to build a solid life for her new baby. More importantly, her focus had moved away from what Martin had been talking about for so long and painted as some sort of vision to strive toward: the merging of their family farms, a shared future as wealthy farmers.

The new baby boy's birthday, as it turned out, would mark the beginning of the end for the couple with the code words "you and me."

14

SABOTAGE

The dog took off without warning from where Annika Karlsson was standing outside her garage. It made a beeline for the mailbox, where a car was just rolling away. The man behind the wheel had stopped to put a note of some kind into her mailbox. He was wearing gloves, which wouldn't have been odd if he were out walking in the middle of winter. But it was early April 2014, and he was in a car.

Annika ran after the dog, primarily so it wouldn't get lost in the woods or get injured attacking the car. The dog actually belonged to her sister; she was dog-sitting. The driver stopped when he noticed both dog and woman were chasing him.

The man behind the wheel was Martin Törnblad, who had been a neighbor of Annika's for a long time. The Törnblad farm was several hundred yards away as the crow flies, but that was still next door in the countryside sense. Ställe Farm, where Martin was registered as residing at that point, was only about five hundred yards away.

Annika, for her part, lived at the end of a three-hundred-foot spur road off the road that led past both Ställe Farm and Mats Råberg's farm, beyond which it wound through the fields on its way to Melby, Förlösa proper, and eventually, the city of Kalmar.

Martin's seven-month-old son, Vince, was asleep in the passenger seat. For unknown reasons, Martin seemed noticeably discomfited by the unexpected meeting.

"I have welding burns on my hands, that's why I'm wearing gloves," he said, even though Annika hadn't asked.

He came across as shamefaced, unfocused, and unsure of how to handle the situation, as though he had been caught red-handed at something. He then told her he had been out putting notes in several local mailboxes. Not everyone's, but some people's. He didn't say what for, or what the notes were about.

Instead, Martin quickly launched into a tirade about how badly Sara and he were being treated by the world at large. Then he composed himself and reeled off what sounded like a well-rehearsed spiel, basically that everything was Mats Råberg's fault and that the man had it out for Martin and Sara.

He told Annika that the Lundblad properties in Stigtomta had been burgled, for example. Mats's farmhand was probably behind it, at his boss's behest, Martin claimed. He continued to slander Mats, who up until Göran's disappearance had rented land from the Lundblads for decades without a hitch.

Supposedly, Mats had deliberately knocked Martin and Sara's mailbox over when he plowed the road last winter. On another occasion, Martin said, he filled their mailbox with manure. He had also reported the Törnblads for cruelty to animals and fed Sara's horses some sort of concentrate to harm them. Moreover, he was secretly colluding with Göran's guardian to secure unfair advantages. Or at least he had been until last autumn, when the most recent guardian had been appointed. This one, Martin noted, was less hostile and more accommodating and willing to compromise than the previous ones.

These accusations, taken separately, in isolation from the history and relationships in and around Norra Förlösa, probably seemed fairly petty, bordering on laughable, to most people.

Manure in the mailbox—who does that? What is to be gained by it? If anything, it seemed like the kind of prank a bored child would pull, not fully cognizant of the impact on others. Or perhaps a severely disturbed individual could potentially think to do it, guided by some twisted form of logic. And trying to harm animals by giving them the wrong feed? That was the same thing—silly, cowardly, petty, and with potentially grave consequences for some innocent animals.

But Annika was well aware that a number of things had happened over the past year that indicated the presence of a madman. A psychopath. Two chainsaws had been stolen from a trailer, for example. Cat feces had been found in a mailbox, a cart intended for animal feed had been moved, an electric fence had been cut four times in the same day, and a combine harvester had gotten a flat tire after someone had opened the valves. Hours after Mats Råberg had taken delivery of expensive concentrate feed, someone had opened the feed bin so most of it had poured out on the ground and been lost.

Another local resident had found two screws in his flat tire, which he was sure couldn't possibly have ended up there on their own. A saboteur must have gotten into his garage.

Each incident on its own wasn't overly disturbing. But taken cumulatively, there was a clear wave of low-key attacks, things that had never happened before in Norra Förlösa. Here, everyone had always gone about their own business in peace, worked hard, paid their bills. Shown respect.

In fact, the one-sided conflict between the Törnblads and the tenant farmer had grown so inflamed that Mats had to do everything he could to avoid Martin. When Mats needed to visit his yearlings on the other side of the Törnblad farm, he never went alone. He always brought a witness, just in case something happened. The tenant farmer was deeply afraid of the unpredictable young man who was very clearly after his livelihood.

In the winter of 2013/2014, Göran's newly appointed guardian, lawyer Knut Lewenhaupt, visited Ställe Farm after inspecting the room where Mats Råberg kept his sacks of manure. Several of the large sacks had been cut open; manure worth hundreds of thousands of kronor covered the floor. While he, Mats, and Mats's partner, Britt-Marie, stood there staring at the devastation, Sara and Martin came home.

"Mats and his partner looked terrified and made themselves scarce," Knut Lewenhaupt said.

Several people tried to talk to Martin, but to no avail.

Daniel Emilsson, one of Mats's employees, was interviewed by the police as early as October 2013, following a couple of reports and counterreports.

"Martin talked a lot of trash about Mats," said Daniel. "He broke Mats's things to force him to close his farm. We have no proof, but it couldn't possibly have been anyone else."

Daniel told the police that everyone in the village believed that Martin had killed Göran. It was clear that Daniel was genuinely upset by his interactions with Martin, whom he had first met soon after starting his employment on Mats's farm in the spring of 2013. One day, Martin simply appeared behind him in the barn.

Martin introduced himself—they had both gone to the same high school, Ingelstorp, but at different times—and they exchanged phone numbers, just the way any professionals in the same business would. But Martin also talked quite a bit about how badly run Mats's farm was, that it was a bad idea to take the job, because it was about to go out of business.

"And that's when it all started," Daniel said.

A curious Martin was suddenly calling him on the phone, all day, every day.

"He would talk for hours."

Martin wanted to know everything that happened on the farm—whether they were investing in new machines, animals, equipment—and was eager to hear what they talked about as well. "He told me Mats was about to have his tenancy terminated," Daniel said. "'You'll be out of here soon,' he said. And he said that he and Sara had been to meetings with various lawyers. Then the sabotage started."

During the winter of 2013/2014, something happened, the full significance of which would not become clear until much later. Daniel Emilsson was a hunter, with a gun license, and Martin Törnblad had been badgering him for a long time to come help him get rid of the pigeons in the Törnblads' barn. The birds perched high up under the ceiling, and their droppings were everywhere. Pigeons are not just untidy, but they are also a health risk and could spread infections and other things to the livestock.

Granted, there was an air rifle on the farm, but according to Martin, it didn't work. When Daniel finally gave in and stopped by to help with the birds, Martin led him up to the small office in the loft, where there was also a bed. On the bed was a gun, a break-action shotgun, the kind where the barrels are hinged open above the trigger to reload.

"Do you know how it works?" Martin asked after picking the rifle up and unlatching it. At the time, Martin had loose shells in his pockets, Daniel noted.

It felt to Daniel like an invitation to use the shotgun to shoot the pigeons. But that would be a rather daft idea, since the weapon would do a lot more harm than good, compared to a small-bore hunting rifle or an air rifle.

It would be perfectly natural for a gun enthusiast to handle some-one else's weapon, assess it, hold it in their hands, maybe even aim and dry-fire it. Or it would be—if they felt comfortable. But Daniel didn't. Martin, who had neither weapons training nor a license, should not be handling a gun, Daniel felt. It was likely his father's, Åke's, rifle, but still.

"I don't handle other people's weapons," Daniel said, and they left the office.

Twenty-two dead pigeons later, Daniel was handed a couple of hundred-krona notes for his trouble, then he left the farm.

If he hadn't already had a bad feeling about Martin, or if he hadn't had time to think twice up in that office, Daniel's fingerprints could easily have ended up on Åke Törnblad's shotgun. That would have complicated things.

The head of the Norra Förlösa Road Association, Lars Melhager, summed up several of the events in the area when he was interviewed by the police in connection with the Göran Lundblad case in January 2014.

Lars's contacts with Martin had mostly been limited to complaints about road maintenance—complaints aimed at Mats, who was con-tracted to plow, sand, and maintain the road through the village.

"I informed him that Mats was performing his duties and that he would not be replaced," Lars said of his conversation with Martin.

He described Martin as rough, undiplomatic, and in the throes of megalomania, particularly when it came to acquiring farming machinery.

"Everyone in the village is afraid of Martin," Lars said. "And they can't think of any other logical explanation than that he's the one doing all those things to Mats."

Several obvious lies made the locals pull away even more. Martin told one of them that he had come across a man in black, skulking around the village.

"It's going to get worse," the man muttered before disappearing, Martin claimed.

One man from Melby recounted an occasion when a group of local men gathered after one particular act of sabotage to help Mats shovel cattle feed back into slashed thousand-pound sacks. Martin showed up, too, but he was asked to leave—the men with the shovels were convinced he had been the one who had cut open the sacks.

"Then he said something about Sara's sister's boyfriend being a commando with a night-vision scope. He said, 'When he gets here, he will put an end to this,'" Stig Karlsson said.

Yet another threat, in other words, but not concrete enough for the police this time either. Even if ten or twenty people had heard it, Martin would be able to find some explanation for his comment on what a soldier with a night-vision scope could do to his enemies.

The supposed commando he referenced was Maria's boyfriend, Owen, the same person Göran's guardian Larz Bimby thought was named Ove Andersson. In fact, Martin had quite a few fanciful notions about Owen.

Mats claimed Martin threatened him with this mercenary in December 2013. "You have until March 12, 2014, to get off the land. After that, Maria's boyfriend is going to come down and plug you," Martin supposedly said.

Martin called him a superhacker, a person who could plant illegal pornography in Larz Bimby's computer, who used several false aliases, and who had been to Iraq with the American Marines, where he had been trained to kill. Martin seemed to think Owen was his own pet mercenary, who—if Martin was to be believed—would do almost anything for him.

The "mercenary" in question, Owen, was born in 1988, lived in Norrköping, and was still dating Maria. He did in fact have a military background in America, but as a dog handler in the Marine Corps. He remained unemployed throughout his relationship with Maria, but he made some money helping people train their dogs.

From a legal perspective, his record in Sweden was clean, aside from a handful of rent defaults. He figured in only one criminal case, but as the victim, after being threatened by a drug addict outside a corner store by the railway station in Norrköping. He was hardly a battle-hardened mercenary or superhacker with the capacity to assassinate anyone at will.

"I'm afraid of what Martin could do; he's out of control," Mats stated when he was interviewed in connection with several reports of intimidation. But when the interviewer asked for something concrete—proof, observations of Martin in the wrong place at the wrong time, witnesses—Mats could only recount his own impressions.

"It's just his manner . . . He has no respect," he said.

The police noted, logged, and then, in practice, ignored report after report. Just like with Göran's disappearance itself, there was nothing tangible for them to work with. Closer scrutiny revealed that the opinions of the Förlösa residents often rested on their own musings, thoughts, and speculations about what other people had told them.

One rumor, for example, had Martin in one of his darker moments supposedly blurting out that "you have to kill a few farmers to get enough land." An alarming statement for any farmer to hear, indeed. And a sign that he really did have a hand in the murder of Göran Lundblad, several listeners concluded.

But the words passed through several people before they reached the police, it would turn out. Martin supposedly said it to a man named Mikael who worked at a garage, who then supposedly repeated it to Stig

Karlsson in Melby, who in turn told a mechanic, possibly going by the name of Billy, who in turn told Mats's farmhand Daniel.

Four times removed from the original utterance. Like a game of telephone, where a whispered phrase is passed from participant to participant. And as every child who has played the game knows, the phrase eventually transforms into something completely different from what was first uttered.

Gossip, hearsay—not the kind of thing a prosecutor could build a case on. They could interview Martin, of course, but he denied everything.

Searching for DNA and fingerprints was another option, but what would it prove in connection with an act of vandalism if Martin's DNA were found in, for example, the machine shed at Ställe Farm? He had unrestricted access to it.

The police were free to install CCTV cameras for a limited time without special permission to catch any future sabotage, but the crime needed to be more serious to justify it. Besides, an awful lot of cameras would be required to cover the whole village.

Patrolling Norra Förlösa around the clock? Not an option. If someone had blown up a building, for example, or systematically killed or harmed animals, fired a handgun, or set fire to houses in Norra Förlösa, it would be a different story. But the criminal acts in this case were so minor and so surreptitiously performed that the police couldn't justify diverting resources to them. What was happening in Norra Förlösa was low-intensity terrorism. Seen from the outside, from the police's perspective, the villain of the piece could not be unequivocally identified. Because accusations were streaming in from all directions.

When Martin was reported to the police for vandalism or intimidation, he responded by making counterclaims, arguing that he himself was the victim of the crime. He claimed that someone had, for example, loosened the lug nuts on the wheels of the car he used. He reported the incident as "endangerment," since he could have lost control of his vehicle and died if he had driven the car somewhere and the wheel had come off. Martin also took pictures of the front wheel with the loosened nuts and sent it to Sara. He also sent her pictures of a padlock that someone had sabotaged with glue and cable ties.

Sara replied via text: "So fucking childish. Is that all—just your car and the lock? Sissies."

She seemed to be unquestioningly on his side, convinced of Martin's innocence. She even encouraged his plans to mess with the neighbors from time to time, urging him at one point to dump big piles of snow at Mats's farm, for instance.

Several of the incidents occurred when she was elsewhere, working in the forest or attending to things up in Stigtomta.

"Almost every time Sara went up to Tängsta on her own, something happened down in Förlösa. There were threatening letters and other things," Henry Nydahl said.

His wife, Doris, who was on increasingly friendly terms with Sara after they moved in during the spring of 2013, had the same impression.

"Something always happened down in Kalmar when Sara was up here," she said.

And every time something happened in Kalmar, Sara had to go back home.

When Annika Karlsson met the gloved Martin Törnblad by her mailbox in April 2014, he had simply recounted things he himself had been accused of by other locals.

Martin, for his part, certainly sounded convinced about his version of things when he was speaking to Annika. After their conversation, he and his infant son had continued along their improvised mail delivery route around Förlösa.

Annika walked back home with the dog, but she found the whole situation so absurd and Martin's behavior so erratic that she took the time to write down an account of the mailbox encounter. The note she brought in from the mailbox further confirmed her impression.

The note turned out to be a copy of a threatening letter that had supposedly been sent to Martin and Sara:

This is what's going to happen now.

Mats is going to be given a multiyear contract.

Mats is not obligated to fix any damages to buildings.

The neighborhood watch asks to be spared from hearing all the nonsense made up about Göran's tenant farmers and former guardians.

The neighborhood watch also doesn't want Sara and Martin to be allowed to stay in or make use of any of Göran's assets.

If these demands are not met, there will be consequences:

Your son, Vince, will come to the same end as Göran . . .

The neighborhood watch will do to you what you have done to Mats.

We just want to let you know that you will never have a moment's peace, so our advice would be to move immediately.

In order to fully understand the contents of the letter, it is necessary to rewind to December 2012, when Mats had received the notice of termination of his tenancy. When he had refused to accept the termination, the contract was renewed by Göran's then-guardian Ann-Kristin Simonsson. The reference to damages in the letter related to Mats, for example, having moved supports in the machine shed that was included in his tenancy.

The threatening letter had supposedly arrived in Ställe Farm's mailbox, unsigned, just over a month earlier, in March, which was when Martin had reported it to the police.

At the time, he told the police the following: Around lunchtime on March 10, Mats Råberg had come to Ställe Farm uninvited and had behaved threateningly. He talked about his tenancy.

"You had better start moving; if you don't, you know what's going to happen to your son," Mats had supposedly said before leaving the farm.

Though upset, Martin continued to work, and didn't react strongly until that evening when he found the threatening letter in the mailbox, he had told the police officer who was recording his report.

The next day, he called Sara to tell her about the incident. She was, as she so often was when something happened at Norra Förlösa, up in Stigtomta. Martin read her the letter and also sent a picture of it to her phone.

Sara was distraught, even terrified, when she read that one or several people wanted to make her son disappear. The letter left her so shaken that she later, in the middle of the night, went over to the home of the tenants she had built a relationship with, Henry and Doris Nydahl.

They listened as she talked through the incident with them. They were supportive and kind, and she calmed down. Over the coming weeks, the friendship between them would grow stronger still.

What neither Sara's nor Martin's relatives knew at the time was that Martin had penned the letter himself. As early as the end of January, he had been writing drafts and considering different versions. He concluded that he needed assistance. The computer had spelling and grammar checks, but he was dyslexic. He turned to Karin Karlberg, a woman his age who had been working on the farm for about a year.

She had training in, among other things, cattle breeding and was very experienced in successfully inseminating cows. When she joined the farm, the proportion of cows impregnated through insemination rose from 60 percent to close to 90 percent. More calves born, simply put, meant more money for a business under severe financial strain.

"Martin came and asked me to help him with the computer, and I went with him to the office," Karin said. "He asked me to spell-check a document for him. I read it through and corrected it, then I asked what he wanted it for. He said it was verbal threats he wanted written down, threats made by Mats Råberg. He wanted to light a fire under the police, because they weren't doing anything."

Martin was, in other words, admitting deliberate lies. Perhaps they could be called white lies, exaggerations for a good cause. He wanted to stir the pot, prod the police into action, so they would finally take action to help him and Sara against the malicious and intimidating Mats.

It is indisputable, then, that Martin had lied to the police in his report about someone else putting the threatening note in his mailbox on the evening of March 10. The letter had been written over a week earlier, which in turn begs the question of whether Mats really had threatened him around lunchtime that same day, using words drawn from the forged letter. It is difficult to see the whole business as anything other than a sloppy framing of Mats.

No one other than Karin Karlberg knew anything about the origins of the letter when Martin reported the purported threats to the police. Only a month or so later, when copies were handed out to local residents, did the police interview the accused. It was indicative of the police's position that Mats was interviewed as a "witness" rather than a "suspect."

"The only person talking about me fixing damages to the machine shed is Martin," he said. "I think Martin and Sara wrote the letter together. The rest of us in the village never talk about neighborhood watch or community. We have no need to talk about it because we're part of the village. The only one who has mentioned there being no sense of community in the village is Martin, since he and Sara are not part of the community nor the neighborhood watch."

The break with the community became ever more obvious in the days after Martin distributed his notes. Martin's father, Åke, turned up at a road-association meeting at the start of April, brandishing a copy of the threatening letter.

He read it aloud and invited comments. Did anyone recognize it? He left the main question unspoken: Which one of you wrote this?

Åke also promised that the Stockholm police were going to investigate the threat, since the Kalmar police were twiddling their thumbs. He had likely been told this by Martin, which revealed the liar's lack of knowledge, because that is simply not how it works. A person reporting a crime is not allowed to choose which police region handles the case.

It was clear that Martin had been wasting a lot of people's time with his litany of lies. Mats's, of course, as well as the other local residents', even his own father's and Sara's. Not to mention the police's, who are legally bound to accept reports of crime, regardless of the context.

It is not easy to put a price on unease, worry, stress, and the violation that being accused of a crime entails, or on the work the police force does recording, logging, and interviewing, but Martin's lies must have cost the police thousands of kronor in wasted work hours alone.

The residents and landowners in Norra Förlösa assumed Martin wanted the land and was terrorizing Mats to make him abandon the property. But who could possibly imagine it would work? The whole affair gave Mats countless sleepless nights, forced him to look over his shoulder wherever he went, and made him feel constantly worried about what was in store for him next. But making Mats leave his farm and a successful business? That would take a lot more than empty threats and serial harassment.

But Martin's motives for what at first glance seemed like petty attacks, lies, and fantasies, were likely not altogether rational. They could also have been the rantings and delusions of an ill or disturbed person.

Martin had had a taste of both powerlessness and isolation in his months-long war with Göran's guardians over the Lundblad lands and fortune, the failed attempt to terminate Mats's tenancy and take over the lease land, and his stress over the poor financial state of his father's farm. Add to that, of course, the fact that he and his girlfriend were murder suspects.

Now, there is a world of difference between cutting up sacks of manure and murdering someone. A more rational motive for him to conduct a campaign of terror against others and to fake his own vulnerability was to create an external enemy. Partly to get Sara back to Ställe Farm in the immediate term, and partly to tie her closer to him in the long term.

This is classic behavior in geopolitical contexts: a government painting another country or people as wicked. In this case, the intention was to amplify the feeling that it was "you and me" against the world, in order to save his relationship with Sara.

Because that relationship was on the rocks, and far more so than Martin realized.

In the summer of 2013, when Sara had been six months pregnant with their child, Martin had been unfaithful. It was confirmed by both him and the woman he slept with a couple of times. Sara didn't learn of this infidelity; if she had, she would likely have left him. She almost left him as early as the year before, in the spring of 2012, after checking Martin's texts and discovering that he was having a fairly romantic relationship with a girl from a gym in Kalmar. She wanted to break up then, but Martin somehow persuaded her to carry on.

She increasingly felt, however, that Martin was changing. Whether it was the constant fighting over the lease land and with the guardians, his father's financial distress, or maybe because he himself made no money and needed to be supported, was unclear. But after Vince had been born, Sara felt Martin trying to seize the reins in the family.

The terror he was accused of spreading in Norra Förlösa was taking another form inside their family home. Martin was clearly jealous of the attention Sara gave their son and also sought to force Sara to stay home at Ställe Farm and look after the house. She felt downtrodden and abused. Not physically—Martin had never gone further than to restrain her—but psychologically, because she could never be sure how he was going to react. His mood changed from day to day when he came home from work—if he was in a bad mood, he would give her a hard time. Several times, mired in a deep depression, he talked about the two of them committing suicide together just to get away from it all.

It was psychologically exhausting to adapt to, she felt. She also felt that Martin was shirking his parental responsibilities. He wouldn't change diapers, refused to cook, and wouldn't do any of the things a parent should. One fight between them ended with Sara getting in her car and driving away from Ställe Farm. Martin climbed into his own car and chased her down the gravel roads, trying to force her off the road, or so it seemed to her. After a couple of miles, he succeeded; she veered onto the shoulder, opened the door, and bolted into the forest before he caught up with her. They eventually reconciled after a lot of talking, at least temporarily.

The young parents at Ställe Farm had been living under immense pressure for quite a long time—both before Göran's disappearance, because he didn't approve of their relationship, and after, being under criminal suspicion and fighting with Göran's guardians. Sometimes external enemies can help hold a relationship together, even if that relationship lacks important components—such as genuine love.

When Göran's third guardian, Knut Lewenhaupt, assumed his position in November 2013, the pressure eased slightly, and Sara started to see that there might be a way out of all this. Granted, not all the Stigtomta tenants thought well of her, but the atmosphere there was nowhere near as toxic as the one down in Norra Förlösa.

Up in Stigtomta, there were no quarrels with tenant farmers, no demanding fathers-in-law who wanted to borrow money, no neighbors throwing sidelong glances. These were just the houses and farms of her childhood. There was pasture for her horses. And just a couple of miles away, in Nyköping, there was the guardian who had literally handed her back her keys.

Sara now had full access to Ställe Farm and the Stigtomta properties again. Knut's view was that she should be able to support herself as she had before, when Göran gave her money from the forestry business or the pipe manufacturing.

Knut saw Sara as "a fragile little girl" and found it impossible to believe that she could have murdered her father. She was easy to work with, he felt, and they stayed in regular, professional, constructive contact.

The long fight with Larz Bimby, the lawyers, and the county court had lasted for over six months, and it had certainly taken its toll on Sara, both mentally and financially. A few months earlier, back in August 2013, Sara had sent an email to her sister, Maria, about Larz:

I want this to end. I'm not exactly someone who wishes people would die, but with him I really do. I wish he would just drop dead, have a heart attack, or something. I hate him!!!!

After Knut assumed his position in November and the external pressure had started to ease for Sara, the problems, injuries, and conflicts that had been lurking under the surface reappeared. Sara's feelings were gradually changing. She was tired of Martin's emotional outbursts, his attempts to dominate her, and his endless harping on about how stupid everyone else was—everyone except him, of course.

Several times during the winter of 2013/2014, she had wanted to break it off. She talked to Maria about seeking a restraining order to get away from Martin. But she went back to him again and again, faced with out-and-out threats about everything, from him taking Vince from her to him killing himself.

The "you and me" pact was crumbling.

There was one other factor contributing to the crumbling of their relationship that Martin, at this point, knew nothing about. His name was Johan Nydahl, and he was the son of tenants Henry and Doris Nydahl, who had been so supportive of Sara over those last few difficult months. He was around the same age as Sara, and he was both kind and responsible, even to children, Sara felt. She had noticed as much when she had brought Vince with her to Stigtomta.

In early 2014, Johan had moved back in with his parents and started working for Sara, making pipes for Patenta. In April, he was allowed to rent an apartment in the Tängsta annex, above the pipe workshop. Their friendly relationship would soon grow into something more.

15

A SINGLE CASE

Night was falling at the pizzeria in Ruda. Stig Karlsson, eighty-three, had been missing for over twenty-four hours. Far too long for an old man to be out in the cold at this time of year.

It was a chilly Sunday in early 2014, and daytime high temperatures had been around forty degrees Fahrenheit that weekend. The previous night it had gone down to freezing before it had started to warm slightly again. There was a morning frost on car windshields and a thin film of ice on the ground.

The factory town of Ruda, with its six hundred or so inhabitants, is located in the countryside about twenty miles southwest of Oskarshamn. At the heart of the town is a combined pizzeria and unmanned gas station that remains open until 8:00 p.m. There is a yellow letter box to the left of the entrance and a sign outside that reads "Café and Dining Ruda" and promises gambling and tobacco in addition to pizzas. At the other end of the building is a small supermarket, and behind that, a rest stop where no one in their right mind would have coffee on this cold day.

Bundled-up volunteers were stomping their feet outside the restaurant. Missing People had announced a search, and many people had come to lend a hand. During the day, the local branch had been in charge, but now, as night started to fall, MPS's Kalmar branch was taking over. COO Therese Tang had taken up a post inside the restaurant, together with her friend and security-officer colleague Anders Lindfors, to prepare the evening's search.

"Over a hundred people came out during the day to help look for the old man, and the evening shift numbered around sixty," Therese said.

There were a lot of people to coordinate, both before and after the actual search, when the organizers had to take stock of which areas had been cleared. Therese liked the responsibility, though; it gave her validation and made her feel as if she was making a real difference.

It was not easy, granted, to find time to juggle everything; she was a working mother of young children, who had now also gone back to school to get her high school diploma. In just a few days, she would be starting a new job, this time with the police.

"They were looking for custody officers, and a police officer I know told me I had to apply," Therese said.

It would only be a part-time job, only 40 percent of full time plus a shift every other weekend, a schedule that would make it much easier to keep her family's everyday life running smoothly. It would also put her in closer contact with the police and, legally speaking, make it easier to gain access to the information her branch of Missing People would need.

The police had been called to the town the night before, when Stig Karlsson had been missing for almost eight hours. Officers on foot and dog teams had done a hasty search, and there had also been helicopters, all to no avail.

The missing man was blind in one eye and his other one was failing. He wore thick glasses and double hearing aids, was about six feet tall, weighed 190 pounds, and might still be wearing his black coat with yellow reflectors.

The search area was large to say the least, about three miles in every direction. The missing man was used to walking long distances for exercise, anything from one to five miles at a time. He preferred flat ground, because he had some trouble lifting his feet. No one knew where he had planned to go this time, and his usual route had already been thoroughly searched. He must have struck out on a new path.

The volunteers were going to head out in their hi-vis vests and march in a straight line, at arm's length, minding each other, the ground, and the trees. The forest drew close to the houses in Ruda and the terrain was difficult in places, but Sweden's Volunteer Automobile Corps was also participating in the search with four-wheelers. Off-road vehicles are not usually allowed in Swedish fields and forests, but emergency provisions for missing-person cases applied here.

In January 2014, Missing People was still having a good run in Sweden in the wake of several notable successes in 2013. As they gained recognition for their work, the organization was building a gleaming reputation for itself.

There had been the discovery of a dead man in the trunk of a car in Billdal in October 2012, a car the police had overlooked during their own search, even though it belonged to the victim. That one had been a suicide.

And in Boden, Missing People's search teams had found the dismembered corpse of twenty-year-old Vatchareeya Bangsuan in an abandoned house in May 2013, a discovery that had made it possible to convict her boyfriend for her murder.

In cities all over Sweden, including Gävle, Norrbotten, and Halland, the police had publicly thanked MPS for successful searches during 2012 and 2013. Starting in 2013, the Gotland police had even incorporated MPS as a permanent resource in their local actions plans.

The attention had encouraged yet more people to join, including specialists of various kinds, such as scouts, orienteers, equestrians, the Sea Rescue Society, and priests. This gave local branches across the country access to valuable competence and experience, both in terms of technical skills—how to conduct a search—but also when it came to dealing with loved ones and their grief, loss, and fear, whether a search ended with sad news or the missing person being found alive.

The successes also led to interest and involvement from companies and organizations of all kinds. Saab, for example, donated an infrared camera worth one hundred thousand kronor (twelve thousand dollars), and a technology company developed a special tracker for the grid search that mapped exactly which areas had been covered.

In the summer of 2013, the organization was renowned enough to be able to drum up close to 1,500 people for a five-day MPS search for a twenty-three-year-old mother of two who had disappeared near Trollhättan.

MPS had clearly met a pent-up demand, both for people who want a worthy cause to contribute to and for society more broadly. The police had quickly gotten used to having access to hosts of volunteers, summoned via a quick Facebook post or a phone chain. Volunteers even contributed their own vehicles, technology, and know-how.

It was, however, also a fine balance for the authorities. Exactly how knowledgeable were these volunteers? How reliable? What we are talking about is, after all, giving a motley crew of people, their backgrounds unknown, access to sensitive information about another person and their closest relatives, personal information that could be injurious and must not be distributed casually—details about their psychological status, illnesses, conflicts, possibly even criminality.

In the case of murder or other crimes, there is also an obvious risk that investigatory information could be leaked, undermining the police investigation. Someone could let something slip, and a perpetrator might get off scot-free.

The ends do justify the means, however—in life-or-death situations, neither the police nor anyone else tends to worry too much about confidentiality regimes, data protection, or anything along those lines. The police are obviously most eager to see results, as well as a lack of detrimental side effects, when they give information to outsiders. And in the case of MPS, they certainly had seen good results.

As Therese sat with the other organizers in the restaurant in Ruda, directing the large group of volunteers, she knew enough to be cautiously proud of their organization's successes. The word *success* is deceptive, though, because in many cases, the circumstances had been deeply tragic.

There was the depressed nineteen-year-old woman in Västervik, for instance, who had a history of suicide attempts. One September day, she tidied her room in her parents' house, and then wrote in her diary that she had gone to a secret place in town where she had decided she would end her life. She was found late that evening, unconscious after an overdose of prescription drugs; her life could not be saved.

"She was still warm when she was discovered," Therese said. "Just fifty yards from our gathering point. The frustration you feel in a situation like that is awful. And the what-ifs. There's obviously no guarantee she would have been alive today if we had started sooner, but maybe. We had people ready to go hours before we were given the green light. The chances of finding her would have been greater if we had been allowed to start sooner."

Therese and her fellow organizers have had to learn to turn their frustration, anger, and despair over unnecessary deaths into energy. Call it stubbornness, a refusal to quit. Instead of being defeated, she and her colleagues studied, discussed, improved.

Another important lesson they had learned from several cases was that people don't always tell you everything when someone goes missing, at least not of their own accord. One might imagine they would. A person close to them disappears; they contact everyone they can think of, search as best they can, volunteer any information that might be useful. But something embarrassing might be lurking. More often than not, there is something or someone that must be protected.

In the early days of 2014, it had been almost two years since Therese had worked in the fashion industry, doing modeling, hairdressing, and design. Now, as a security officer, she was in a completely different world. On a daily basis, she was in direct contact with violence and evil. Once, when she was on loan to Visby during 2012, she noticed something that looked like a fight break out some distance from the building she was protecting together with a colleague.

"It was definitely assault, seven people kicking a guy who was on the ground," Therese said.

"I didn't really stop to think. I just hurled myself over the fence, pulled my nightstick out, and ran toward them. I guess I counted on them being scared. Nine out of ten people who see a person in uniform, brandishing a nightstick, should be scared."

"When I got involved in the fight," Therese said, "one guy was just about to have his head kicked in. He would've died. The assailants moved off when they realized there were more of us coming, but we were able to identify them to the police later. It was experiences like that one that helped foster a kind of general security awareness in me."

Even in her work for the volunteer organization Missing People, she needed that kind of broad perspective on security. With Missing People, the topics of discussion included survival times in various temperatures, segmentation of high-resolution maps to maximize search efficiency, search lines, and methods of communication.

And there was all too often cause to ponder the darkest depths of the human psyche: mental illness, depression, substance abuse, suicide—and murder.

One single missing-person case remained unsolved in Kalmar County since Missing People had established a local branch there. The very first case they'd had: missing multimillionaire Göran Lundblad, sixty-two, who never normally went anywhere and always kept his appointments until one day, he vanished without a trace.

On an October day the previous fall, in 2013, it had been Therese's colleague Anders who had made the first calls to reopen the search for Göran Lundblad. In the summer of 2013, Missing People's national headquarters had urged all local branches to review their cold cases, which is to say cases where the missing person had not been found, dead or alive. At the same time, Therese and her fellow organizers were discussing the need to better train both their members and themselves, as well as streamline the organization to be able to launch a professional search as quickly as possible. They considered various training efforts like practice searches: in other words, they simulated searches with no missing person, to get used to the situation, identify shortcomings, and improve.

Now there was an opportunity to hit two birds with one stone—a practice search based on a cold case. If Kalmar had had more of a backlog, Therese would probably have chosen the most recent one, one where public interest could be expected to still be high. But there was only one unsolved case in the county at that time: Göran Lundblad's.

In this case, Missing People's first search had been limited to an urban environment and smaller patches of forest. What could be better than to run a practice search out in Norra Förlösa? Woods and fields—searching bigger swaths of terrain—made for a more useful practice search than a fragmented cityscape, for both humans and dogs.

An enthusiastic Therese declared that Missing People Kalmar was going to be the best in the country, or at least conduct the best training effort ever. They would pull together all the K9 teams from across the country that had participated in successful searches, work with other local branches, and have everyone involved learn from each other's experiences. And they would do it all as soon as possible.

It always falls to the group leader to contact the police and any relatives if they are hoping to undertake a search, so in October, Anders Lindfors sat with a phone in his hand. In front of him on the table were handwritten notes, written with a pen on a letter-size notepad picked up from a security-officer training course. At the top of the page was the name Göran Lundblad, with the notation "Förlösa farm."

Then a list:

* Daughter 1, Sara Lundblad, approximately twenty-five years old.
* Daughter 2, Maria Lundblad, approximately twenty years old. Not the same mother. Lives in Norrköping.

The next name on the page was Ulf Martinsson, the detective in charge.

Had the two daughters been listed inversely, things may have turned out differently. But Anders had simply copied down what he had been told during the organization's previous search for Göran. Sara was "daughter 1."

But he decided to start with the detective.

"I introduced myself and told him who we were and said we were planning a search," Anders said. "I asked if there was anything we needed to know, if there had been any developments since the last search. Which is to say whether the police thought we might be better off searching somewhere else. It had been over a year, and if someone doesn't turn up in that time, they never will. That was my thinking.

There didn't seem to be anything out of the ordinary. A straightforward training search."

He was told that there had been no new developments. The Göran Lundblad case was ice-cold.

"I know the police can't always tell us everything—in an earlier case, a man disappeared and was later found dead, but for various reasons, the police couldn't tell us that straight out. But they can at least word things differently, such as, 'There's no need for you to be out there anymore.' We know what that really means. I mentioned that to Martinsson, but he just replied that he had no information to give."

It was a short call, three minutes at most, and the first minute was spent on Anders introducing himself properly. Now, having cleared it with the police, everything was good to go, as far as Missing People was concerned. They were unlikely to find anything, but they could at least proceed with the training as planned. The only thing remaining was to contact the relatives, of course.

"I called the oldest daughter, Sara, first, because she was the first on the list," Anders said. "That was when things changed for me."

"Her first words were, 'What? I don't want to talk to you, I've told you.' So I tried to counter that she was the one who called us. 'No, that was my sister,' she replied."

When Anders apologized, Sara calmed down slightly and explained that she was trying to put her father's disappearance behind her and move on.

Odd, Anders felt, given that it had only been a year. But he ended the call and tried to call Maria next, only her number had been disconnected.

"So I had no choice but to call Sara back and explain my predicament," said Anders. "And she exclaimed: 'It's the fucking guardian: he's had them disconnected.'"

"I had no idea what she meant; I've been a guardian myself and know what guardians can and can't do. But it wasn't the time to ask her more about that, though I did feel everything about this was off. Then she asked me what we were planning to do. And when I told her about the dogs, she explained that the police had already been to her house. Several times. That they were still out there on occasion, snooping around. She was conspicuously aggressive. Normally, relatives are extremely helpful, verging on impossible to get rid of. This was the complete opposite."

During the conversation, Anders was given Maria's new number. Her reaction was very different. An eager Maria asked whether Missing People had any news and explained that she hadn't heard from them or the police in a long time.

"She seemed incredibly relieved just to have a chance to talk about it," Anders said. "It seemed as though she hadn't been able to with anyone else. Not even with her sister, as far as I could gather."

After finishing the call and pausing to think for a few moments, he picked up the phone and called Detective Martinsson back.

"'You think the oldest daughter did it,' I said. And the other end went dead silent."

Martinsson had not in any way confirmed that a prosecutor had taken over the investigation as early as November 2012, that the case was being treated as a suspected murder, or that Sara Lundblad was in fact formally under suspicion for the murder of her father, together with her boyfriend, Martin Törnblad.

These were all perfectly natural things to withhold, since the suspicions were based on circumstantial evidence, evidence that would never hold up in court. The police were quite certain but couldn't prove anything. There was, after all, no crime scene, no blood, no body.

When an external individual, who can't possibly have all the information, calls and confirms your suspicions, what does one say to that? Martinsson didn't say a word.

"I tried to explain that we didn't want to cause any problems," Anders said, "and that if the police were in the middle of doing something, it would be a shame for Missing People to come bumbling in. Maybe he could just say something about us holding off or something."

Anders pointed out that the organization's searches often brought a lot of media attention and that things like that can leave potential suspects badly shaken, make them act unpredictably, and thus muddle a police investigation—in other words, that Missing People's search could hurt more than it helped.

"In the end," said Anders, "he asked me to call him back two weeks later, since they were experiencing an unusually large caseload at the time. And that it might be for the best if we were to hold off for a while. I took that as confirmation of my suspicions about Sara being involved. But we simply had to wait. Because something seemed to be in the works. We thought the police were on top of things and working on it since Sara had told me they were out there with dogs from time to time."

Three weeks later, he called the detective back.

"Martinsson told me they were in shock over the double homicide in Flakeböle," Anders said. "They were still busy with that and were short-staffed. They wanted us to wait a little longer."

In December 2013, Anders made yet another push.

"It's almost Christmas," Martinsson told him. He had only managed to free up one officer to work on the Lundblad case and that wasn't enough. But he was careful to point out that he wanted to be on board when Missing People did the search. The organization didn't want to mess anything up for the investigators, so they postponed their training search yet again.

As the January evening turned into night in Ruda, the proprietor of the restaurant started serving volunteers free pizza between search rounds. Police vehicles and four-wheelers crisscrossed the village between patches of forest. Missing man Stig Karlsson must have been somewhere.

The last verified observation was just over twenty-four hours earlier, outside the old station house in Ruda, no more than fifteen minutes after he had left his home on Saturday. But even though the search went on well into the night, he was not found. The search continued for another few days, with police involvement and helicopters, before the old man's body was finally discovered, just about a mile from his house.

"He walked the same route every day, but he had gone a different way this time for some reason," Therese said. "Then he fell into a hole by the road and wasn't strong enough to get back up. It wasn't even a hole, more like a hollow, but he wasn't able to get out of it. You could see that he had struggled. He must have had a terrible final night."

16

REWIND AND RESTART

By early 2014, the situation at the Kalmar Police Authority had finally started to improve somewhat, after having been so strained for such a long time. The double homicide and arson in Flakeböle on Öland in the winter of 2012 had been a constant drain on their resources, even though a suspect had been arrested as early as April. At long last, carpenter Pierre Karlsson, who had been remanded in custody throughout the summer, was formally charged in August 2013.

When Missing People's Anders Lindfors had contacted the police back in the autumn of 2013 to open up the discussion on the Göran Lundblad case again, the Flakeböle case and its after-effects had still been weighing heavily on the Kalmar police. The appeal process was not concluded until March 2014, when Pierre Karlsson was placed behind bars for the foreseeable future.

They were now finally ready to turn their full attention back to their old cold case: the still-missing Göran Lundblad. Although the case had never been far from their minds, there were several interesting leads that had surfaced in the intervening months that had yet to be fully examined.

For example, the new guardian in the Lundblad case, lawyer Knut Lewenhaupt, who had been in charge of Göran's affairs since November 2013, had now informed the police about Bäckebo Sawmill paying Sara one and a half million kronor (180 thousand dollars) for lumber back in September 2012.

This had also now come to the attention of the Swedish Tax Authority, which was demanding that tax be paid on the income; to be precise, the government was owed four hundred thousand kronor (forty-eight thousand dollars), which Knut was planning to pay using Göran's money, and drafting an IOU so that everything would come out right when Göran's will was executed in the future. Finally, the police had some new evidence to chase.

Over the past year, while the police's attention and resources had been so focused elsewhere, Sara had been spending a lot of time in Stigtomta, especially since late 2013 and early 2014. Martin had not been accompanying her as much as he used to, and there were rumors circulating about their relationship foundering. But so far, they were just rumors.

Sara had, for months, been spotted dragging things out of the main house at Tängsta and burning it all. No wonder, according to tenant Doris Nydahl, considering the house was jam-packed with junk.

"Göran was a real hoarder," Doris said in a police interview. "The house was full of stacked boxes—boxes everywhere—full of several generations' worth of clothes. Göran seems to have collected everything—whether big or small. For instance, we found his grandfather's old gold teeth."

The idea was to clear out the house to make it possible to renovate it and rent it out, although the landlord situation in Stigtomta wasn't going perfectly smoothly either. Some of the Stigtomta tenants found Sara bossy, compared to how lenient her father had been with rents and fees. Other tenants were unfairly favored, according to the local gossip, as reported in police interviews.

As the investigation picked up speed again, the police also took another turn interviewing some of Göran's relatives in early 2014, as well as some of the residents of Norra Förlösa, where Sara and Martin were consumed in an all-out war with their neighbors. No one had any new facts to contribute, but everyone had pondered and reflected on the disappearance, and more than a few had things to say about Sara's behavior. Some perceived her as cold and aloof, unfeeling; for example, she called her father "the old geezer" in a conversation with Eva Sterner in Stigtomta.

The police also sat down with Göran's elderly aunt Stina. Great Aunt Stina, now over ninety years old, was so hard of hearing the police had to write their questions to her on a laptop. She said Sara hadn't been in touch with her for over a year, that she had many things she wanted to ask Sara, and that she thought the boyfriend, Martin, was behind everything somehow.

> Stina then said: I think they want Sara's money and Göran was standing in their way.

> When asked what she meant by that, Stina said that is how she sees it, and that Sara is the one who would know.

The bulk of the interviews in early 2014 at least still seemed to corroborate the police's view: Sara and Martin killed Göran and got rid of the body. But as more and more time had passed since the disappearance, the observations of the people involved carried less and less probative weight. Prejudice, suppression, reevaluations, and wishful thinking affect our memory. Gaps are filled with conscious or unconscious confabulation, because humans crave logic and connections.

Aunt Stina had, naturally, been talking to other people in the family, all of whom had already shared their views after being interviewed soon after the disappearance. Stina had then mulled everything over, recreating meetings with her missing nephew, Göran, augmenting them with what other people had told her. She and others were also likely to have been influenced by the media reporting on this case and others.

Taken together, this is termed *postevent information* and is vehemently loathed by every prosecutor looking to have a suspect convicted.

It is just as eagerly searched for by every defense lawyer who wishes to question the reliability of a witness.

The interviewees have rationalized, to find answers to the questions haunting them. And by the same token, they have undermined their own credibility as witnesses.

The perceptions of the interviewees are also colored by their own views on how a bereaved daughter ought to behave if she were innocent. But what do people really know about that? What do we know about the suffering of others, their loss, and their grief? And what do we know about how other people rationalize to survive?

More interviews and more evidence continued to be added to the once-again-growing pile of documentation in the Kalmar police's files, like the report from the Swiss bank. Credit Suisse had finally handed over lists of Göran's accounts and investments. This clarified, in writing, that he had four and a half million kronor (540 thousand dollars) in various assets in Switzerland, even after withdrawing that two million (240 thousand dollars) himself back in the spring of 2012.

Around the same time as the Swiss bank report finally came in, the company MaskinGruppen confirmed an impression of Åke Törnblad's finances. They were in a very poor state indeed.

"He has had a few close shaves," said Per-Olof Svensson from MaskinGruppen.

In 2014, Åke's debt amounted to 120 thousand kronor (fourteen thousand dollars), and several unpaid invoices had been passed to the Enforcement Authority. All this was well after Sara had let Åke borrow over a million kronor (120 thousand dollars) without even a written agreement.

In mid-February 2014, the last of the scheduled interviews of the investigation took place. On February 18, Göran's old friend Rodney Ahlstrand was given his chance to speak. He seemed to be the only interviewee with any degree of hope left. Not a lot, but still, he had hope.

"Göran could definitely have gotten on a plane. I wouldn't be surprised if he had rented a whole plane just to get away," he said.

But even he seemed to know, in his heart of hearts, the truth. Göran had asked Rodney to design a new logo for the distinguished Dollar Pipe, Gustav "Jösse" Lundblad's invention, patented in the 1960s. He had planned for the pipes to be marketed using a new logo in 2013. Göran would never have skipped out on an event of such magnitude, not the Göran Lundblad that Rodney knew, at least.

By this time, the police had used every tool available to them, but they were no closer to a solution. Missing People was finally given the go-ahead to plan their search.

Therese and her Missing People colleagues started to concretize their search plans in April, just over four months after Martinsson had asked Anders to hold off because the police were understaffed.

"'Make it as big as you can,' Martinsson told me when we met to discuss it," Therese said. "He wanted as much attention as possible, of course. He was probably hoping the suspects would react in one way or another."

It is an age-old, very simple police tactic to use when things have ground to a halt—figure out a way to shake things up, then hang back and observe, and hope something happens. That old loyalties have changed, that guilty consciences might start to bubble over, or that a suspect starts to feel anxious and sets about checking that all their tracks are truly covered. This time, however, the police would have no phone tapping in place, so they would have to observe carefully.

Several media outlets reported on the Göran Lundblad case and made it known that Missing People was about to conduct another search. As it turned out, the disappearance of a multimillionaire was still newsworthy two years after the fact.

"Our motto is to never give up," Therese told local paper *Barometern*. "For the sake of the relatives, we are giving it another shot."

But the enthusiasm of the volunteers was not what they'd hoped—less than thirty showed up, nowhere near enough to do a big grid search. But you have to work with what you have. Therese rallied the group, divided people up, gave them hi-vis vests and maps, and sent them out into the terrain.

The police had flagged two areas as especially interesting—the fields around Norra Förlösa, but also Göran Lundblad's land in Balebo, further inland. This was where Knut Lundblad, the man who panned for gold in Alaska and established the family fortune, had been born. Several relatives were buried here too. It is to the Balebo forests that both Göran and Sara would go when they wanted to be alone.

As luck would have it, one of Missing People's organizers had a contact in the area: a relative who ran a mushroom farm in a closed-down petrol station. It became the gathering point for one of the groups on the search day, May 17. The other group gathered by a biogas installation in Läckeby, north of Norra Förlösa.

"It was mostly locals from Norra Förlösa who joined the search," said Marie-Louice Strannemark, who had joined the organization's management team in early 2014, around the time of the search for Stig Karlsson in Ruda. That day, she was the responsible field organizer in Läckeby.

"The sense of community among the volunteers was palpable; most were from the village. Many seemed anxious. They were huddling in small groups, talking about what might have happened to Göran," she said.

Marie-Louice noted that one of the volunteers seemed particularly enthusiastic. She did so with a measure of suspicion, since it was not unheard of for perpetrators or colluders to participate in searches or other efforts to find missing people. The volunteer in question was Mats.

"I obviously didn't know that then, in Läckeby," Marie-Louice said. "It took us a few days to get a handle on who everyone was and what had been happening in the area."

The volunteers were sent out to walk in long lines through the terrain, following predistributed maps. As they set out, a few more volunteers joined them.

"One of the women who turned up was talking very loudly," said Marie-Louice. "We tried to separate her from the rest. She talked a lot and wanted to be seen and heard and to speak her mind and give her account of what she thought had happened."

Marie-Louice and the other field organizers ushered the woman into the gathering room. Her name turned out to be Eva Sterner, the tenant from one of Göran's Stigtomta properties, and she had brought her partner, Kurt Jädersten.

"She said she was a friend of Göran's, that they were close, and that she was convinced something had happened to him, that it wasn't like him to disappear," said Marie-Louice. "It is not unusual for all kinds of peculiar information to surface when we do a search. But this was special. I didn't know anything about Martin and Sara being suspects, but considering what the police told Anders and how the sisters reacted when we contacted them, it really confirmed my feeling that something was amiss."

Marie-Louice sent the determined Eva and her partner to Balebo so that Therese could hear the story for herself.

"They called to tell me they had a woman there talking incessantly, to anyone who would listen, about how Göran must have been murdered and that everything has to come out," Therese said. "She continued talking when she arrived in Balebo. It was hard to focus properly, because she was telling me so many things at once. From time to time, her partner managed to get a word in, correcting or curbing her a little."

Therese asked a colleague to take notes while she listened, asked questions, and nodded attentively, because it quickly became clear that these two knew quite a bit about the Göran Lundblad case.

Eva revealed that Göran had been in Stigtomta for work just a few days before he disappeared in 2012. He was supposed to come back again quickly to continue the drainage work he had started there.

That is not the kind of thing a person leaves once it is begun, with the ground dug up around the house, piles of pea gravel and drainage pipes, machines left sitting outside. But after two weeks, there had still been no sign of Göran in Stigtomta. At that point, Eva called his daughter Sara, who told her Göran might have gone to Italy. The next time she called, Sara mentioned Thailand.

Odd, Eva felt, considering that Göran got heat rash and was afraid of flying. In addition, Eva had heard from a tenant farmer in Stigtomta that Sara had claimed her father had gone to a rest home abroad. Even stranger behavior from a man Eva had always thought of as organized, who would never leave things unfinished.

Eva went on to tell them everything she knew, thought, felt, and to some degree, assumed. That Göran didn't like Martin Törnblad—"a guy who had no limits and was in possession of a shotgun." That Sara was spoiled, but that Göran had taken the properties away from her. She also told them a little about the business, about the convoluted quarrel with the guardian, and a great many other details she had ferreted out. She told them that Sara was virtually unreachable these days, staying holed up with a couple of other Stigtomta tenants—Henry and Doris Nydahl.

If Therese and her colleagues were not suspicious before, they certainly were now. Not to mention more than a little confused; there were so many twists and turns to keep track of.

Eva had been in touch with several other interested parties, such as Sara's sister, Maria, some Stigtomta tenants, and people in Norra Förlösa. This was far from ideal, with regard to her credibility, given that her views and information could be influenced by both her own agitation and the interpretations of other people. Moreover, several of the things she reported were not entirely factual, strictly speaking.

A game of telephone again, impossible to avoid in criminal investigations, when the police must provide a certain amount of information to be able to ask relevant questions. The information is naturally interpreted by the interviewee and then tends to get passed along, often in a new form.

But that didn't matter too much here and now at the mushroom farm in Balebo. These people were not the police, who need to back up every claim they make, but a group of volunteers who were gradually turning into something else—a tiny army of makeshift private investigators, detectives without badges and guns, wielding their inquisitiveness as a weapon.

They could completely disregard that some of what Eva was telling them was postevent information and just absorb it. It might come in handy at some point. They could arm themselves with this information to sound a little bit more informed than they really were once they came into contact with the principal players in the Norra Förlösa intrigues—for example, when they finally met Martin and Sara.

With their relatively small number of volunteers, MPS was not able to cover much ground on Saturday, May 17, and nothing was found. That afternoon, they packed it up to start afresh the next day. As they set off toward Kalmar, Therese decided to give Sara Lundblad another call. They were passing through Norra Förlösa anyway. Forensic dogs were available. So why not try to get into Ställe Farm, Göran's last known location, just to check?

"I got it in my head that I had to get into that house," Therese said. "We had gone there two weeks before to tell Sara that we were planning a search, but there had been no one there."

In hindsight, she was unsure what it was that drew her there; she had no police checklist to work through, no clear strategy, only a mental list of interesting circumstances that she felt should be checked out, a list that had been changing constantly as she and her colleagues spoke to people. She simply wanted to have a look at the place for herself and get a sense for the context, as though she could absorb the truth through osmosis. Maybe she would see something others have missed.

She had tried unsuccessfully to reach Sara on her cell phone several times. Now, in the car on the way back from the mushroom farm, she decided to try a bluff. She had been given a few different contacts, names, and numbers by Eva Sterner. So she dialed the number for Doris Nydahl, Sara's confidante.

"I just said, 'Hi there, this is Therese, Sara's friend. She's not answering her phone, but she's at your place, right?' 'Yep, hold on,' Doris replied and handed over the phone," Therese said.

"She went completely quiet when I introduced myself and mentioned Missing People. I pressed on with an update, but I really talked up the search to make her think there were a lot of people going out. Then I asked her when she was coming back, because we wanted to search the house with dogs if she would let us."

To persuade her, Therese mentioned that Missing People had specially trained cadaver dogs. She told Sara that she didn't think the dogs would find anything dodgy at Ställe Farm, but that after the search, she would be able to tell the locals that the house was "clean" and that there were no signs of death and horror. That could take the edge off the speculation and smearing, Therese argued.

Sara said that it would be fine, but that she was in Stigtomta and didn't know when she would be back in Norra Förlösa next. Unfortunately, she had the keys with her, so it would have to be some other time.

"Her tone was curt and anxious," Therese said. "I knew straight away that she was lying, and everyone else listening in that car did too."

So where did that leave Missing People's efforts on that Saturday afternoon? Put plainly: they were back to square one. No finds. No clues. Just a set of puzzle pieces consisting of bad vibes, suspicions, rumors, interpretations, and gossip. Hardly any corner pieces, and only one or two edge pieces to help try to complete the rest of the puzzle.

Yet at the same time, no one could ignore the growing feeling that something was clearly wrong. It was the same feeling the first officer on the scene, Jonas Blomgren, formally noted in his report in 2012. The gnawing suspicion that there was more to know meant Therese wanted to do some more digging. She was going to have a chance to prove that she'd meant what she had told the local paper just a week earlier: "Our motto is to never give up."

Either way, further searches were planned for the next day, and the car she was driving in was rolling toward Norra Förlösa. The landowners in the area needed to be contacted, to make sure they were comfortable with volunteers moving across their property. Her next call was to someone who had clearly been significantly affected by the events in Norra Förlösa. She dialed Åke Törnblad.

"Even as she was picking her phone up, she said, 'We're going to solve this damn case,'" Anders said.

It was time to prod the bubble around the Göran Lundblad case, to see if it would burst.

"See that stand of trees over there?" Åke said, pointing. "That's where I'd look; Mats Råberg has been moving around there quite a bit. It's a very interesting place."

He had just told Therese that he was sure Göran had been killed by his tenant farmer Mats.

"So what did he do with the body, then?" Therese asked.

"Well, I suppose the best way to get rid of a body is to cut it up in the kitchen, wrap up the parts, and dump them in various places. Then no one would be able to find the corpse."

Therese and her colleagues Anders Lindfors and Morgan Lifberg were sitting on Åke's porch, listening to him talk. She had called Åke to tell him that Missing People would like to check in with him, introduce themselves, and ask permission for the volunteers to move across his land. They would also love to hear anything he had to say that could help them in their search, she told him. And more importantly: they were very interested in hearing another point of view from a local. He had welcomed them in.

Therese, who recorded over half an hour of the conversation, did everything she could to win his trust. She repeatedly underscored that she and Missing People didn't take sides; they simply wanted to help, and that they were there for Sara's sake.

The story she and her colleagues were told on Åke's porch was miles apart from the one told by the other villagers, let alone by Eva Sterner from Stigtomta. According to Åke, he and Göran were fast friends. Furthermore, he assured them that Göran had begun to accept Sara and Martin's relationship and to wish them both well.

They were told quite a bit about the mood in the village—how so many people had it in for the Törnblads, but that it was really Mats Råberg who was behind everything because he was so desperate to keep his lease land.

Åke also showed them the threatening letter that had supposedly been placed in the Ställe Farm mailbox just a month earlier, the one in which "the neighborhood watch" threatened Martin, Sara, and their son, Vince, if they didn't move.

The convoluted logic of the imagined intrigue—let alone the potential contradictions in the purported motives for murdering and dismembering a person and hiding the body parts, then for sending threatening letters—was not discussed in any detail. The three Missing People organizers merely nodded their heads in agreement and asked some more questions.

During the conversation, they were also told that Åke had a couple of extra sets of keys to Ställe Farm. Which meant, Therese noted, that Sara had lied on the phone to her just a little while earlier.

"When I told him I had spoken to Sara and that she had told me she had the only keys, he reacted like, 'Really? She said that? Well, I don't want to speak out of turn,'" Therese recounted.

It was with decidedly mixed feelings that the three Missing People organizers left the Törnblad farm and drove south. The more they heard, the more questions they had, the more layers the Göran Lundblad case turned out to have.

The Missing People management team gathered at their Kalmar hotel later that evening. Together, they decided to discontinue the Balebo search and instead focus all their resources on Norra Förlösa. That was where the conflict was; that was where people stood accused of murder. They needed to maximize the effectiveness of their small number of volunteers, and they wanted to focus on a particularly interesting place to search.

"Therese took a phone call that evening," Anders remembered, "and she came running over to the rest of us after she'd hung up, saying, 'I have the solution, I have the solution.'"

Therese refused to say much more than that she had had a tip-off, that she wasn't allowed to say more, but that they would see soon enough. It wasn't until the next morning, Sunday, May 18, that she finally revealed she was going to let the spirit world direct Missing People's work.

The tip-off she had received over the phone at the hotel the previous evening was from Mats Råberg's partner, Britt-Marie Einarsson, who had been in contact with a medium. Britt-Marie had, over the past few months, come to trust Missing People's COO, who seemed so confident, focused, and bright.

It was with a degree of desperation and anguish that Britt-Marie had called Therese about the medium's information. She didn't know who else to turn to. She could hardly speak to the police about it, that much Britt-Marie was adamant about. She knew if she did, she would likely be branded as simple at best, someone who believed in fairy tales.

Granted, the police had been known to use information from fortune-tellers and mediums before. A formal collaboration of that nature had been initiated as early as the 1950s by policeman Tore Hedin in Skåne, Sweden, in connection with a murder case. The national police had called in fortune-teller Olof Jönsson in an effort to unstick the so-called Tjörnarp Murder in 1951.

The way that story had ended was that the policeman Hedin himself, later known as the Hurva killer, was tied to the murder. The killer himself had guided Olof Jönsson around the crime scene for a whole day without the spirits telling Jönsson the truth.

By August 1952, Tore Hedin had killed nine more people, including his parents and ex-girlfriend, before drowning himself in Bosarp Lake, at twenty-five years of age. The police in Sweden had never warmed up to listening carefully to tips from mediums after that debacle.

But Britt-Marie had been living for so long with the terror and mistrust in Norra Förlösa, and like so many other locals, she was frustrated about Göran having simply vanished. Under those circumstances, no information could be casually dismissed, she maintained. All avenues should be explored. Also, the medium's information was eerily detailed:

> *Göran Lundblad was killed and dragged down a flight of stairs. Paint and wallpaper have been scraped off the walls in the house where he was murdered. And the body is supposedly hidden near water or somewhere wet, next to a red house built on a slope. Down the hill and to the right.*

Britt-Marie told Therese that her house on the outskirts of Norra Förlösa fit that description perfectly. It was next to a body of water as well—a pond.

17

THE POND

Behind that red house on the western outskirts of Norra Förlösa ran something that could only generously be described as a brook. It was more of a dirty brown stream that trickled rather than flowed over stones along the ground drain that appeared out of the undergrowth about ten yards from the house.

It was the runoff from the forest to the north and from the fields beyond, where drainage pipes had been laid down to absorb and redirect moisture, drying the soil out enough for the plants to grow better. The drainage system started in a triangular patch of dirt a little over a mile away, a small patch of land that would soon become the focus of a lot of attention.

The pipes led to a pond, a pool of water that, after a particularly wet period, could swell to about six or seven yards in diameter. The pond was waist-deep at most, just a depression in the forest floor, muddy and rocky. A few thick tree branches had fallen into it and gone black with damp.

On this day, May 18, 2014, it was raining in that way you never see coming. The damp rises inexplicably up your pant legs while finding its way in from above at the same time, as though the atmosphere has been laden with something for far too long and suddenly decides to let it all out at once. It's like being in a shower.

Two cars drove up toward the house by the pond and stopped. The house had been extended with a conservatory; from inside that room, sheltered from the rain and damp, a handful of people watched as the car doors opened.

Three men climbed out of the nearest vehicle; first out was Detective Martinsson from the Kalmar police, inappropriately dressed for the weather. He wore a jacket and brogue-style shoes instead of a raincoat and rubber boots. The detective used a small umbrella to shield himself minimally as he scanned the scene to take it all in.

From down by the pond, two people in waders were looking up at Martinsson and his colleagues, Ulf Einarsson, also an investigator, and Anders Elmqvist, the county's chief forensic technician.

It was just after lunch that Sunday afternoon when two of the three dogs participating in the search indicated in the same spot by the edge of the pond. At least one of the two dogs was specially trained to find dead bodies. In other words, this was likely real. There could be a body, or body parts, submerged in this shallow pool.

As far as graves go, the pond was perhaps a little too close to the house. A person would have run a high risk of being seen if they were trying to bury a corpse here. At the same time, the location was ideal for a murderer who might want to cast suspicion on, for example, the owner of the house. As it happened, that owner was Britt-Marie Einarsson, the partner of Mats Råberg. Both Mats and Britt-Marie were sitting in the conservatory with friends and acquaintances, watching the scene outside unfold.

Although Britt-Marie was not suspected of any involvement in Göran's disappearance in any formal sense, having civilians with their own agendas and motivations near a crime scene was not something any detective would consider desirable.

The Missing People management team climbed out of the other car with Therese in the lead. They had guided the police to the scene. She summarized the situation for the investigators: the forest had been searched with specially trained dogs, and two of them had reacted.

After that, Therese had called in a couple of members to search the small pool, without immediate results. They had raked and cleared out leaves, branches, and other junk. They had also found a pump to drain the pool of water but then decided to pause to await further orders from the police.

It would be enough to give a forensic technician a heart attack. Trampling around a potential crime scene, where a body might be buried? Jumbling potential tracks and clues? This was a job for professionals, the archaeologists of crime with their brushes and trowels, who sift and sieve every grain of soil, sand, and clay before moving on to the next patch. But what was done was done.

Martinsson wanted Missing People to repeat the search with one of the dogs. Forensic technician Anders Elmqvist filmed Wilma the cadaver dog doing another lap around the pond with her handler. The dog indicated again.

Martinsson exchanged a few words with his colleagues. There was only one thing to do before this got even messier and more insurmountable: take charge. He would call in more staff and follow the checklist.

"You're going to have to move back, everyone. Clear the scene. We are cordoning it off," he said.

Formally speaking, a police officer's word carries as much weight as blue-and-white tape around a location. Martinsson's decision was time-stamped 2:30 p.m. that Sunday.

Shortly thereafter, actual police tape was put up around the pond and the house. The police also called in a security officer to guard the scene at night while they waited for a group of technicians with the appropriate equipment to pump the pond dry and go through it with a fine-toothed comb.

Anders Lindfors had gnashed his teeth, at least inwardly, when Therese told him that they had been guided to the area by supernatural forces. Missing People had their own experiences of such things, like in the case of the young woman whose body was found, at a troublingly opportune time, by a relative, supposedly thanks to a medium.

"I don't believe in stuff like that," Anders said. "So I was very skeptical when Therese told me. I wouldn't have come if I had known. But then we released one of the dogs and it started right away. Ran over to the water and barked. It was incredible. A pool no more than three feet deep at most, and there was supposed to be a corpse in it."

They sent out the other dog, which walked past the pond at first but then turned back and barked as well.

"If the dogs had come there and indicated, without any talk of a medium, I wouldn't have said anything," Anders said. "But this all seemed very suspicious. When someone identifies a spot like this, it's because they know something or have overheard something; this nonsense about mediums seeing things is just that—nonsense."

But the result of the nonsense was undeniable: two dogs had indicated for possible cadaver scent in the same spot. This was not going to turn out to be a dead animal in the pond. The dogs are trained to sniff out humans, using, among other things, materials from morgues. Besides, both dogs had been tested next to a dunghill with several dead calves in the vicinity, and neither had reacted.

Missing People rooted about the pond for clues for a while before Therese contacted the police to ask for advice and was told to immediately cease activity and wait for the police.

"It must have been an absurd situation for them, arriving at the house," Anders said. "Dragged out there by civilians who had in turn been guided by a medium, as far from proper procedure as you can get as a detective. And you're told Göran Lundblad is supposed to be at the bottom of that damn puddle."

When the police arrived, no one mentioned the medium. After Missing People dog Wilma had shown what she could do, and Martinsson had ordered the area be cordoned off and got back in his car, the deluge finally stopped in Norra Förlösa. There was a drizzle in the air, but the skies slowly cleared as Therese and her colleagues packed up.

They had done their part now. No point sending volunteers out on a grid search or running around the woods with the dogs, because there were no locations of particular interest to search.

Or—wait. There was actually *one* place left Therese wished to search.

Martin Törnblad looked surprised, almost like he had just woken up, when he opened the door to Ställe Farm, the house where he didn't really belong, not if Göran Lundblad could have anything to say about it. But now he lived there, together with Sara and their son, Vince, unless they were away in Stigtomta.

Now a beautiful blonde in jeans and a windbreaker was standing before him on the steps. She was wearing a name tag and had a determined look on her face. She was nine years older than Martin, who was turning twenty-three that summer.

The woman shook his hand politely and introduced herself as the chief operating officer of Missing People Kalmar. She said she would like to come inside with her colleague Agneta, who was standing next to her with a leashed forensic dog.

Martin knew something had been going on that day over at the neighbor's house. Just a few hours earlier, one of Missing People's cars had been here at Ställe Farm, meeting up with another car that it then led over that way.

Three people had been in the car—maybe they were police, maybe other volunteers. He couldn't be sure, but he was aware that something had been going on, and that was not usually good news. The police had been around several times with dogs and technicians and interviews and accusations over the past many months. And now these two. With a dog.

Therese and her colleague had decided to drive over to try their luck after talking to the police by the pond. When they rolled up toward Ställe Farm, they had noticed a pickup truck parked outside and decided to check if anyone was in. If Sara was home, it was a done deal—she had already promised on the phone to let them in, dog and all, as long as she was home.

On the way to the front door, they passed the double doors to the basement garage and Wilma the dog stopped by the crack under the door, pulled on her lead, and sniffed. She had to be yanked away from the scent she seemed to have picked up.

On the other side of the house, they knocked on the front door.

"Martin was skeptical and curt throughout our conversation," Therese said. "*Uncomfortable* is probably the right word. At first, he didn't want to let us in because he said the police dogs had broken things when they were there, his stereo and several other things. He hadn't been compensated for any of it."

Therese promised to accompany the dog at all times and pay for any damages out of her own pocket. She also asked him to contact Sara, who had given her halfhearted promises the day before. But Martin first claimed not to have Sara's number, then that his phone needed charging, and finally that he didn't want to bother her.

"Between questions, I offered to let him use my phone," Therese said. "I had her number and everything, after all. But he just said no, and we left. As we got back in the car, we suddenly exclaimed at the same time: 'What a liar!' We should have called Sara's cell phone to see how he would have reacted if it suddenly started ringing in the living room behind him. We had a feeling she was in the house all along."

Feelings don't solve crimes, but they can guide an investigation. And things were crystal clear, as far as Therese was concerned, regardless of what the police may find in the shallow pond in the forest: Martin and Sara murdered Göran, probably at Ställe Farm. Her gut and her intuition were sure of it, and Therese had long since learned to listen to them.

What remained was to prove it. And the best way to do so was to find Göran Lundblad's body.

18

SCENT

"Isn't that Martin?"

"That's Sara!"

Therese Tang and Anders Lindfors shouted over each other when they spotted two people walking along the gravel road up ahead of them. Her colleague's exclamation made Therese jump, but she kept the car on the road and continued to roll slowly northward.

She was driving her black BMW with detachable magnetic signs along the car's sides reading "Team Organizer." Only a blind person could miss who was coming. Anders Lindfors was in the passenger seat, and another member of the management team, Maria Nilsson, was in the back.

Martin and Sara were walking side by side along the shoulder, the very couple that everything revolved around. The rumors and half-truths, but also the cold, hard facts in the puzzle, swirled around Therese's head.

"All our eyes met as we passed them, as if in slow motion," she said.

"I smiled and gave them a friendly wave," Therese said. "It was the first time I'd seen Sara in real life. She looked nothing like the pictures I'd seen. We obviously wondered what she and Martin were doing there. And they had to be asking themselves why we were there."

Sara and Martin were walking south, in the direction of the pond. Even if they were every bit as guilty as people thought, they would hardly be on their way to cover their tracks. But it was nevertheless interesting that they were here, the three people in the car agreed.

Hours earlier, Therese and her colleagues had left their hotel in central Kalmar to make their way back to the red house. They knew the police had pumped the water out of the pond, and they wanted to see what it looked like dry.

"I knew straight away that his body wouldn't be there," Therese said, "but I wanted to keep focusing on the pond and its surroundings." The extensive drainage system that had been put in place in the surrounding land meant that there were likely many other wells up among the trees where the water might be draining from.

That same morning, several news outlets reported on the potential success of the search. On *Barometern*'s front page:

> Missing People may have made a pivotal discovery. Two forensic dogs have indicated in an area the police deem interesting in the search for missing local man Göran Lundblad.

Therese was quoted in the article: "We contacted the police, who have now cordoned off an area, so we discontinued our search." She didn't reveal any details—that was for the police to cover, if and when it became appropriate.

There wasn't a lot to see among the trees. The police had indeed been back to pump the water out. A rocky bottom could be glimpsed beyond the police tape, with old leaves, branches, and litter scattered about. A security officer was posted out by the road to make sure no unauthorized people got in and rummaged around, not until the dogs had done their jobs.

Two cadaver dogs that had been requisitioned from the Skåne police would arrive the next day, Tuesday. Scents indicated that Göran's body could be nearby, perhaps farther up the drainage system, stuffed into a well, a basin, or a dunghill. Or he might have been, through sheer coincidence, buried next to one of the area's drainage pipes.

The three members of Missing People chatted for a while with the security officer, whom they knew. He wasn't sure what he was guarding, so they filled him in on what was going on. Just after 5:00 p.m. they headed out for one last drive around the neighborhood to look for potential search sites for next time.

They had to do something. This was going to be solved, as Therese had already made clear. She was sure the body was somewhere nearby. Whether it was her strong desire to succeed that had tipped over into conviction, or whether gut feelings and intuition really did exist, she didn't know. But Therese was sure that Göran Lundblad was close at hand. It was at this point, on their drive away from the pond, that they met Sara and Martin walking down the side of the road.

The gravel road was too narrow to turn around on. It was only when they got to the next bend, near a dilapidated barn full of hay bales, next to a concrete slurry pit several yards tall, that they were able to turn back, the dust from the gravel road billowing around them.

When the Missing People car passed the young couple on its way back, Sara and Martin were standing in the middle of a field.

"It was like they were posing, to have an excuse to be in that exact location and seem unperturbed," Therese said. "Sara was looking up at Martin, who had picked up stalks or blades of grass and was releasing them. As though he was checking the direction of the wind or what the harvest would be like or some such."

When they got back to the security officer at the pond, they informed him that two people of great interest to the investigation were on their way. Then they took up a post next to the car out on the gravel road and waited.

The members of the management team had an established division of labor: Therese did the talking while Anders and Maria stayed in the background, listening, observing, and thinking, preparing the craftiest possible interventions should Therese lose her train of thought or the conversation slow.

Maria's role was to focus entirely on body language, noting what people react to, how they react. It was similar to what the police do during their more structured interviews, except that Missing People was not allowed to detain the two people who were, at that moment, walking toward them. They were not allowed to put them in separate interview rooms and bombard them with all sorts of questions. They were not allowed to overwhelm them with anything but words.

Because for all intents and purposes, Missing People was nothing but a congregation of interested—some would say nosy—private citizens with no further jurisdiction than any other stranger on the street. They didn't have police rights; they didn't even have the powers of a security guard. Only the good name of MPS, built up by several successful searches during its short existence, gave them authority, paired with the official benevolence that police chiefs in several parts of the country had bestowed upon the organization. But still, fundamentally, MPS had no particular authority or jurisdiction. They were just a bunch of ordinary citizens with yellow vests.

The birds were singing among the trees around Britt-Marie's red house. It was an early summer's evening in the Swedish countryside, idyllic. Sara and Martin were walking toward the car where the three Missing People organizers were pretending to be engaged in casual conversation. Therese hit the record button on her phone.

She knew she would have only a few fractions of a second to establish trust, to lure them in with something to make them open up, if only ever so little.

"You weren't wearing glasses yesterday."

It was as much a question as a statement from Martin, who had just shaken Therese's hand. Good recall for someone who claimed not to be able to remember his partner's phone number, or at least hadn't been able to the day before when Therese had tried to get into Ställe Farm with Wilma the forensic dog.

Therese had stepped across the road, hand outstretched, to introduce herself to Sara. They shook hands as Anders and Maria joined them. Sara and Martin seemed nervous about the meeting at first, uncomfortable.

There could be many explanations for that—one being that the couple was in deep conflict with practically the whole world and didn't trust anyone. They might also have been in deep conflict with each other. The first problem was obvious to Therese and her colleagues. The second was not.

A conversation slowly got under way.

"Martin kept tapping his foot," said Maria. "He was talking about the area and pointing to the interesting parts of the fields. Sara mostly just stood there glaring; my impression was that she was trying to catch Martin's eye to make him stop talking. But Therese managed to get him going again and again. This seemed to annoy Sara."

Therese was taking the lead. She kept circling back to the topic of the dogs indicating by the pond and talked up Wilma—the corpse expert—as much as she could.

"If she indicates, there is something to be found," she declared. "But there's nothing to say it happened here; it could be farther away, upstream. If the police don't find anything here, we'll have to look for the other location. We have to figure out what the indication means."

Anders cut in, saying that they were going to search the entire area. He pointed out across the fields, asking who owned what, and where a body could be buried. He nodded as Martin responded, then continued to ask more questions.

The subject soon shifted to the local conflicts, and Therese was quick to position herself on Martin and Sara's side against the world. She implied that the other villagers might have an interest in messing with them. She almost exclusively addressed Martin, once again led by her gut. Sara had been dismissive on the phone, so attempting to push beyond her hard shell would likely be pointless.

Therese angled for Martin's version of the situation, after having heard "everyone else's" in the village. She wanted accusations. They were quick in coming, along with an unexpected anecdote.

"We actually had two people over at the house a while ago," Martin said. "I think it was late April. They said they were from Missing People. They had a key and everything."

The visit had supposedly happened when he was home alone at Ställe Farm.

"I wasn't too keen on letting them in. One of them was about forty-five, your height, beard, just like you," he told Anders. "I'm almost sure I've seen him before. I could almost swear he was one of Mats Råberg's relatives."

The tenant farmer again, their nemesis, being fingered for a possible involvement in Göran's disappearance.

"I wouldn't want Göran found if I were him," Martin said. "Then he would be declared dead, and we would take over, and he [Mats] would be given notice and made to leave."

It must have been Mats who had provided the key to Ställe Farm, Martin claimed. He used to have a key to the main house and had probably made copies. The Missing People imposters must have been acting on his orders, for unknown reasons, but they must have been up to something.

In hindsight, it fit perfectly into the preexisting pattern of lies—something malicious happening when Sara was away. Yet another lie to fortify the wall against the world, to keep anything or anyone from undermining their pact.

Furthermore, Martin seemed to be copying the exact scene from yesterday—when Therese knocked on his door with her colleague and a dog. He even included a character who looked like Anders.

Therese didn't believe him, but she was unsure how to interpret the story. What could Martin possibly gain from telling it? Other than further damaging Mats's reputation. As was the case with most of his stories, there were no witnesses to verify his claims. For the moment, they just had to swallow it.

"Ah, I hadn't considered that. Interesting," Therese interjected during Martin's narration.

Spontaneous questioning—back away, play dumb, but not too dumb. Ask, but don't question. Play along to make your interlocutor take the bait.

One detail of the story that would turn out to be unexpectedly significant: the claim that there were keys to Ställe Farm floating about. According to Martin's story, there may have been copies as early as 2012. Therese committed the information to memory and improvised.

She said that she and her members always wore vests and badges to identify themselves, and that Martin should report the incident.

"Sure—but that never does anything," he replied.

And then the infamous threatening letter came up, the one Mats had supposedly put in their mailbox, or possibly delivered verbally, in person, the one that Martin later made copies of and distributed. The story behind the threatening letter was, as they knew, full of contradictions.

"The police never do anything," Martin said. "They take our reports, but then they don't give a shit."

Therese tried to offer a shoulder to lean on.

"I feel for you, I really do," she said. "I'm impressed you can bear living like this."

A white lie? Of course. But unlike the police, she didn't need to bother with objectivity, regulations, and interview procedures. This wasn't an interview at all, just a regular conversation between two civilians, a conversation that Therese continued to push back to the subject of Göran, to the fact that his body must be somewhere close by.

She opened up a broader perspective by talking about other missing people. Like the Linda Chen case, the missing woman in Falun where a cause of death couldn't be established because by the time they had found the corpse, animals had disturbed the body. That could be the case here too.

Which is to say: even if Göran was found dead, there was a significant risk that no one could be tied to the crime. It might not even be possible to prove there was a crime at all. It was a candy-coated way out for a murderer with a lively imagination: the body is found, the inheritance gets paid out, and whoever committed the murder gets off scot-free.

Therese wanted to shake things loose. Not just to find out more, hear more, and hope that Martin let something incriminating slip, but also to make the couple think about things differently, to offer them the hope of a way out.

A private investigator looking for openings, however small. But the hunt was what mattered, the truth that Therese knew could be found somewhere nearby. If she had not been so firmly convinced of that, she wouldn't have spent the past few days here, in this godforsaken backwater; she would have stayed home with her family in Oskarshamn.

She pressed on, using her most authoritative voice.

"Regardless, we're going to keep working on this. We have clear indications; they point to something. We are going to figure out what it means. We have scheduled more searches in late June, no matter what happens with the police investigation and the dogs and everything."

After about forty-five minutes, Therese reckoned it would be too pushy to keep Martin and Sara any longer. Better to retain the initiative and break it off herself before they did.

"Right, well, I suppose this has to be today's big news in the village," she said conspiratorially. Then, to her colleagues: "Let's go, we have to get something to eat. If you think of anything, Martin, just call me, that would be great."

The Missing People car drove off in the direction of Boatorp, where the road curved in an arc to the east through the fields before narrowing further and turning back down toward Norra Förlösa, Åke Törnblad's farm, the main road, then eastward toward the Lindsdal Junction and the E22 highway.

Excerpt from memo regarding the K9 search, undertaken the next day, written by dog handler Johan Esbjörnsson, Skåne police:

> We were informed that the organization Missing People had been searching for a missing person in the area in question, and that one of their dogs had indicated a find in a water-filled natural dam.
>
> According to Missing People, their dog is trained to find dead bodies.
>
> The area in question measures approximately twenty by ten yards. The technicians from Kalmar had drained the pond to help with the search.
>
> We decided to search both the pond and the adjacent wooded area. In conducting the search, one dog

team searched the forest first while the other searched the pond, then we switched search areas.

This is done to maximize the efficacy of the search.

Neither one of our forensic dogs indicated. Not in the drained pond nor in the nearby forest.

"Police suspend search," local paper *Barometern* noted on page four on Wednesday, May 21, 2014. It was a brief article, but in a prominent spot.

Back to square one. Or it would have been, if not for one woman who refused to give up.

Two cars rolled into Norra Förlösa on the same morning that the news about the failed K9 search was made public. Missing People was back, though in smaller numbers.

The four people in two cars were led by Therese Tang. They visited both Åke Törnblad and Mats Råberg to talk to them about continuing their search in the area. They wanted to be extra cautious to avoid being reported for anything—trespassing or criminal damages. It was a litigious neighborhood, as they had come to understand. Now they would like to go out and climb hunting blinds, search abandoned buildings, wells, dams, burn piles, everything, so they were careful to request permission first. It was time to shake the tree and see what fell out.

Over the next few days, members of Missing People moved about Norra Förlösa constantly. They were not doing grid searches—there were no official searches at all—just a handful of people, the organizers. They did what they could to make themselves as visible as possible.

"Drive by and stress them out," Therese told everyone.

"Drive through the village whenever you're in the area," Anders said. "And make sure you have the Missing People signs on your cars."

They undertook all this with the tacit approval of the police.

"'Go out there and stir the pot; it's good you're keeping at it,' they said," recounted Marie-Louice Strannemark. "We decided internally that we were going to drive around as much as possible."

"Don't lose heart," Therese told tenant farmer Mats Råberg and his partner during one of their conversations. "Things are just getting started."

People in the area were hugely disappointed that nothing had been found in the pond behind the house. After the police packed it in and left, people started to turn to Therese and her private investigators. She was the one who received the tip-offs, ideas, and suggestions. The neighbors were eager to keep the search alive and, as always, the people involved in a missing-person case seemed to find it easier to talk to Missing People than to the police. They felt free to air their wildest theories and notions. Therese encouraged this; she wanted to shake out every last theory, every possible clue she could.

"As a child, I wanted to be a police officer," Therese said. "I suppose that never went away. I wanted everything neat and orderly. Plus, I found the police exciting, but I suppose all children do."

She refused to give up. She was filled with determination, bordering on obsession—the locals in Norra Förlösa could clearly see that. She herself put it this way: "I have my opinions—I've always been like that—and if they're not welcome, I'm out. I'd rather be alone."

Although she didn't have much in the way of a formal education, what she did have in spades was drive—to see justice done, to be proven right. She also had experience of a lot of other things—including naked violence.

"I was fifteen when I first fell in love. He was a few years older and so cool. My mom would barely allow me to have sleepovers with my girlfriends, but I lied and stayed out with him."

She carved the first letter of her boyfriend's name, an *A*, into her arm, by scraping and cutting to make scar tissue.

"But he wasn't well, and it took me a while to realize it. He was jealous and beat me up several times. The third time he nearly killed me."

One night in the 1990s, the relationship went off the rails. Therese had been helping a badly intoxicated male friend get on a bus. Her boyfriend had seen her with her friend's arm around her shoulders. Jealous, he confronted her when they were back in his bedroom.

"His eyes were black. He grabbed me by the shoulders and shook me."

Then it got worse.

She tried to get away, half-dressed, together with a girlfriend who was staying over in the same apartment. But the boyfriend wouldn't let them leave. He threw their clothes out the fifth-floor window and went to fetch his baseball bat.

The night no longer smelled of drunkenness and alcohol; it reeked of fear, blood, and death, as the teenaged Therese dodged her boyfriend's bat again and again. She was shaken by the ringing noise of the bat hitting the sink. In the end, when her back was literally against the wall, she had no other choice than to fight back. She used one or two judo techniques she had learned, to punch, kick, pull, and wrest the bat from his hands.

The episode ended with a police intervention; the girls were eventually taken from the apartment by officers. The boyfriend was convicted of assault on Therese's testimony. She came out of the affair with a scar on her arm that will never fade and emotional wounds she consciously chose to transform into energy rather than self-pity.

Regardless of what the psychiatric term is for handling setbacks and horrible events the way Therese had, she had always felt she had the ability to channel her experiences into something good, and to always, no matter what, stand by her opinion.

Therese was now working as a jail guard—the security officer who works in the police station and wears a police uniform, but is not in fact a police officer. In this job, she had access to every police station in Kalmar County in the spring of 2014, but she was still a private citizen, unencumbered with the regulations restraining the police. She was beholden to no handbook telling her how she had to treat suspects, no preliminary investigation regulations dictating how an investigation must be run to hold water in court.

She answered only to herself. She could lie, fib, spice up stories, and angle things as much as she liked, without putting the investigation in jeopardy. The end—getting closer to the truth—justified the means, she decided.

Her methods could potentially cause trouble down the line if she and her colleagues were to uncover important information, statements, or claims. If they hadn't followed protocol, they could accidentally invalidate potential evidence and testimony in a future trial.

On the other hand, Swedish jurisprudence is based on the so-called free sifting of evidence. It doesn't matter if the material was obtained using shady methods; the prosecution can still use it. In effect, a police officer could steal, bribe, threaten, or use any other questionable techniques to get information or gather evidence against a defendant, and it would still be accepted in a court of law. The officer in question would have to answer for any and all possible crimes committed in the course of getting that evidence, and possibly even be sentenced for it, but the evidence would nevertheless be admissible.

In the US, the exclusionary rule states that evidence collected or analyzed in violation of the constitution is inadmissible for a criminal prosecution in a court of law. But while a Swedish court would obviously downplay the value of evidence beaten out of a subject, to put it bluntly, the more tangible pieces of evidence—objects or other corpus delicti—would be deemed to be as valuable as any other piece of evidence, notwithstanding the manner by which it was brought into the investigation.

If you were to record an acquaintance with a secret microphone, and he revealed himself to be a thief, embezzler, or murderer, you could be charged with illegal surveillance. That said, the recording could still be used against him in a court of law.

On the flip side, Therese didn't have any of the rights granted to the police either, like the ability to interview anyone at will, either as a suspect or an "other." She would have to rely on her ability to connect with people, her ability to seem more knowledgeable than she really was.

The Missing People management team did all they could to proceed with the search. One example was the dilapidated barn in Boatorp—Therese entered the ramshackle building wearing climbing gear.

"We searched the gaps between the hay bales on the top floor—no one had looked there before—mostly just to show that we were doing something. The aim was to be seen, after all," she said. "I wanted to scare them as much as possible by keeping up our patrols and making sure we were seen around the village."

Martin rolled around the area in his tractor every day. He could hardly avoid noticing Missing People wandering all around. Therese had also been in touch with his father, Åke, on the subject: Where do you think someone could have buried a body? Where were the wells, ditches, drain pipes?

The dilapidated barn was located some distance north of the pond. Next to the building was a slurry pit—like a cement tub dug into the ground, three feet deep and filled to the brim with manure. They dragged the muck and, on the possibility that there might be something down there, Therese arranged for help emptying the pit, acquired permission to dump the manure in an adjacent field, and persuaded a volunteer to come slosh around the bottom with a rake, dressed in a full-body suit and a gas mask.

"All that was just for show," Therese said. "I wanted to show we were serious about never giving up, checking everything we could."

It was actually Therese's ex—the father of her oldest daughter—who helped her drain the slurry pit, a useful tidbit Martin caught wind of when he rubbernecked on the way past in his tractor. He even learned that Therese had once lived with the man on a farm up near Mönsterås, yet another piece of information he set to work fitting into a new possible version of reality.

Nothing turned up in the slurry pit. Therese was left at the scene with only her colleagues, the powerful smell of excrement, and a very well-fertilized field on the other side of the road.

Marie-Louice Strannemark often went by Norra Förlösa when she was taking her dogs out. She liked to drive an extra lap through the village with the magnetic signs on the sides of her car to alert the locals about the presence of Missing People, certain everyone would soon have heard about it through the grapevine.

One day, going down a spur road, she came across something that appeared to be bone fragments, a garbage bag, and a pair of plastic gloves. She had brought her camera, so she took some pictures to show her colleagues. They informed the police, but after an examination of the pieces, it was determined that they were animal bones.

Some distance from the house by the pond, a set of items that did not belong in nature, and may therefore have held some interest, were found, so Therese turned them in. The police listed the items as: "fan belt, small rubber mat, soil with plant parts (slightly spongy), and pieces of something hard she describes as desiccated skin." But when forensic technician Anders Elmqvist examined the items, the skin-like substance turned out to be "either a large fish scale or a piece of plastic."

It would be easy to scoff at the amateur detectives out there searching, climbing, and snooping, or to dismiss the whole thing as shadow chasing, as if Therese and her colleagues were merely out on a ghost hunt, looking for shapeless bogeymen and imagined perpetrators, dreaming up convoluted conspiracy theories.

Yes, they could be dismissed as civilians without any level of insight into murder investigations, who enjoyed playing detective and feeling as if they mattered. It would be just as easy to speculate about how the figments of their imaginations were amplified by the attention they got whenever they meddled in things, through the media, and also from the local residents, who had no one else to turn to. But they carried on.

The playing field in the Göran Lundblad case looked different now than it had just a few months earlier, when the police had been conducting their additional interviews in early 2014. And it was virtually unrecognizable from when the original interviews and phone tapping were being conducted back in the fall of 2012.

During the spring of 2014, several of the people involved had been mulling things over, speculating, and working together to add up the facts in new ways. The main suspects, meanwhile, had undergone quite a few changes as well.

Only a few days after her conversation with Martin and Sara and the search of the pond, Therese's conviction regarding who killed Göran was confirmed beyond doubt.

"We were checking out the last place of the day, beyond Boatorp. As we were parking, Martin arrived in his tractor," she said.

Therese had been telling anyone who would listen that Göran's body must be buried somewhere nearby, that the cadaver smell must have traveled along the drain pipes. Without more precise information, it would be a Sisyphean task to search all the covered ditches, wells, and pipes that had been dug over the decades without ever being recorded on a map.

Therese, who on this day was accompanied by colleagues Marie-Louice Strannemark and Fredrik Mundt, wanted to approach the search systematically. They drove past the dilapidated barn in Boatorp in the direction of Skyttelund, then they parked the car.

Fredrik walked down across the field to the wooded area to have a look at a spot where one of their dogs had indicated in the past. The other two were joined by Martin Törnblad in his tractor.

"He was very nervous and couldn't sit still, but he stayed and talked to us for over an hour," Marie-Louice said. "He tugged on his ear, scratched his arm, wouldn't look us in the eye, things like that. He seemed to have a lot on his mind. I'm no doctor, but his behavior was not that of a healthy person. There was something in his eyes, too, that I couldn't put my finger on."

Marie-Louice kept a low profile during the conversation, observing while Therese talked. It was a strangely gory conversation that was nevertheless conducted in dry, neutral tones. Therese and Martin talked about whether body parts really would decompose in a slurry pit or would be preserved.

"I rambled on as best I could," Therese said, "though I interspersed my suppositions with things I knew for sure, and I could tell he believed me."

She mentioned Switzerland and the millions of kronor that Göran had stashed there. "I told him my dad used to have money there, but that he moved it to somewhere else because it was so difficult to get money out of Switzerland," Therese said. "Around that time, Fredrik came back and heard what I was saying. He added something about how there were people still struggling to extract the money that belonged to relatives who died in the Second World War. His spontaneous comment somehow finally convinced Martin I was credible."

They could see the cogs turning in the mind of a shaken Martin. In front of them was a twenty-three-year-old man without much education or experience of life or society outside the two hundred fifty acres that made up Norra Förlösa. Therese realized it could be eminently possible to help him redirect his thinking in many different directions, to persuade him of any number of things, as long as she didn't stray too far from the truth.

"I explained to him that the reason they're seeing us about so much is that I've been told the time frame for declaring a missing person dead is set to change in 2015, that they are raising it to fifteen years."

This was a vitally important consideration for Martin. All Göran's assets would remain frozen for as long as he remained missing. There would be no execution of the fifty-million-kronor (six-million-dollar) will until he was declared dead. And there were only two paths to that outcome: that the body was found or that a court ruled him to be deceased.

It was, in fact, true that a death certificate could be a long time coming. In the case of a man named Carl-Eric Björkegren, who had disappeared from his luxury villa in Viken in Skåne in the nineties, it took two decades before the Stockholm District Court declared him dead.

But for anyone who knew where to look for information, it would be easy to expose Therese as a liar. According to a Swedish statute about declaring a missing person dead, a missing person can in fact be declared dead immediately under certain conditions—like after a natural disaster or major incident. Under other circumstances, a motion can't be filed until five years have passed, at the earliest. And the Ministry of Justice had not proposed any changes to that time frame in the spring of 2014.

"I also told him that the new time frame was going to be evaluated in 2017 and potentially raised even more," Therese said. "That riled Martin."

"What the fuck?! Why are they doing this to us when we're already having such a hard time?" he roared. He mentioned that criminals were murdering each other all the time. In those cases, he could buy their argument, but here, when Göran was just missing? Why couldn't he and Sara be allowed to move on? He told Therese he didn't think much of the police. He said they did everything they could to make life a misery for him and Sara.

Martin then started to ask her some very specific and rather odd questions. Therese played along, continuing to build the image of herself as an inexhaustible private investigator, a person who knew a little bit more than most, a woman who could predict things, see around corners.

In response to a specific question, she told Martin that, no, the police couldn't track shotgun bullets back to specific guns. She managed not to let on how strange it was for the young man to be asking her that. Yes, she told him, it was the same with fingerprints—there would hardly be any of those to find on or around a body after such a long time. She used her most soothing voice. She was a shoulder to lean on.

Who except a murderer or an accessory to murder would need to ask about identifying ammunition and fingerprints? But Martin had most definitely taken the bait. He clearly had no one to talk to about these things, and he just as clearly needed to talk, think, and make plans. She could tell that more things were waiting to come out of him, and she planned on being there, right next to him, when they did.

The only way for her to get in close to him would be to show him even more of herself, to give him more details he could build his elaborate fantasies on, his slightly tweaked details, like that thing about her father's bank account. Personal information, presented with feeling.

"I was surprised by how much she revealed about herself to him, that she would give him such intimate details," Marie-Louice noted.

The best lies always contain a grain of truth. That also makes them easier to keep track of. Therese wanted to keep shaking the tree, as the fruits of this particular tree felt ripe for the picking. She suspected—rather than knew—that this tree was not just shaking; it was about to be completely uprooted by the storm that was brewing.

19

NO ONE MAY KNOW

I would like to talk to you but without anyone knowing. And I mean no one . . .

It was exactly 22 minutes and 48 seconds past 11:00 p.m. on June 17 when Therese's phone buzzed. She saw the message pop up on her screen.

She had already turned her brain off for the night and was lying in bed at home with her youngest children. It was time for everyone to go to sleep.

It was far too late for her kids to be awake, but June nights in Sweden are as bright as day, and school was out for the summer. In her house, that meant the kids got to stay up late and sleep until lunchtime if that was what they wanted. Mother and children were chatting among pillows and blankets while their eyelids grew heavier and the day came to a close. They were half dozing, warm and snug.

Until now. The message woke her up instantly; she was suddenly icy cold. She started to disentangle herself from the children. The message was from Martin Törnblad, and there was only one possible way to interpret it: He had been broken. She had won. She felt as if she had just scratched off the winning combination on a lottery card and was sensing the first whiff of all those millions.

Winning might be overstating it. But she did feel somewhat victorious; he had something he wanted to share. The only question was how to make him take the final step, how to wring the details out of him. She wanted the location—the grave. That was the most important thing.

A few weeks earlier, a day or two after the pivotal conversation by the tractor, Martin had added her as a friend on Facebook. She assumed he had already found out most of what there was to know about her. Therese was not a private person, quite the opposite. She had long been making a living by exposing herself and her work.

Photographs of her as a model or stylist were publicly available online. As were pictures of herself, her children, her husband, her entire private life on the popular wedding and maternity blog she had written for years. They hadn't been updated in years, but the material was all online, out there for the world to see.

As anyone with online experience knows, a general impression of when a person was born and in what part of the country they live is enough to get quite a lot of their personal information with just a few clicks of the mouse. What someone paid for their house, who they vote for, where they live, what kind of cars they have, etc. The process is even more straightforward if a person has an unusual name.

Like Tang. Not a common name in Sweden at all.

The personal identity number is the key to every public database in Sweden. It is similar to a social security number in the US, except that instead of hiding it away, you use it everywhere—in the grocery store, in the bank, in the schools, at the hospital—everywhere. All your interactions with the authorities can be collated in less than a day—run-ins with the law, fines and sentences, debts and incomes, your benefits, even the complaint you sent to the Swedish Consumer Agency about your hairdresser.

It was with a sudden sense of vertigo that Therese replied to Martin's text that night. She had to assume that he had found out everything from her home address to the names of her children. As far as she knew, he could be parked in the street outside her house, texting her, right now. It was imperative that she choose her words carefully going forward. Therese, it appeared, had found herself a stalker. A stalker she suspected of being a murderer.

On the other hand, she knew a lot about him and his situation too. Not only what the police had told her, but also what she had read and what he and Sara had told her themselves. Therese had spies in the field as well.

"It felt like everyone would call me all the time," she said. Both from Norra Förlösa and Stigtomta. The locals reported everything they had seen and heard.

"We're a lot more like detectives than a group looking for a missing person," Therese wrote in Missing People's closed Facebook group as early as late May. She had, at that point, handed over the surreptitious recording of her conversation with Martin and Sara to the police upon their request. It was yet another tiny piece of the puzzle.

Missing People's next large search was planned for the weekend of June 19 and 20. That information, too, had been disseminated in the area to ratchet up the pressure and sow seeds of doubt and discord.

On May 28, the day he first contacted her on Facebook, Martin had also called Therese. There was this medium who sees and knows things, he told her. The medium in question supposedly saw Göran's body close to a stone wall. There might be more information, but the medium didn't want to draw any attention, or end up in some police register.

"How do you deal with something like that?" he had asked Therese.

Therese had explained that a person could tell her anonymously about his or her visions, then she could go out and have a look with her colleagues. There was no need for the police to get involved, at least not until it became clear what they were dealing with. It was a bit like it had been with the pond, she had explained. They would just get a couple of dogs out to have a sniff around.

It didn't take Therese long to figure out where Martin's questions were coming from. Here was a murder suspect suddenly talking about fortune-tellers who could help locate the missing body. She texted in a group chat with the rest of the management team:

> We have to make it obvious we're around. Martin is coming along; he's going to talk "through" a medium. This is coming to a head now.

At Ställe Farm, just over a week before Midsummer 2014, an engine revved and someone screamed. The words could not be made out from a distance, but there was fear in that voice. Despair. The car drove off.

Sara Lundblad had trailered her horses and carefully placed her son, Vince, in his car seat. Martin was running behind the vehicle across the farmyard, chasing her.

He watched his future disappear as his partner drove off toward the E22 highway and the road north, to Stigtomta. After twenty or thirty yards, he slowed down, stopped, turned around, and walked back to the house. It was June 11. Martin had been left alone with his thoughts and dreams.

The problems in their relationship had always been worked out before. After a few rounds of texting and calling, Sara's tone would change, overwhelmed by Martin's energy and powers of persuasion, by his nagging. Then she would start including hearts and pet names in her messages again. She'd come back to him. "You and me."

But this time, it was not enough. She had actually left him. It was final, she said. She wanted to move on, to be left alone. She repeated that again and again when he called, begging and pleading for her to come home.

So he went after her.

Martin turned in between the Tängsta houses a little after three in the morning. It was not a calm and collected man who climbed out of the car after the 180-mile drive from Norra Förlösa. The main house was undergoing renovations, he knew that, so he marched over to the annex. The pipe manufacturing equipment was housed on the ground floor, and there was an apartment above it. Martin made a racket entering. He banged and pounded on the front door at first, before realizing that Sara had forgotten to lock it.

The scene that played out next was straight from a tragic relationship drama. The rejected man who turns up unexpectedly in the middle of the night. The woman and infant rudely awakened. And in the living room, on the couch, the lover. The new leading man.

That was how it played out in Martin's mind, anyway. Johan Nydahl, the young man whose parents were tenants, who had been helping out with the pipe-making, was in the apartment. As part of his salary, he was permitted to stay in the apartment when Sara wasn't there. But now stronger feelings seemed to have developed between them.

Where Johan Nydahl had been sleeping is open to debate. Both he and Sara claimed afterward that he had been on the couch when Martin arrived. But by the time Martin had entered, he was already on his feet and on his way out the door. He could certainly have been laying his head elsewhere.

Even so, there was no violent reckoning, only a verbal one. With Martin hurling insults after him, Johan headed over to his parents' house across the road and waited. He wanted to give them the space to work out whatever it was Martin had come to discuss.

The couple had quarreled before. Many times, especially over the past few months. But Sara couldn't ever seem to break free. She had even gone so far as to consult Göran's guardian, Knut Lewenhaupt, to see whether he could help her get a restraining order. Perhaps formal measures could keep Martin from dragging her back every time she decided to break it off. But that would be very difficult to secure, Sara had been told. She couldn't point to a risk of violence, because Martin had never assaulted her physically, not even close.

That she felt psychologically abused and stalked might have helped with a restraining order, but it would require a manic slew of texts, emails, and other messages to persuade a prosecutor to take up the case.

Everything was also made more complicated by the child they had together. It would be easier to slap a restraining order on a person who had committed a violent crime. But Martin was innocent as a baby lamb, legally speaking. Granted, he was still officially registered as a suspect in an ongoing, if low-key, murder investigation. But that was a long way from a formal charge and even further from a conviction in court.

Sara would simply have to manage her own breakup.

After several hours, Martin brought his baby son over to the neighbors, asking them to look after him. Sara and he had more things to work through, he told them.

When he returned to Tängsta without Vince, Sara tried to escape. She ran from the house at full speed, out into the fields, with Martin hard on her heels. Her head start lasted for about a hundred yards, then she slowed down, and he caught up, refusing to let her go. Talking and more talking and more talking.

To Sara, it was the same old rhetoric—about how they belonged together, how he couldn't live without her. On previous occasions, Martin had even talked about a suicide pact, so they could be together forever. But she had moved on. New friends, a new job. A different life. She wanted to look to the future, not bury herself in the past.

The two young parents talked for hours over the following days. The endless conversations associated with the breakup of a long-term love affair is something most people who have ever ended a relationship can relate to, even without the added complication of being suspected of murder in the case of a missing multimillionaire.

You weigh your options, for and against, more or less rationally. Maybe remember first encounters. The hand-holding, hugging, closeness, the first kiss. The feeling of being invincible together. You and me against the world.

But that is set against everything that has stagnated over time. Everything that has been eroded. Wrecked. Broken promises, harsh words.

Later that same summer, Sara said, "Dad told me Martin would, like, ruin me and turn a lot of people against me, kind of exploit me. I feel like I should have listened to him. But that's how it goes when you're in love; you don't see the flaws."

After three days, Sara finally relented, or at least claimed to. The only way to get Martin to leave was to promise to come back to Norra Förlösa. She just had to sort out a few things in Stigtomta first, she told him. Top priority was an order of Dollar Pipes for Swedish Match.

With Sara's words in his ears, Martin finally calmed down and drove back home. Holding the steering wheel was painful because he had injured his hand. He had punched a wall during one of his long conversations with Sara. No major damage, just swelling, but it was a stinging reminder of his own helplessness.

During the drive home, he slowly realized that their relationship was over. Truly over. Sara was done with him and with life in Norra Förlösa in general. It was a pale June day, with Midsummer just around the corner. There was nothing left.

Martin needed a new plan. And there happened to be a certain woman who had been on his mind for some time now.

Therese fumbled with her phone. Her eyes were roving around the bedroom without really seeing it. Her thoughts were racing. It was almost midnight on an ordinary Tuesday.

Something must have happened. Something had triggered Martin. The main suspect in a murder case was texting her in the middle of the night. Therese knew she had to seize this chance. She needed to reply quickly, kindly, and invitingly.

Therese: Ok, do you mean call or what?

Martin: Not sure. Having some personal problems I think and no one to talk to. Just thought you were a nice lady but don't know if I can trust you, without you telling for example my girlfriend or anyone else. I don't actually know you.

T: I can promise you complete secrecy. What you want to talk about will stay between us.

M: My head is playing some weird trick on me. I keep thinking about how you're doing and what you're doing.

Don't know why and I don't want to wreck anything, for you or myself. But I don't want to wait for an answer anymore.

Really don't want you to tell anyone that I'm telling you this. You thought I was going to have big news. Right?

T: I feel like you think I could be helpful and listen, so I'm here! I have felt for the two of you from day one and feel that your dad really welcomed us and I'm here for you whatever way I can be.

A few minutes passed between messages. The game was on. Her tactic: invite, but don't exaggerate. She signaled familiarity by mentioning Martin's father, for example. Not flirty, but still promising to be there in "whatever way" he needs. And the secrecy, the secret-making—they shared something now.

While texting, she logged onto Facebook and the group chat with the Missing People management team to update them.

"Maria Nilsson immediately said he was in love with me," Therese said. "Not a chance, I reckoned, but he had some kind of plan. 'This is as close as we're going to get,' I argued. This was our chance. Marie-Louice was worried, viewed him as unstable, and started talking about my safety."

The texting continued. It soon sounded as if Maria might be right. Martin was flirting with Therese.

M: My head isn't thinking about finding Göran when it thinks about Therese but about how she's doing and what her life is like. Because I'm guessing it's not always easy. You came from nowhere and suddenly I feel like you could mean more than a regular person.

Feel a bit stupid writing this and a bit scared of how you're going to take it.

After just under an hour of texting back and forth, while Therese was simultaneously group-chatting with her colleagues, Therese and Martin switched over to a phone call. The conversation would go more quickly that way, and it would be easier for Therese to hear undertones, hesitation, and pausing, which might help lull him into a sense of security. She left the bedroom so as not to wake the children. Then she set things up to record the call.

The day of Wednesday, June 18, 2014, was only fifteen or sixteen minutes old when Therese sank into an armchair to have what might turn out to be the most important phone call of her life.

To Therese, the person on the other end of the phone sounded less like a man than a boy. Under the surface, she could sense the violence and fury she would need to work with, harness, preserve. Otherwise she wouldn't get anywhere. His suppressed rage would boil over somehow, she knew.

Therese was not a psychologist or therapist, even though some of her experiences had made her feel like one. And it was probably impossible to predict or train yourself for, let alone fully understand, situations like this one.

Now, in this moment, in the middle of the night, she knew Martin was a murderer. Not in that formal sense—she could never prove such a thing beyond a reasonable doubt. But she *knew* it. She could tell as much from what he said as from what he left unsaid.

He was a little boy with immense difficulties in his relationship with the world, a mere child hidden inside a grown man. A little boy in big shoes. Could she trip him up, make him fall on his face, unmask himself—tell her exactly how it happened?

Possibly, but she would only be able to do so by being open in return. By going along with the conversation, with nothing but intuition—gut feeling—to help her predict what he wanted to hear.

Open. She would need to lie and make things up, in order to give him exactly the image he was looking for, the exact building blocks that fit into his mental construct, without knowing what that construct looked like.

At that moment, she knew, his construct was swaying precariously. The fundamentals of Martin's very existence were creaking. When he shouted "you and me" into the void, there was no echo.

Therese could pretend to be the soul mate he needed, the sounding board he could use to make himself feel significant again, important and strong.

Therese knew that the objective truth about Göran's death was probably already lost forever. No one would ever find the whole truth.

That is not how it works, as Therese was well aware. But she could come close. Close enough for it to be decisive. Close enough to find the body.

The transcript of what Therese and Martin said to one another that particular night would end up being 166 pages long. A verbal wrestling match. Therese rambled on about herself and her own invented relationship problems. She lied and told him she was getting divorced, but that she and her husband were staying together until after Christmas, for the children. She and Martin were in similar situations, she told him, though they were playing opposite parts.

Then she changed the subject to a more everyday topic—pointed out that she was on his side, on his family's side. She didn't care about the gossip in Norra Förlösa. She also joined in Martin's cursing of his neighbors, mirroring his disdain.

The police investigation was a completely separate thing, she argued. The police could run or misrun that as they please. She represented a volunteer organization with a single purpose: finding missing people. And she could help with whatever he needed help with.

He was open but cautious. Martin was very aware of the fact that his phones could be tapped. The police had already done that to him and Sara, he let her know.

Therese kept carefully homing in on the core question. That he knew something big and important. And he was skilled at concealing it, at playing along without being caught out.

> *Therese: But you screw up on certain things. Like your body language, for example.*
>
> *Martin: I screw that up?*
>
> *T: Yes, you do.*
>
> *M: Like how, for example?*

T: (Laughs) So you're saying I should teach you?

M: Yeah.

T: Yeah. Yes. Well, it's mostly when Sara's around. Then you screw up all the time.

M: What?

T: Yeah. Your whole body language and everything. How you act around her. The looks you exchange.

M: I had no idea.

Therese pointed out a flaw—nothing big, nothing he could really take exception to. A statement, immediately followed by good advice—she could help him do better. She was on his side.

Martin was in his home—the deserted Ställe Farm—with his phone pressed to his ear. For the first time in several years, he was talking to someone who wasn't dismissing him as a liar, braggart, or saboteur. A woman, to boot, and older than he. A beautiful woman who knew her stuff. Unlike Sara, she was helping him, providing solutions.

And her dreams matched his, he felt. She talked about having a farm in the country, horses—because she missed the horses of her childhood—and somewhere for her children to play, with fresh air and green grass.

She wanted it to be a big place where large companies could hold conferences. That's a moneymaker, she said. A hotel section, a small restaurant. Horse riding for guests who want to have a go. Clay pigeon shooting. Like a playhouse for adults. Therese implied that she had a tidy sum of money tucked away. She could easily start something up.

T: You know, having worked in the modeling industry, I make two, three calls, and I get strippers to come over. Guys can come for bachelor parties and shoot guns with half-naked girls and stuff. Do you think you could make money that way?

Again, the best lies contain a grain of truth. The idea was real—the dream of a hotel and conference facility in the countryside. And the modeling thing, well, it was true: she had been one. The rest were lies, of course. But she was counting on him buying them.

What else was Martin supposed to do? Call various modeling agencies and ask if Therese had contacts in the stripper business? It is always easier to believe what you want to believe. She could almost hear the cogs turning in his head. Indeed, after they hung up, the farm idea would take deeper root than Therese could possibly have imagined.

Intuitive interrogation strategy: validate the other person, then present alternatives. That is what makes people talk. And some talk more than others.

"I talked about things I knew," said Therese, "but I took them further and made them bigger and better. Among the first things I told him was that I'd had a glass of wine. It wasn't true, but it gave him the upper hand a little."

Martin told her that he and Sara had gone through the safe-deposit boxes since Göran disappeared.

"I've never seen that kind of money before," he said.

He also implied that he knew what had really happened to Göran. Or no, that he had a theory. "They" might be behind it. A group of people in and around Förlösa who had been laundering money since the 1970s.

A conspiracy theory! One that fit in with a lot of the things he had said when they met by the pond, that crazy story about a mysterious couple claiming to work for Missing People, but who were more likely friends with Göran's tenant farmer.

This made Therese wary: Where was he going with this? But she accepted his statement without question. She played along, as though she instantly got who "they" were.

T: *Mm. Mm. I was just thinking. If maybe we could just nail all of them.*

M: *No. Yes. I have no idea. I guess you need proof . . .*

T: *What did you say?*

M: *And stuff. You have to have evidence.*

T: *Well, evidence. There isn't any. That's what I'm saying. There's hardly going to be any evidence after two years.*

M: *You mean Göran?*

T: *Yeah.*

M: *But . . . well, then they'd have to find him in that case.*

T: *Mm.*

M: *Before anything.*

T: *Mm.*

M: *Yes. And that's not exactly easy, maybe.*

T: *No. Well, I wouldn't know.*

M: *But I feel like . . . I feel like that's impossible. Because then . . . I mean, I don't know if they've done anything. I actually don't want to judge them. And it's just as likely to be Mats Råberg, I reckon, given that his tenancy had been terminated.*

She was so close.

Martin was on the verge of being concrete several times. But every time, he backed away. As though he was just testing the waters, gauging reactions. Then he got personal again, told her that he had fallen for her that time they had talked by the tractor.

She remained noncommittal but didn't reject him out of hand. Instead, she continued to talk about the case and her job. Her loyalty was with the missing person, his family.

The closest Therese got that night was when Martin suddenly started talking about how one of the employees at the farm had had visions. The medium.

Anyone who believes in this kind of supernatural phenomena might by now be excused for thinking Kalmar County was crawling with people with paranormal abilities. Or that Göran's spirit was particularly powerful in its restlessness.

But this was not the time to argue. Keep him going, whatever he said. Sooner or later, it would come out. Martin claimed that the employee had seen signs that Göran's body was buried in the fields south and east of Ställe Farm.

M: And that's right in front of our house. Those hills over there, you know, that stand of oaks with the hunting hide.

An identified location. Was this a test? Was Martin checking to see what she would do? Call the police straight away, or go out and look? Or was it all nonsense? Words strung together to keep the conversation going while he planned his next attempt to get in behind her guard.

The wrestling match continued as night drifted into early morning, those hours after 3:00 a.m. when humans are at their most slow-witted.

At that hour, our levels of the sleep hormone melatonin are elevated, our digestion is at its slowest, and our body temperature and blood pressure are at their lowest, whether our body has been pumping out adrenaline during a potentially pivotal phone call or not.

Film director Ingmar Bergman called it "the hour when most people die, when sleep is deepest, when nightmares are most real. It is the hour when the sleepless are haunted by their deepest fear, when ghosts and demons are at their most powerful."

As the sun started edging up in the east a few minutes before 4:00 a.m. on this summer morning, and a pale light started to break through the windows in Therese's house, she was utterly drained. Stiff, her ears and throat exhausted. A happy coincidence, then, that her iPhone felt exactly the same way. The display had shown one percent battery for a while. The phone beeped, and the call cut out.

The call had lasted for many hours. At the end, the conversation had just been moving in slow circles. Until the two of them could meet in person, there was nothing more she could do, she realized.

The rest of that Wednesday, June 18, was a blur of calls, texts, and Facebook messages for Therese, who had only gotten a couple of hours of sleep. The nocturnal speculations, those castles in the air, had turned into harsh, bleak reality.

She knew she had to contact the police, because things were getting out of hand. But she had nothing other than hunches and convictions to give them. No coordinates, no confession, no proof.

She also had to keep any police involvement covert, without Martin even coming close to suspecting it, if she wanted to get further. He mustn't stop trusting her.

At the same time, she needed to keep her colleagues at Missing People abreast. She owed them that. They were a team, pulling at this tangled web from different directions. But she also needed to keep them informed for her own sake. If things heated up somehow, Martin might snap, fetch his father's shotgun, and come after her, or, god forbid, her husband, children, and friends. That was the nightmare scenario. If it happened, she needed to be able to call for help. Better safe than sorry.

Texts from Martin started flowing in before ten that morning.

M: It might be stupid for someone in my situation to have these kinds of feelings for you. To think about how pretty your lips and eyebrows are, for example. You're such a nice, bubbly girl. I've become really curious and want to get to know you. But if you don't want anything to do with me, that's just the way it is, I suppose.

Therese was not just convinced that Martin was a murderer and that Sara was deeply involved, too, but she was also increasingly certain that Martin was sick. Not in a clinical sense, necessarily; she didn't have the training to judge that. But she did have enough experience to realize his worldview was completely warped.

But then, he was under intense emotional pressure, and burdened with guilt of epic proportions. One wrong move on her part or a twisted conclusion on his, and this could end really badly.

"I called Detective Martinsson and told him Martin had his sights on me," Therese said. "And that the whole thing was unsettling. 'He's not well and he's going to come after me. I need your help!' I told him."

Martinsson told Therese he would call back later that evening, but he never did.

It is not difficult to imagine Detective Martinsson's dilemma on that June day. A private individual was poking around inside the head of a suspected murderer. She seemed to have managed to get him on the ropes using borderline interviewing techniques, or more accurately, *conversational* techniques.

Theoretically speaking, it could be helpful to the investigation. Therese had tools unavailable to him and his colleagues. In practice, she was now Martinsson's mole in an otherwise utterly stalled murder investigation where the body was still missing.

On the other hand, he couldn't instruct her to act. That would make him guilty of professional misconduct. He also, both as a fellow human and as a professional, needed to be mindful of her safety.

"What had happened did give them a new opening," Therese said. "His spontaneous reaction was 'be careful and abort.' He told me not to contact Martin, but that I could respond if he contacted me."

Martin got in touch with her again later that evening:

M: I was thinking about this thing that's important to me, which is that if something happens between us, I want to think of your children almost as mine, because I could never imagine being without children. XO

This text unsettled her. Therese was no longer sure who was holding the reins in their interactions. She was not dumb enough to miss that Martin wanted to sleep with her. That much had been made painfully clear from his many hints over the phone and via text. She had dealt with things like that before and had no problem keeping him at bay. But that a guy would, after half a day's pondering and fantasizing, be talking about building a new future with her and helping to father her children was something else entirely.

"He had implied before that he knew where I lived," Therese said. "He knew the registration number of my car, and then he started talking about my children. It felt like he had a good grasp of my life and knew a lot about me. And he kept saying he had to see me in person. Martinsson told me I couldn't meet up with him. But here Martin was, wanting to come over that same night. What was I supposed to do?"

20

THE TRUTH

In the early hours of June 19, 2014, a champagne-colored Saab 9-5 turned off the northbound E22 highway. The car set its course for the second-largest town in Västervik Municipality, Gamleby, home to just under three thousand people. Then it roared past Baggetorp with the shores of the Baltic Sea just a few hundred yards to the east.

Farther out is Ullevi Island, and if you were to follow the inlet south-eastward, you would soon see Västervik. There is a jumble of islands before you reach open water, and the next stop on an easterly trajectory is Gotland. Gamleby is very close to the coast, a bit like the Stockholm archipelago, but without the ferryboats and outrageous property prices.

Martin Törnblad was driving his mother's car. He had borrowed it under the pretext of meeting friends on Öland later in the day. At 7:35 a.m., the Swedish summer sun had already been up for hours, and Martin had been on the phone to Therese for the last forty-two minutes.

Only a smattering of people were out and about on this Thursday morning, the day before Midsummer's Eve in 2014. Martin rolled along Östra Ringvägen toward Varvsgatan and up around Garpedan Hill, the home, according to local lore, of the giant Garpe.

One of the stories about the giant says that one day, lovelorn and grumpy, he came across the humans in his search for a giantess to marry.

Employing various kinds of trickery, the humans made him eat hundreds of unproofed bits of bread dough. Later, when Garpe was dancing, the dough swelled and he burst. The dead dough-filled body of the giant continued to rise until it hardened into the rocky outcrop that looms over Gamleby. A wicked creature brought down by human cunning.

A little before eight in the morning, Martin parked the car outside Anders Lindfors's house on Loftagatan and was welcomed in by Therese.

"I had decided not to seem weak," Therese said. "Because that's never a good thing in these kinds of situations. Martin came in and took off his shoes and jacket. Then we went up to my bedroom. He wanted us to sleep together and hang out and watch a film. But I asked him what it was he wanted to tell me, the thing he didn't want to say over the phone. At first he replied that I was in Missing People and security-guard mode. I told him again I was not a police officer. That I was there for support if he wanted to tell me something."

Martin wasn't too keen on playing that part. He wanted something else—more validation. Someone who understood him.

"He told me several times that he had things to say," Therese said. "But that he didn't know if he could trust me. He was anxious and veered pretty wildly between subjects. He kept coming back to me. How I was doing and who I was privately. I could tell I wouldn't be able to push him on the topics I was interested in, so we started talking about his dad and my dad, who had something in common—they had both been diagnosed with cancer."

It was a slightly more neutral subject than her private life, but still a way to share intimate details, the way people do when they're forming a friendship. Or a romantic relationship, for that matter.

But nothing could happen between them. Not the way things stood, she stressed to Martin. She worked as a security guard for the police and was the head of Missing People Kalmar. She could not date a person who figured in a murder investigation. She couldn't build a future with a suspect. He had to understand that.

The enormous elephant in the room, the big secret, was a palpable presence between the two people on the second floor of the 1940s detached house in Gamleby. It emerged as a crucial obstacle, a road-block on Martin's road to salvation.

Therese was careful to avoid the name Göran. She talked about *the case* and said that she and her colleagues were going to keep on searching. She waited for another opening.

It was clear to her that Martin had reached his limits. The psychological pressure was so strong, it was manifesting physically. Even when he first arrived, he was more nervous than anyone she had ever met.

"He was sad, too, because his relationship with Sara was tricky," Therese said. "She would nag Martin that she didn't think he was taking care of Vince. Sara had said that she felt more like Martin's mother than his partner. I replied by saying what I thought he wanted to hear, rather than what I really thought. I told him I was there for him."

When Martin recounted the story of catching Sara with her new boyfriend, Johan, he told Therese that he had punched him. Therese immediately called him out, telling him he was a liar. She pointed to his knuckles, which were unharmed as far as she could tell. No teeth marks. No swelling, like there normally would be after you hit someone.

She was taking a chance. But it worked. Because she was right, he had punched a wall, not a person. Once again, to him, she became the mystical creature who noticed what others missed, who could see around corners and read Martin like an open book.

The one who could take away his pain.

"He thought I'd looked him up in the police database because I told him that if he had punched someone in the face, he would have been reported, but no report had been filed. I didn't answer when he asked about it; I just smiled at him."

The first rule of a skillful liar is to stick as close to the truth as possible. The second is to avoid statements that are too easily checked. The third: to let your dupe's imagination feed the lie.

"When I just smiled and didn't answer, his pupils exploded and got incredibly big. So I told him I knew he was lying. That I've seen him do it before. He wanted to know how I could tell. I replied that Sara was in the house the entire time when I was there with Agneta and the dog and he wouldn't let us in. His pupils dilated again."

He admitted she was right. When the two members of Missing People had rung the doorbell, Sara had run upstairs, covering Vince's mouth so he wouldn't give them away.

Whether the poetic turn of phrase that "the eyes are the windows to the soul" is true or not, there is scientifically proven data demonstrating that our eyes react involuntarily to both feelings and thoughts.

When we are working on solving a problem, our eyes try to take in as much light as possible to find the solution. More light, more details. If the problem is too thorny or terrifying, on the other hand, when our processing capacity is insufficient, we switch off. Our pupils contract. Our subconscious is telling us: "avoid, move on."

The apertures of our eyes open and close as ancient animalistic mechanisms are activated in our brains. The same is true in cases of overwhelming tension or emotional stress. When faced with something terrifying, dangerous, our pupils go supersized. Our bodies prepare for fight or flight and need as many impressions as possible to perceive threats and obstacles, to act.

Therese hadn't made a particular study of how to detect a lie, but she had no trouble reading Martin's reactions based on, among other things, the way his eyes changed.

"Martin asked how I could read him so well when the police had been unable to for two years. I told him we were more relaxed together, that maybe that was the reason."

And then, finally:

"He asked: 'Do you think I had something to do with Göran as well?' I said I *knew* he did, and his pupils went big again."

From time to time, over the course of their long conversation, there was a faint knocking sound from the ground floor. Likely a bird, coming to perch on the windowsill, looking for food, pecking with its beak.

Several hours had ticked by when the moment of truth finally came. Lina's Pantry down in Gamleby town center had opened a long time ago. Therese was hungry, but she knew this was not the time to interrupt the conversation. That would break the spell.

Then her phone rang. The screen of her phone was in full view; the caller's name was clearly shown: "Ulf Martinsson, Kalmar Police." The detective, the lead investigator in the Göran Lundblad case, was calling her as she sat right next to his prime suspect. He was supposed to have called her back the night before but never had.

Therese had a quick decision to make. If she picked up and Martin realized that Martinsson knew about their long conversation the night before, if he figured out that Therese was basically a double agent, it could turn everything on its head.

Martin could snap and attack her. He was, at that moment, sitting between her and the stairs. There was no easy way out. Martinsson would probably be able to hear if there were a ruckus on the other end of the line, but Martin could beat her to death many times over before the detective could get a patrol car there. In the meantime, Martin could kill her in his own good time, set fire to the house, and slowly roll away in his Saab, long before anyone could arrive to save her. On the way back to Norra Förlösa, he might stop by her house in Oskarshamn. The children might be home.

If she didn't pick up, Martin could be suspicious anyway. Even if he didn't lunge at her, the moment, their cocoon of trust, might disappear. The chance of getting a confession from him would be lost.

She just had to roll with it. She could not be seen to hesitate.

"Well now, speak of the devil," she said, holding up her phone.

She had just finished telling him a made-up story about Missing People's forensic dogs being out searching that particular day. She referred back to that, telling Martin that the police probably wanted to know whether the dogs had found anything.

"He's always calling me to check up on us. But let's ignore him, okay? He can keep his snooping to himself."

She put the phone down and looked Martin straight in the eye without blinking. Now it was just the two of them again. No police, no neighbors, no partners, and no parents. No one to lie to.

"He said, 'Maybe I know more than I should,'" Therese recounted. "He started talking about how Sara was psychologically terrorized by her dad. About how that was the reason Göran was missing. 'But what do you mean, missing? People don't just vanish, do they?' I asked. 'I know you know where he is, and I know you're involved somehow,' I told him."

Martin went in and out of the bathroom several times during their conversation. Quick visits, never longer than a minute, but long enough to lean over the sink and stare into the mirror with empty eyes and nausea gripping the back of his throat. To spit a little as saliva filled his mouth and he felt the vomit rising up. Breathe deeply, take stock, then make a decision, splash water on his face to snap out of it, then return to the conversation.

When he came back, Therese decided to push one more time.

"I can read you. Haven't you realized that?"

Martin was painted into a corner, by his own actions and everything else that had happened since August 2012. Now she had blocked his last escape routes, doggedly and stubbornly. She was not going to give up. There was nowhere for him to run. That left only two options for him: fighting or giving up.

"It just all came rushing out of him," Therese said. "He told me Sara had wanted to kill Göran on an earlier occasion with a forestry vehicle when they were out working in the woods. It was supposed to look like an accident. But she was unable to do it for emotional reasons. Instead, they planned for Martin to shoot Göran. Sara wanted it to happen at night, but Martin thought early morning would be better, because then it would just look like regular farmwork when they buried the corpse."

Simple, direct, and clear. We killed him. I killed him. Therese had succeeded. But she had yet to solve anything. All she had done was find the first loose end in a quickly unraveling tangle.

Martin contracted on the bed in a fetal position. He complained that his stomach hurt, leaning against Therese as if to draw strength. She could no longer see his pupils or facial expressions. She couldn't see his face at all, but she put her arm around his shoulders, bringing her other hand up to his head. She massaged his scalp, stroking him like a mother does with her child when he is in pain.

"Everything's going to be okay," she said. "It must have been awful carrying that around for so long."

The murder had been meticulously planned. The grave had been dug the day before. On the morning of the crime, Sara was already at Ställe Farm to let him in.

Martin took one of his father's shotguns from the weapon cabinet and loaded it with two kinds of ammunition, both 3s and 5s. One kind is bigger than the other, but he was unsure which one he would need.

Might as well load up both kinds. He was not an experienced shot; he didn't even have a hunting license.

Therese said, "He told me how he walked up to Göran, who was on his side with his face to the wall. When Martin was about five feet away, Göran turned around and was about to cry out. So he fired."

What had happened next looked nothing like films or video games; it was so much gorier. One of Göran's eyes almost flew out of its socket. And the smell; he cannot forget the horrible smell that filled the room.

Martin relived the retching, the stabbing pain in his gut. It was not the shot itself that haunted him, not the blood or even the knowledge that he had killed someone.

"It's his eyes," Martin said. "Those eyes still haunt me."

He visited the bathroom yet again. But now the floodgates had opened. All his inhibitions were gone, and getting it all out in the open seemed to make him feel better. Like cleansing himself of something foul that had been putrefying inside him for years.

"It is really hard to say how long it took Martin to confess," Therese said. "I lied to him and said Anders and another person would be home at four, even though they weren't due until six, just to have a fixed end point. I was focused on memorizing everything Martin was telling me. It turned into a long narrative that lasted for hours. It was tough for him, but he didn't cry once."

His phone rang several times while he was talking. It was Sara. But he didn't pick up.

It was midday on June 19, 2014, and Therese now knew everything. She knew everything about how Martin and Sara had discussed, planned, prepared, and then gone ahead and killed Göran Lundblad.

In that moment, she was a coconspirator. Martin had told her about pulling the trigger, about all the blood. About the tarpaulin Sara had to fetch to wrap her dead father in. About the dragging, carrying, and heaving they did to get the body down to the basement. About all the blood that had trickled out of the package, down the garage floor drain. And about how they had gotten the body into the flatbed of the pickup truck together to transport it to the grave. Just the two of them. Against the world.

Therese knew everything. And yet it was unusable in practice. Without a body—no crime.

Martin and Sara cleaned up the same day. The body had been done away with and the bedroom cleaned by 2:00 p.m. on August 30, 2012. It was clean enough that dog handler Jonas Blomgren did not notice anything amiss when he visited about a week later.

Among the first things Martin got rid of was the shotgun shell. Just to make extra sure, he drove farther inland, to the village of Trekanten, and threw the shell into a stream. He smashed Göran's cell phone with a sledgehammer and discarded the pieces in a slurry pit. He burned the dead man's passport in the wood-fired stove at his father's farm. Other private possessions ended up in a burn pile in the forest.

Since then, he and Sara had also renovated the bedroom thoroughly. Burned furniture and smaller items. Cleaned and washed the floors and walls with pint after pint of industrial cleaner. Sanded, scraped, and put up new wallpaper to get rid of the blood spatter on the walls and ceiling.

They had ripped up the vinyl floor in the room, only to find dried-in blood on the subfloor—they scrubbed that with more cleaner. They had even taken the shotgun apart, cleaned it with a strong cleaning solution, rinsed it with water, and let the weapon air-dry. The basement drain had been hosed clean.

Therese had been given a narrative and a context so detailed and precise, she couldn't help but believe all of it. But Martin could deny every word in a police interview or in front of a judge and be released the same day he was called in. No matter how convincing Therese's recounting of his confession might be, or how convinced *she* might be, it was of no use.

Maybe the forensic technicians would be able to find some evidence in the renovated bedroom, now that they knew where to look. Perhaps they would even find traces of blood matching the DNA from Göran's toothbrush.

But what would that prove? That Göran Lundblad had, at some point in the past, bled a lot in his own house. When? Determining the age of blood stains is a difficult science, easily challenged and called into question. There remained both unreasonable and reasonable doubt.

It is true that people have been convicted of crimes without a body being found, but that has only happened on the basis of more substantive evidence than the claims of a notoriously untruthful, boasting, and now jilted farm boy, made to a security guard during a secret meeting. A meeting that, moreover, occurred contrary to the express orders of a Kalmar police detective.

As much as Therese was sure she was right, that she finally knew exactly how it happened, she was well aware that there were still too many unsubstantiated aspects here. Most importantly: Where was the grave?

It was clear from their conversation that Göran was buried somewhere higher up in that drainage system that trickled down to the searched pond. One of Martin's fears was that Missing People would eventually reach the spot just by continuing to search their grid, area by area. Which meant he might as well confess. And with Therese's help, perhaps he could get off scot-free.

He might have to spend a while in jail, a few days, a week or so. But there wouldn't be any fingerprints on the plastic tarp after two years, she had assured him of that. And there was no way of telling which gun the bird shot had been fired from.

He would be a major suspect. But he would not be convicted, that much she could promise him. As long as he and Sara acted in unison, despite the wobbles in their relationship, things would work out.

"Of course," Martin said. They had agreed on what to say years ago.

There were a few loose ends left to deal with. There was the small metal chip from Göran's passport that had been left over after the rest was burned. And the boots Martin had been wearing when he fired the rifle were still in the barn back home.

"I explained to him that he had to get rid of those things," Therese said. "It all had to go. He had to go home and clear things out after we finished talking. Burn the boots. Get rid of everything."

Her ulterior motive for this piece of advice was of course to continue to build on their shared secret, to play along even more. Pretend to be useful to him. She felt it was needed. So far, he had shown that he believed every word she said. Now it was time to test that trust and demand an answer to the pivotal question.

"I told him the only thing left to do was the worst part," Therese said. "I have to know where Göran is to help you. Otherwise he will never be found, and it will never end."

She used her most neutral voice, as though what she had found out was completely natural, and only confirmed what she already knew. She was the woman who could see around corners, read everyone, who knew everything about everything. Who could solve all his problems.

There were maps in the office downstairs, she told him. She asked him to show her where the body was buried, then it would all be over. Then they could go and get something to eat.

Martin's stomach was rumbling—either from stress or hunger—so Therese took a chance that her plan might work. She made a point not to lead the way down the stairs. She didn't want a foot between her shoulder blades to be the last thing she felt in this life. Landing face-first on the floor downstairs, him on top of her, fingers tightening around her throat. Helpless.

The steps creaked under his weight. Therese pulled out her phone and managed to start recording without him noticing. The knife was still hidden under the crime novel by her bed. Martin went to the bathroom one more time as Therese walked over to the office with a determined stride. Her back was straight, her shoulders pulled back. Just one more thing. The last thing.

She found detailed maps of Norra Förlösa and spread them out on the desk. It was only at that point that she noticed what was hanging on the wall. Two gleaming green metallic ice axes, at perfect grabbing height. Serrated with tapered points and razor-sharp. As if made to hack someone to death with.

Fuck.

She heard Martin unlock the bathroom door.

21

SELF-DEFENSE

Anders Lindfors instinctively crouched low as he entered his own house. Not that it would help much, but at least it would make him a smaller target. It was early evening on June 19, 2014, and he wasn't exactly sure what awaited him inside. He moved extremely cautiously. He had no desire to be killed with one of his own guns.

He had loaded the 9 mm rounds in his guns himself. The bullets were the same model as the police standard, Gold Dot, but half a gram or so heavier. Hollow-point ammunition. Banned for use in war by The Hague Convention. The kind of bullet that expands and tears a hole of at least half an inch in diameter through whatever body it hits.

The objective: maximum stopping power, as well as controlled penetration and a decreased risk of collateral damage. A straight hit on target, in the chest, is instantly lethal, as confirmed by the Swedish Defense Research Agency.

Anders couldn't be sure that Therese had done what he had told her to do when he gave her the code to his weapon cabinet in the basement. In it, he kept a veritable arsenal. A shotgun and two revolvers of .357 and .44 caliber, respectively, both magnum. Like cannons, to an untrained hand. There were also two semiautomatic pistols, a CZ and a Glock.

The Glock was easiest to handle for someone who was scared and stressed: less of a kick, fewer stoppages, and no safety to fumble with. The security mechanism, designed to prevent misfiring, was built into the trigger. You just had to push the magazine in, pump the slide once to feed a round into the barrel, then pull the trigger. Simple. Painless. At least for the person holding the gun.

He had told her to put three rounds into the magazine, no more, for her own safety. If she was unable to eliminate the threat with three bullets, the enemy might still be alive and powerful enough to take the weapon and aim it at her. If that happened, it had better be empty.

Anders couldn't smell any lingering gunpowder scent in his house, but there were no sounds, no signs of life. The living room was empty. He called out to identify himself, then quickly popped his head into the next room and scanned it. Therese was crouched on the floor by the bed with the Glock in her hands.

"It's just me," he said. "Put the gun down."

When Therese finally put the gun down, she let out a deep and shaky breath. Several hours had passed since Martin had confessed to the murder of Göran Lundblad and gone downstairs with Therese to point out the grave on a map.

When faced with the potential murder weapons, the ice axes on the wall, Therese had decided to deliberately draw attention to them when Martin came out of the bathroom. That seemed a safer option than him starting to furtively contemplate what he could do with them.

Her cell phone was lying screen-side down on the nightstand, recording. There was always a risk of Martin wanting to check it. She had to make sure his focus remained on something else. He had to stay inside his bubble of fantasies, in the world where everything would work out, so long as he tells Therese everything.

Next to the ice axes was an archery bow and an enlarged photograph of the Troll Wall, a 5,500-foot rock face in the Trolltindene massif in Norway, every climber's fever dream, the kind of thing Anders Lindfors got up to in his spare time. Adventures.

When Martin came into the room, she pointed at the axes and started talking.

> *Therese: Yeah, so those are ice axes. Because he has . . . I think he might even have won the ice climbing national championships . . .*
>
> *Martin: That's his?*
>
> *T: It's pretty cool.*
>
> *M: It's heavy.*
>
> *T: Mm. What is he . . . One of fourteen Swedes to have scaled the Troll Wall, I think. And he did one of the hardest routes too. You'd almost have to be an idiot to go to places like that to climb.*

Therese chitchatted as casually as she was able. The message: We are in this together. We are on the same side.

She spread the maps open on the desk, as far away from the ice axes and compound bow as possible. Side by side, they leaned over the map and pointed, finding their way from the slightly larger town of Läckeby to Norra Förlösa, the Törnblad farm, and then the road where he had stopped his tractor and they'd had their first long talk, not even a month ago. But at first, they had a hard time picking their way through the patchwork of properties that had been sold, subdivided, and leased over the years.

Martin also had his own names for the landmarks, different from the ones on the map. They tried digital maps on his phone, but the screen was too small and it was difficult to zoom in.

So they started over with the paper maps, following the road from the slurry pit, the barn, and on toward Skyttelund. Once Martin understood the compass directions, he finally located the spot.

M: *The ditch is there.*

T: *The ditch is there. Is there water in it?*

M: *Well. I think so.*

T: *Yes.*

M: *And then over there . . .*

T: *Yes.*

M: *That's the boundary.*

T: *Yes.*

M: *And this is just a fence . . . like barbed wire.*

T: *Okay.*

M: *But that barbed wire is up against a bunch of . . . trees and rocks and whatever . . .*

T: *Over there it's like . . . Yeah . . .*

M: *So it's fifteen to twenty yards out.*

T: *And how deep did you say?*

M: *Yes. Five . . . maybe six and a half feet.*

It was done. The final piece of the puzzle, just like that. And a depth as well. Five or six and a half feet down. All the straws Therese had been reaching for, cajoling loose, and collecting over the past few months now formed a respectable pile. Enough to build a straw man. One wearing a prison jumpsuit.

Martin had pointed out a spot on his own father's land, at the tip of the triangular field. Next to it, the map read *Skyttelund*. The tip of his finger was resting on the map, some distance from the boundary line marking the next property, at a right angle from where an overgrown stone wall met barbed wire. More precisely: 56 degrees, 46 minutes, and 5.5 seconds north and 16 degrees, 6 minutes, and 30.5 seconds east.

"That's when I circled the spot on my map," Therese said. "Martin wanted to know why; I told him it was for me. I said we had dogs out that very day and that they were on their way to that field. Martin retorted that it was lucky he had told me today, because maybe he would have been caught regardless."

It should be okay for Missing People to go to the location and start digging, Martin said. But they had to hold off a little longer, he insisted. One or two weeks, because the grass was tall over there at the moment. His dad had to have a chance to harvest it. It was worth money.

In this situation, it is difficult to understand how Martin, who had kept silent for over a year and a half, had suddenly gotten the idea that it was okay to reveal, so openly and naively, exactly where he had buried the victim of the murder he had committed. Corpus delicti. Given what he had said about firing the killing shot and how they had gone about covering their tracks, Martin had just put the final nail in his own coffin, and very likely in Sara's too.

How could anyone be so stupid?

But that would be the wrong question to ask, as anyone able to put themselves in Martin's shoes must realize. He seemed, under the influence of sustained wheedling, to have decided to completely trust one person with the most important secret he had ever kept. He had tricked himself into believing that he could get away with it, now that Therese was on his side.

If, and only if, what he said was true, of course—totally, unambiguously true—Therese could kick up a fuss and point to the recording. She could recount Martin's story down to the smallest detail and get Missing People colleagues, the police, diggers, and everyone she could think of to this small field in the middle of nowhere.

But if she does all that, and it all turns out to be another one of Martin's delusions, if all they find in the ground is rocks and dirt, if everything is in order in the bedroom at Ställe Farm, sanded, painted, neat, and blood-free, then she is finished. Both as a professional and as a person. Her credibility will be shot, on a level with Martin's.

But she could hear his stomach rumbling and twisting, not only from hunger, but from fear. She was sure of it. His entire body language, his pupillary responses, his constant bathroom visits, the whimpering in her arms—he seemed to be a man on the edge of a nervous breakdown. And what he had told her about his relationship and his feelings for her. It must all be true. Or was it really all an act?

Criminologist Leif G. W. Persson talks about three main rules for a successful murder investigation. They are quite simple:

1. Go with it.
2. Nothing happens by chance.
3. Don't complicate things.

Therese had complicated things, for both herself and others, quite severely. But considering the results so far, she thought it might well have been worth it.

She had ignored chance since the first moment she became involved in the Göran Lundblad case. There had been too many strange coincidences she could not ignore, like the purported threats that he only received when Sara was in Stigtomta. The termination notice for Mats

Råberg's lease, which hadn't turned up until after Göran's disappearance. The cadaver molecules in the pond. It all had to mean something.

Sheer instinct told her how it had happened, from conversations with witnesses and residents, supported by Sara's and Martin's odd behavior, as well as the fact that the police had also settled on the two of them as their main suspects based on experience alone.

Instinct and gut feeling are not, as we are well aware, enough, but now she had a detailed confession that was coherent and fit into the theories that had already been put forward regarding the course of events. Given this, the time had come to stop vacillating. Go with it. And make sure that body gets dug up.

But first: she had to get out of the house. She had to get rid of Martin as quickly as possible. This was far too big for her to handle on her own.

"Hey. Let's get out of here," she said. "We need something to eat."

Lina's Pantry was a perfectly ordinary lunch café in the middle of Gamleby town center, next to the supermarket. The daily specials were things like beef stew or house-made stuffed cabbage, and there was always a fish of the day. Salad, bread, and coffee were included, and regulars always got a discount.

The Gamleby town center had everything the average person would need. In addition to the supermarket, there was a liquor store, clothing retailer, a pizzeria, the pharmacy, a store for electrical supplies, and a corner store.

No one recognized Martin, who was sitting alone at one of the tables with a black coffee and an untouched cheese sandwich in front of him, staring vacantly at the passersby. Next to him was a crumb-covered plate with the remains of a curry chicken salad baguette and a half-empty cup of cold cappuccino. Therese was in the bathroom.

The chilling story he had told her was just starting to sink in. Her fear was creeping up again, now that her curiosity had been satisfied. During the ride from the house to the town center, no more than about a mile, Martin had changed.

"The mood was almost jolly in the car when we set off," Therese said. "He seemed happy about having told me, about us 'getting through this together.' He had already found a farm he thought we should live on and where we would raise our children. He thought I would make a great mother for Vince."

This was hardly what she had expected after the long hours of self-pity and anxiety. He had somehow shoved down all the bad feelings and was now playing the role of first lover, a real man. True, she had only met him a handful of times, but they had talked for over twenty-four hours in all. She should have had a decent sense for how he worked by now, but she could not figure out how or why his mood had changed so abruptly.

When they got to the café, he changed the subject and started boasting. He told her how inept the police had been, bringing him and Sara in for questioning but failing to see through them. He also told her he had a police contact, a mole, who had helped him acquire a couple of handguns, three pistols. Ready to use, stashed away back home on the farm. For self-defense. He had fired them several times and knew they worked.

A confabulation? Maybe he did in fact have a gun. Was it in his car? Was it on his person right now? Nothing seemed entirely inconceivable with this man who seemed comfortable talking about things like this here, surrounded by regular people doing their week-end shopping.

"Before we headed downtown, I felt like I had the upper hand, because he was in such a terrible state," Therese said. "But then his mood changed, and things started to feel awfully unpleasant. So I went to the bathroom and called Marie-Louice, asking her to contact Anders so he could go get my family somewhere safe straight away. It needed to happen now, not later."

Anders was at work at the nuclear plant that day and couldn't use his cell phone. Instead, Marie-Louice had to chase down central operations, who in turn had to chase him down via radio. It was a process that took a while, but at least it had been set in motion.

Therese went to the bathroom three times in just a short while. It would be suspicious in most contexts, but not compared to Martin's many visits back at the house. Therese's final call from the stall was to her husband, Richard. She had already tried him several times without getting through.

"I told him to just listen to me and trust me. He was to take the children someplace safe and stay there until the police or I called. I didn't want Martin to pass by my house with my family in it. Richard was livid, but that was going to have to wait."

Back at the table, the boasting continued. Martin, who had been in such a bad state before, was now beating his chest over what he had done and how dangerous he was.

"It was like he was expecting a medal," Therese said. "Like, we're so damn clever and no one can catch us. He asked what I thought about him now, now that I knew everything. I was quiet for a bit. I couldn't tell him he was an idiot, even though that was my first thought. Then I said 'crazy.' But that there's good crazy and bad crazy. And that I supposed women were always drawn to dangerous men."

In a way, his phone saved the situation. More specifically: Sara did, by continually trying to reach Martin. In just over ten minutes, she called him seven times; he didn't answer. But the repeated calls made him restless, stressed, defensive again.

Therese stood up.

"Anders is going to be back any minute; you have to leave, like I told you. And I promised the guys at the station I would bring a Midsummer cake to work. I have to bake. Let's go."

In the car, Martin went on and on about tarps. He wouldn't stop talking; he wanted them to go to the nearest hardware store so he could show her exactly what kind of tarp he and Sara had wrapped Göran in. Could the body have decomposed, or would it still be there? Therese refused to go to the store with him. It was time to break up this powwow.

They drove past a motorcycle covered in a tarp. No, not that kind. He had used a green one. Thinner. When Therese turned down the driveway to Anders's house, it had started raining. Heavy, scattered drops.

She was not about to turn her back on Martin, and she was not about to go back inside the house. Not without some kind of backup. Not while he was still there—acting unpredictably, odd. Not a chance.

Now that the adrenaline, the curiosity, the energy of his confession had faded, only the surreal realization remained: Martin was a murderer who had shot a defenseless old man in the head. He had dragged the dead body downstairs, through the woods, and out into the middle of a field to bury it.

This man should be locked up, not walking around here in Anders's backyard. He was talking about guns in the café, three of them. Had he brought any of them with him? Were they in his car?

"That's the kind of tarp it was. Thin and flimsy, that's why it leaked so much," he said, pointing at a tarp in Anders's yard. It was a cheap, green plastic tarpaulin with a visible weave. He would be fine then, Therese assured him. That would hardly have been enough to protect the body. It would have had time to decompose quite a bit since Göran's death.

She ducked in under the eaves of the garage. Martin walked over to her and moved in for a hug. A kiss. Like a teenager on his first date, after the movie. Awkward.

"No, we can't do things like that in public," she replied, smiling carefully while turning away.

She was back in her role, the security guard, the head of Missing People. The official Therese.

"What if the neighbors saw us? It'll have to wait."

As they stood side by side next to the garage, Martin reached out a hand and patted her stomach. Pleadingly. Maybe, someday, they'll have a baby together?

Enough is enough.

"Oh shit! I forgot the strawberries," Therese said. "I have to go to the store. And Anders will be here any minute. I told you. You have to leave. Just do what we agreed. And I'll see you later."

She set off toward her car. Her mind was a blank as she covered the short distance from the garage to her black BMW. She opened the door and climbed in. She looked over at Martin and smiled as she started the engine, then she pulled out of the driveway.

Right away, she noticed that he was tailing her. Out onto the road, then southward toward Gamleby, past the veterinarian by the harbor. She took quick glances in the rearview mirror, hoping he wouldn't notice her watching. When she turned off toward the town center, she watched as the Saab continued on, going past her in the direction of Kalmar.

"But did he go home? How far did he go? I had no way of knowing. He might have stopped, turned around. Gone back to the house to lie in wait for me there," Therese said.

At this point, she could simply drive away, head straight to the nearest police station, sound the alarm, shout, scream, call. But no.

"All I could think about were the damn strawberries. I really did go to the shops. Paid for them in a daze, I think, and then back out to my car."

There, in the parking lot, with a pint of strawberries in a flimsy plastic bag on the passenger seat, everything finally sank in. What had really just happened. And what she had managed to pull off.

"I sat in my car for quite a while, just staring at the rain beating against the windshield," she said. "It all washed over me at once. A million thoughts."

Her stunned epiphany couldn't have lasted more than a few minutes before she started the engine. Her priorities were clear in her mind: make sure her family was safe, avoid continued contact with Martin, and find a safe place for herself. Then she must let the police know.

The first three points could be ticked off quickly, once she finally got through to Anders. He had been summoned via radio, checked his phone, and started making his way home. His assessment was that his colleague Therese was in a self-defense situation. Simply put, self-defense is your legal right to defend yourself using the same level of violence as the person attacking you. Fists against fists, knife against knife. If you are strongly emotionally affected and have reason to be in a great state of fear, an added emphasis—the official term is *self-defense in excess*—applied. In such situations, you can use more violence, and fight back to eliminate the threat against your person. Permanently.

Anders had given Therese the code to his weapon cabinet in the basement. It contained enough firepower to knock out a stampeding herd of cattle.

On her way back to the house, she double-checked that her husband and children were safe before calling Martin again, despite having promised herself she wouldn't. But she had to be sure.

Where was he? She made him describe his surroundings and was persuaded, in part, because she could hear the sound of the moving car over the phone. She hung up with Martin, then it was time to tackle the most difficult call: the police. She could now give them all the puzzle pieces they would need to conclude an open murder investigation. If, that is, they believed her.

None of her contacts were on duty, she was told. They were all out of the office until after the Midsummer holiday. Detective Martinsson was off as well, the on-call officer informed her when she got through to the central switchboard in Kalmar.

"I told him they were probably going to have to postpone their time off for a bit," Therese said. "Then I told him what I had to say. The on-call officer promised to make sure to get hold of Martinsson."

It took him fifteen minutes. At exactly 4:58 p.m. on Thursday, June 19, 2014, Therese made phone contact with Lead Investigator Martinsson.

His report, typed up the same night, summarized the call:

> Therese told me that she met with Martin Törnblad privately for a number of hours today in a house in Gamleby to which he had driven from Kalmar. During their long conversation, Martin told her that he killed Göran Lundblad by shooting him.
>
> Therese stated that Martin was upset as he recounted how both he and Sara spent several months during 2012 planning to kill Göran Lundblad. A few days before the murder, they had planned for Sara to run Göran over.
>
> This didn't happen because Sara was unable to go through with it. Instead, Martin fetched a rifle from his father's weapon cabinet.
>
> With that weapon, Martin then shot Göran in his bed. He and Sara then wrapped the body in a tarpaulin together and buried it in a hole they had dug with a wheel loader.
>
> The hole is supposedly on Göran Lundblad's land. Therese claimed to have a map showing the location of Göran's body.

It took Ulf Martinsson just over half an hour to cover the most salient points, as well as to assess and process the information. The broad strokes of the Göran Lundblad case were already clear to him. What the woman from Missing People was telling him fit in neatly with his own existing theories. He came to the simple conclusion that he needn't complicate things unnecessarily. Just go with it.

Sara and Martin were already under formal suspicion, a decision dating back to 2012, and now he had an identified murder scene, as well as directions to where the body, corpus delicti, was buried.

Unless Therese had suddenly lost her mind. After all, something like this had never happened before in Sweden, that some sort of private investigator had cracked a murder case.

He ordered Therese to cease all contact with Martin, to not answer if he calls, to lock her doors and windows, and to sit tight. She could expect to be interviewed by the police shortly.

At 5:30 p.m., Martinsson made the formal decision to bring Martin Törnblad in for questioning. He would be found at one of three addresses, which he gave to the on-call commander. A patrol would be released from regular duty and sent to collect the young man. By force, if necessary. And quickly, before he had a chance to destroy anything else.

22

CIRCUMSTANTIAL EVIDENCE

A patrol car was cruising through Norra Förlösa at a leisurely pace. It would be impossible to miss for anyone who was still up and about and not yet curled up on the couch after dinner.

Police vehicle 9420, carrying Police Sergeant Möller and Police Constables Corlin and Jonasson, had been given three addresses where the wanted man, Martin Törnblad, twenty-three, might be found. They had already been to the first, Ställe Farm, but there was no one there. Now, as they drove up toward the Törnblad farm, they spotted a Saab 9-5 parked in the middle of the yard, the exact vehicle they had been told he was currently using.

The charge was murder, but the three officers in the car had not been sent out to apprehend an armed and dangerous madman who could be expected to put up a fight or attack them. If that had been the case, they would have turned up in force. More cars, weapons at the ready. Bulletproof vests, maybe K9 units. They would have staked out the location from a distance, waited for the right moment, and tried to get through to the suspect via a police negotiator, even used force if gentler methods had failed.

No one in patrol car 9420 brandished their weapon or readied their pepper spray. If the information they had been given was correct, this was a routine pickup. A legally enforceable measure, yes; the man would have to get in the car with them and that was final. If they found him, he would end up in the backseat. But pickups like this one were rarely contentious.

At around 6:00 p.m. on June 19, Constable Corlin checked the barn. He found a woman milking cows. Martin was around, she said, but she didn't know exactly where. The farm consisted of a number of buildings, and people did not keep track of each other during the workday.

Corlin took a look around the rest of the barn. Empty.

When he came back outside, his colleague Möller was speaking to a man who appeared to be the owner of the farm, Åke Törnblad. That very moment, the heavens opened up. Corlin quickly strode over to the patrol car to fetch his jacket. At that point, someone came jogging across the farmyard in the rain.

Not a good sign, as every police officer knows. People running in the presence of the police could be trying to hide things, destroy something important, escape. But not this one. This man was running toward them.

Excerpt from Police Constable Andreas Corlin's report:

> The person, a young man, seemed to match the description we had been given for Martin Törnblad. He went over to stand next to the man I assumed was his father.
>
> I went over to the younger man who had come running and asked him whether he was Martin; he said yes.
>
> I asked to see his ID, which he showed me. Once we had ascertained that this was the person we were looking for, we explained to him that he was coming with us to the police station for questioning.

In the car, Martin Törnblad asked what this was about; we explained again that he was going to be questioned and that we didn't know exactly what it was regarding, but that the investigators would explain everything to him.

Martin Törnblad was put in the back of the patrol car with a police officer next to him. No handcuffs, no fuss, although the doors to the car could not be opened from the inside.

Through the windows, he watched as the familiar scenes of his hometown glided past. Off toward Ställe Farm, turning right at Mats Råberg's farm, left in Melby, down the gravel road toward Mosekrog, and then the E22 highway south for twelve miles or so.

He had been brought in for questioning before. It had always gone well, and he had been allowed to return home. On this day, he showed no particular signs of concern about having his Midsummer ruined. Therese had told him this could happen. He might have to spend some time in prison, but surely only a couple of days.

He was hungry, though, and repeatedly asked for a sandwich during the ride. Maybe he should have eaten that cheese sandwich in Gamleby this morning after all.

To the police officers, their passenger seemed strangely unperturbed at being picked up. He clearly didn't grasp that it was game over for him, that he could write this Midsummer weekend off altogether, along with a great many subsequent holidays. Or perhaps he believed in miracles.

By 6:55 p.m., Martin had been unloaded at the Kalmar Police Station and placed in an interview room along with violent-crime detectives Marcus Tinnert and Ulf Einarsson, both of whom had been briefed on the situation by their colleague Martinsson.

It was a so-called 23:6 interview. The numbers refer to the Swedish Code of Judicial Procedure, chapter 23, section 6, which states that "anyone who is reasonably likely to possess information relevant to the inquiry" may be interviewed.

He was informed of what he was suspected of. "Murder or manslaughter in Kalmar in late 2012 of Göran Lundblad." But he did not possess any information relevant to the inquiry, he told them. Or any other inquiry, for that matter. He had already told them everything he knew, he insisted. And he stuck to that statement. He told them nothing.

Marcus Tinnert and his colleagues wrapped up the preliminary interview thirty minutes later without any boastful confessions, and Martin was taken away to a cell. Meanwhile, two police officers were stepping out of their car one hundred miles farther north, on Loftagatan in Gamleby.

Martin emptied his pockets, handing over his cell phone, driver's license, debit card, and 1,500 kronor (180 dollars) in cash. The custody staff always relieved detainees of loose items, as well as belts and shoelaces, to prevent suicides in the cells.

By the time the metal door shut behind Martin, police officers Ingrid Kristoffersson and Lena Ingesson had entered the house on Loftagatan and introduced themselves to Therese Tang and Anders Lindfors. They really only needed to speak to Therese.

Interviews are best conducted in a controlled environment without potentially distracting secondary characters, who should, in fact, perhaps be questioned about various things themselves. But everything about this story was exceptional. They could hardly kick the owner out of his own house, and time was short. This was not the time to be fastidious.

It took the police officers an hour and twenty minutes to navigate through the main points of Therese's narrative and get from her what they needed to take back to the detective in charge. As they had no detailed knowledge of the people, locations, or events, Therese had to go back and explain things several times over and disentangle the chronology, especially since she herself had been jumping back and forth between things she and Martin had talked about in the past few days.

This is a common phenomenon in witness statements, especially if the information is fresh and has not yet been processed by the witness, tidied up in their mind. All the information rises to the top of the person's awareness. Everything is felt to be of equal importance. They have to get everything out. Immediately.

But the fresher a statement is, the better, from a strictly legal point of view. The witness will have had less opportunity to adapt events to his or her own preconceived notions or experience, and the statement will be more credible in a court of law.

The two police officers rarely intervened during their interview with Therese. They mostly nodded in understanding and asked questions only when something seemed incoherent.

The result of the interview, also conducted in accordance with the Code of Judicial Proceedings 23:6, was, in the end, chillingly clear. Martin had given a detailed account of how he had shot Göran, something a pathologist could easily verify if the body were recovered in a relatively decent state.

He had also identified the supposed location of the body with remarkable precision. With the help of Google Maps, Therese found the longitude and latitude for the police officers. She handed over the paper map where she had marked the spot. Now the machinery of justice could start grinding away in earnest.

Just before 9:00 p.m., on the night before Midsummer's Eve, the two police officers thanked Therese and Anders Lindfors for speaking with them and left. They took Therese's cell phone with the recording of Martin's confession with them.

In Kalmar, the latest developments in the Göran Lundblad case had been recounted to the prosecutor on call, Anna Landner, who had just made the decision to charge Martin. Half an hour before midnight, when the results of Therese's interview had come in and been evaluated, the same prosecutor decided to also charge Sara in her absence. The story was so detailed and coherent that it could be considered sufficient evidence to bring a charge.

Several paths were open to the investigators and prosecutors now. They could choose to not detain the suspects and to attempt first to confirm the veracity of the purported confession by digging in the field. Or they could ask for a warrant to search Ställe Farm and conduct a crime-scene investigation. If they found something first, they could detain the alleged suspects afterward.

On the other hand, none of those measures could reasonably be taken without the main suspects finding out. That meant running the risk of them absconding, harming themselves or others, or undermining the investigation in some other way, before the police had found what they needed.

It would be safer, then, to round them up and see if their interviews led anywhere, perhaps even to full or partial confessions.

During the night, the Södermanland police were informed that Sara needed to be brought in as soon as possible. Probable address: Tängsta Farm in Stigtomta, outside Nyköping. The prosecutor also granted a formal warrant for searching Tängsta and Ställe Farm, as well as the suspects themselves.

And thus, the clock started ticking. Loudly. The arrest of alleged offenders is a temporary measure while awaiting a free and impartial hearing in court. People are locked up in order to allow the police to investigate things at their own pace, to keep suspects from leaving the country to evade a future hearing and potential punishment, or to prevent new crimes from being committed. The reasons for detention are defined as "risk of tampering with evidence, risk of absconding, and risk of continued criminal activity."

In the Swedish legal system, the police can normally detain you as a suspect for six hours. After that time, a prosecutor needs to assess the evidentiary situation. If things are looking bleak for you, you can be formally charged, which allows investigators an extra seventy-two hours to strengthen the case or dismiss it. They may, for example, want to interview people before you have had a chance to persuade them to provide an alibi. Or search for blood in the room where you stand accused of having shot someone, before you or anyone else has a chance to clean up more.

When the seventy-two hours are up, the prosecutor has to either release you or, if the case against you is strong, arrest you. Once that happens, a court has another twenty-four hours to hold a hearing, where you will have the assistance of a lawyer to counter the claims of the prosecutor, unless, of course, you prefer to handle it yourself.

In other words, the Kalmar police had around one hundred hours, just under four days, over the Midsummer weekend to solve this case. They must find something to confirm the gory charges or they would have to open the cell doors, tail between their legs, and inform Martin and Sara that they have a right to apply for damages for unlawful detention. The police could even be charged with misconduct for believing the woman from Missing People so easily.

Just before 10:00 p.m. on the same night that Martin was brought in for questioning, a police patrol arrived at the alleged murder scene, Ställe Farm. They used Martin's keys to unlock the doors, then they had the locks changed and sealed the house tight.

The basement door facing the road was cordoned off with police tape and a yellow and red sign: "Closed in accordance with Code of Judicial Procedure 27:15. Do not enter."

The intention was to secure the scene until forensic technicians could get to it with their solutions, brushes, hammers, chisels, cadaver dogs, and whatever else they needed to start verifying the confession.

For those who like to keep an open mind, the case was by no means closed when the sun rose on Midsummer's Eve and a police patrol up in Södermanland prepared to go pick up Sara.

Let us suppose a blood-spattered murder scene was found at Ställe Farm, but no buried corpse turned up—the confession would then be considered false, at least in part. Under those circumstances, no one would likely be convicted, not after two years of rumors, lies, and accusations, during which various witnesses' own conclusions had become entrenched.

The body of the crime, the corpus delicti, was still missing.

Or vice versa. What if the missing multimillionaire was found exactly where Therese said Martin had pointed on the map, but there is no proven murder scene? What if the bedroom turned out to be spotless?

That would open several possible routes, all equally disagreeable. The best-case scenario would be, of course, that both Martin and Sara were convicted. But how could their involvement be proven without blood spatter and damage inside the house?

Bird shot in the body would be a significant piece of circumstantial proof, as it would correlate with Martin's confession to Therese. That the body was buried locally, on the Törnblads' land even, would be fantastically awkward in and of itself. But theoretically speaking, Göran could have shot himself. The rifle in his mouth, his thumb on the trigger. Such things had certainly happened before in these parts, as everyone knew. The daughter and her boyfriend could have come across the body somewhere in the woods. They'd panicked and buried it. Implausible. But beyond a reasonable doubt?

Sara could, furthermore, hardly be implicated in a crime based on a secondhand accusation alone. Conspiratorially speaking, the main witness, Therese, could be involved herself. She said she had playacted with Martin to get him to open up. But could they have been playacting together? Could they have planned the confession to get their hands on the millions by as-yet-unknown means?

That would certainly be complicating things unnecessarily, true. But Sara could not be convicted without some kind of technical evidence, which meant Martin would stand to gain nothing by falsifying the confession. Not as things seemed to stand at first glance, anyway. But what do we really know about our fellow humans or their fantasies?

As dawn broke on Midsummer's Eve, almost all the balls were up in the air. It was time to start collecting them.

According to the patrol's own notes, Sara Lundblad was picked up at 12:41 p.m. on Midsummer's Eve by Police Constables Jimmy Gustmark and Per-Emil Engström. She left her son, Vince, with her neighbors for the time being.

Half an hour later, she was put in cell number 12 in the Nyköping custody suite to await transfer to Kalmar. Her car, the Ford Ranger her father's body was transported in according to Martin, was seized for forensic examination.

After almost two years, the chances of finding blood, or any other evidence, in the flatbed were small, but the Murder Bible checklist must be followed. Every chance of finding something to strengthen the case must be seized.

About an hour before lunchtime on Midsummer's Day, a demolition crew arrived at Ställe Farm in Norra Förlösa. To the untrained eye, they must have looked odd. They wore thin white overalls and carried aluminum toolboxes into the main house. Several cars were parked outside Göran Lundblad's machine shed. The forensic technicians had also arrived, led by Anders Elmqvist. The demo crew intended to utterly disassemble the relatively recently renovated dining room, so that the forensic technicians could finally analyze the purported scene of the crime.

If this tragic drama unfolded exactly the way Martin had claimed in his confession, there must be evidence to find at Ställe Farm. Blood tends to linger. Not just in the nightmares of murderers, but on objects, walls, ceilings. Ställe Farm was the police's best chance.

A bouquet of purple cloth flowers hung upside down from the dining room ceiling when the police officers entered. There were three small pictures on the wall and a wall sconce of frosted glass. A vacuum cleaner was sitting on the floor. Two dying plants wilted in the window.

The police cleared the room, boarded up the windows, and turned on an ultraviolet light. On the west wall, a clearly visible stain, approximately a foot in diameter, emerged, though it was covered by a layer of wallpaper. A first box could be checked: this really was a bedroom, or at least it was before it was redone. The stain consisted of sweat and grease from the head of whoever it was who used to sleep here. No one had been able to remove that. The question was whether the murderers had missed anything else.

The technicians dug deeper. There was no visible blood, though they discovered some darker patches behind the wallpaper. As a presumptive test, the police technicians coated those spots with leucomalachite green, a solution that turns blood stains fluorescent green under special lighting. To no avail.

If a couple of amateurs had cleaned this room after murdering someone with a shotgun, and if they had used as many cleaning products as they could think of—water, soap, chlorine, or something even heavier duty—they had probably succeeded in scrubbing any visible surface clean. But blood was also likely to have had time to seep into all kinds of places, into the subfloor and other nooks and crannies.

It was an old house. The interior walls were not covered in plaster or plywood, but Treetex, a porous, airy material that provides excellent insulation. Treetex walls are smooth and highly suitable for wallpapering, but they are also highly flammable and therefore rarely used in newer buildings. Furthermore, and more importantly in this context, a Treetex board will absorb moisture like a sponge.

The last chance of finding enough blood to match it with the DNA of presumed murder victim Göran Lundblad lay, therefore, in tearing up the floor to reach the possibly drenched parts of the Treetex that would have come off the walls before the floor was built.

To the investigators, it looked a bit odd that only one section of the floor had been smoothed down. Consequently, the police started breaking off pieces of Masonite board around the spackled surface.

At that point, a visitor arrived.

Excerpt from report:

> At this stage, a dog handler from the Skåne police arrives with a blood-detection dog.
>
> The dog is let into the room to search for traces of blood. The dog immediately indicates on the floor by the broken-off piece of Masonite board.
>
> The dog indicates only in this spot. The board is removed to determine whether it is the floor or the Masonite board that makes the dog indicate.
>
> The dog is asked to search again.
>
> The dog now indicates by the hole where the board was removed instead.

The dog didn't indicate anywhere else in the house. When the broken-off piece of Masonite board was brushed with leucomalachite green, the hoped-for fluorescent light finally appeared. Blood. Blood in a location where someone seemed to have done their best to conceal it.

There were traces of dried-in cleaner. Signs of tool use, possibly pincers, on the Masonite board, probably made by chipping away a bloody floorboard piece by piece. Then the entire surface had been spackled over.

Further down into the floor, the traces became more abundant. Diluted blood had seeped in under the floorboards and been absorbed by the Treetex board, leaving behind a large dark-red, nearly black, stain, running about twelve inches from the radiator along the floor.

OBTI (a rapid screening test) confirmed that it was human blood, and a considerable amount of it. Another box could be checked. Therese's story was looking increasingly credible.

Within a few weeks, the Swedish National Forensic Center in Linköping would confirm, with the highest level of probability, +4, that what had seeped into the wall was indeed Göran Lundblad's blood, mixed with a cleaning agent. Already, even now in June, well before any DNA results came back, there was enough compromising material to easily extend those one hundred hours of respite.

As the technicians in their white suits wrapped things up in the demolished, or at least severely stripped-down, bedroom, the main events of the past few days had already become widely known. First and foremost, no one in the area could have missed the police tape cordoning off Ställe Farm.

Martin and Sara had also been appointed public defense counsels to accompany them during police interviews. Defense lawyers are routinely appointed by district and county courts and when they are, those appointments are made public. The media checks this information from the county courts daily to glean the identities of alleged offenders. Beyond all that, a prosecutor's request to have someone arrested is almost always public news.

From national newspaper *Dagens Nyheter*'s website on the afternoon of June 21, 2014:

> A man born 1991 and a woman born 1988 have been charged with the murder of the sixty-two-year-old. Both hail from Kalmar and were charged on good grounds on Thursday, Robin Simonsson from the Swedish Prosecution Authority's press office informs *Dagens Nyheter*.

The police also told the media that they had a recorded confession and that Missing People was involved. Therese refused to say a word when asked about it by journalists, referring to a police request for secrecy.

During the first few days, the media was cautious about revealing details about the two suspects. It was not made clear that the alleged offenders were Göran's own daughter and her partner; they were only identified as "a young couple," "both without prior convictions and both known to the sixty-two-year-old, as his close family members."

On first inspection, the police found no signs of a grave in the identified location. No outline of a hole, no mound like in cemeteries after a funeral.

They did note that the bucket of Åke Törnblad's wheel loader was about eight feet wide, well-suited for grave digging. With only a couple of scoops, you would have a hole of six feet, the standard depth for burial. Under nearly six and a half feet of soil, gravel, and loam, a body could easily be buried somewhere down there. But if so, then there should have been soil left over after the hole got filled in, and there should also be color striations in the ground.

But Martin could have topped it up with fresh soil, driven back and forth a couple of times, and smoothed the mound out with the bucket. Then he might have run a plow over it, going back and forth, this way and that, smoothing it over again and again during those late-August days back in 2012.

Since then, the field had been harrowed, cultivated, harvested, and then harrowed again several times. Even if Martin had given the correct location and the grave was here, about twenty-five yards in from the barbed wire, it was something of a mission to move all that soil, especially since it had to be done carefully, more archaeological dig than construction site. Every stone had to be brushed out of the ground, and the soil should preferably be sifted. After all, there could be something in it, however small and insignificant, to tie a perpetrator to the scene.

Given that thirty-five cubic feet of soil weighs something like 2,600 pounds, close to five and a half tons of it would need to be shifted by this method just to examine an area the size of a grave. Suppose the location was less precise; then the police might need to cover an area four times that size. The amount of earth they would need to move would be closer to twenty-two tons.

If the only objective were to identify the grave and not bother to sift the soil, the task would become much easier. A team of archaeologists from the closest university could, with the aid of a skilled machinist, peel back the topsoil from half the field in under two days.

Underneath, at a depth of maybe sixteen to twenty inches, the hardpan begins. That is the unplowed part of the uppermost layer of soil, which is normally lighter than the topsoil. Even an untrained eye can normally see if anyone has been rooting around in it, since that would cause the humus-rich topsoil to mix into the hardpan like a dark ripple.

But in this case, the police decided to choose a different method. A few days into July, something that looked like a lawn mower rolled over the freshly mown meadow near Skyttelund Farm. The man who was pushing the handles wore a yellow hi-vis vest. The man, Lars Winroth, worked at the Swedish National Heritage Board, and his mower-like device was a GeoRadar.

It is an invaluable machine for anyone examining, for example, historical battlefields. The GeoRadar is moved over the area in question, sending signals into the ground that bounce back, which are then interpreted. If there is a sword, a coin, or even a body in the ground, it shows up on a screen. The result is a simplified X-ray image of the terrain, a cross section of the different layers of soil and anything contained in them.

Lars Winroth was not alone. A whole gaggle of police officers was watching him curiously. They had measured out an area of twenty-seven by twenty-seven yards for him to examine with the machine. A cadaver dog had already sniffed around but given no indication whatsoever. Hardly surprising. The soil would have been packed tightly around the body by now.

The images from the GeoRadar were not easily interpreted. They looked like old black-and-white photographs of the Milky Way, a jumble of lights against a black background. But two interesting areas emerged right next to one another, both in the area Martin Törnblad had pointed out. Closer examination revealed that one was a cluster of stones, moraine, and glacial debris from the most recent ice age. The second area was smaller, and the cross section showed that all the layers of soil had been broken through here not too long ago.

Next to it, no more than a few yards away, was a cement drainage pipe. The drainage system that began here stretched out to the southwest, in the direction of the forest, on toward Boatorp and on to a certain pond, a rather shallow pool of water near the road through Norra Förlösa. Whoever had dug the hole here was either well aware of the location of the pipe or very lucky not to disturb it.

A wheel loader was called in. After careful scraping, inch by inch, a clearly visible dark rectangle appeared in the ground. It was the afternoon of July 3, 2014, when the hunt for missing man Göran Lundblad appeared to have, at long last, come to an end.

After a few more scoops with the loader, police technicians in white overalls, hairnets, face masks, latex gloves, and shovels continued the work by hand. At a depth of almost exactly six feet, a green tarpaulin emerged, a package still neatly wrapped in blue nylon rope. More boxes on the list, checked off.

When the police carefully folded back the flaps of the tarpaulin, the uncertainty was over, if anyone was, indeed, still unsure about what the package might contain.

Göran Lundblad was lying in the same position as when he had been shot. On his side, but with his head turned back as if to look. So many things can be deduced from tracing the outlines of what otherwise looks like one big fleshy, compressed mass. If you didn't know it was a human, it might take you a while to figure it out. Without a DNA analysis, no one would be able to say for sure who it was.

With the pivotal find secured, all the police could do was repackage the body in a body bag and send it off for a forensic autopsy at Linköping University Hospital.

23

THE INHERITANCE

Date: Wednesday, November 26, 2014

Time: 1:04 p.m.

Location: Kalmar County Court, Room E

Witness: Forensic Pathologist Erik Edston, The Swedish National Board of Forensic Medicine

Topic of testimony: Autopsy findings

When Göran's body was recovered, a police technician was present when we opened the tarpaulin.

The body was fairly well preserved on account of low temperatures and the wrapping. There was no presence of worms. The body was, however, radically transformed. Gray and pliable.

The discoloration made it impossible to assess minor injuries, but it was immediately apparent that there were head injuries.

There was substantial fracturing of the skull and up. Bird shot was found in the brain.

In his right cheek were small plastic fragments, presumably from a plastic wad from a shotgun shell. The rest was subsequently discovered wedged under his right ear.

Wads are not usually found in heads; this indicates a close-range shot. What would have smelled bad in connection with the shooting is urine and feces; evacuation occurs immediately.

His left eye was hanging out of its socket. That was because of the extensive fracturing of the face—the eye was pushed out.

The skin on his back was cracking, which I ascribe to the body being moved after it was found. The body was dissolving. It takes a few hours for rigor mortis to set in.

Before that happens, the body would have been limp and difficult to move. Under these conditions, I believe it would have taken approximately two hours for rigor mortis to set in. It would have been fully developed after six to eight hours.

Considering the injuries, there ought to have been a lot of blood. Bleeding ceases when the heart stops beating, but due to the pressure, two to four pints are lost during the first minute. The blood flow will, however, continue if the body is moved.

Pathologist Erik Edston had thirty years' experience with autopsies. He had performed something like five thousand in his career, he told the court, which lent considerable weight to his statement.

The many days of the trial were eagerly followed by a curious general public, witnesses, the plaintiffs—such as Göran's daughter Maria, her half sister Eleonora, and their mother, Irina—as well as a number of journalists.

There was a great deal of coverage of this trial. A dark and deranged Romeo and Juliet story about star-crossed lovers in a rural setting. Lovers who murdered the girl's father. All the money added a bit of extra spice, as those are the kinds of things that naturally stoke curiosity. But how the case was solved—thanks to a private investigator who put herself in harm's way to find the truth and convict the perpetrators—really raised the interest from mere curiosity to public frenzy.

On this late November day in 2014, when the pathologist told the court about the autopsy of Göran Lundblad and drew conclusions about how the murder had taken place, Sara Lundblad was in a separate room. The court required her to listen to accounts of how her father's remains had dissolved, as well as the injuries on his body. But she didn't have to look at the pictures the pathologist showed.

Was it a sign of her guilt—that she couldn't bear to look? Or of grief, a feeling she didn't want augmented further by images she would probably never be able to forget? It was open to interpretation. Nothing was settled yet. It was the fifth day of a twelve-day trial.

Five months had passed since Martin and Sara were arrested and Göran's body was recovered from the hole in the field next to the ground drain. It had been an intense time for the police, who had checked every box in the Murder Bible checklist before the case had gone to trial.

They ran new interviews with all relevant people: relatives, tenants, neighbors, and friends. The reactions ranged from "I told you so" to shock, distress, and skepticism. The interviewees still didn't have any pivotal information to give, only their persistent hunches, their opinions about how the alleged offenders had behaved: Martin's sudden presence in all Stigtomta contexts, something Göran would never have accepted. Sara's coldness and lack of reaction. That she didn't look, call, search. But also, her exaggerated reaction in the first few days. That she cried so much on the phone to her stepmother, Irina. Melodrama? Grief? Remorse over the horrific crime? Paradoxical. Plenty of both reasonable and unreasonable doubt.

The probable murder weapon was quickly identified. One of Åke Törnblad's shotguns showed signs of amateurish cleaning. The weapon had been rinsed, likely with both cleaner and water. Having then been left to air-dry, it had begun to rust. This was bad for the weapon, but actually good for the killer, if there had ever been blood on the barrel. The police were not, in other words, as lucky as they had been with Pierre Karlsson, the double murderer in the Flakeböle case, who had left dried-on blood stains on his rifle. But the incompetent cleaning of Åke Törnblad's weapon could, at the very least, be considered circumstantial evidence.

The technicians also came across an interesting puzzle piece when they carefully combed through the burn pile behind the Törnblad farm. Everything from defective briar pipe bowls and plastic to foam and metal furniture was discarded there to be burned in due course. But a pair of sooty, cracked glasses were also found among the debris. They had been there a long time and were a perfect match for the model Göran used to wear.

Why would an innocent daughter and an equally nonplussed son-in-law throw something like that away? Only someone who knew that the owner was never coming back would do that, no?

There was no help to be had from the suspects, who were both interviewed a handful of times before the trial.

Sara denied everything from the outset. She and her dad quarreled before he disappeared, but that wasn't unusual. When she entered Ställe Farm a few days later, she didn't notice anything unusual. Not that she was a hundred percent familiar with the place, since she didn't really live there, but, rather, with Martin.

And Göran was her rock. She would never have hurt him.

Confronted with the blood stains in the bedroom, she was completely uncomprehending. Yes, she had renovated recently, but she never saw any blood. The spot in the corner, by the Treetex board and the spackled subfloor, that was mostly Martin's area, she claimed.

And fine, she had forged her father's signature on the company's annual report, but only because she wanted to keep the business running as smoothly as she could manage until he came back.

The only explanation she could see as to why Martin would point the finger at her is that he wanted to get back at her for breaking off their relationship. He must have done it all himself.

The resentment she felt toward Martin was palpable in a message she wrote to him in the exercise yard of the pretrial detention center, a well-known way for inmates to communicate:

Thanks for ruining my life, Martin. I have nothing to give Vince now. Disinherited. Thanks!

One might expect different behavior from an innocent young woman, locked up on false charges.

Such as: "Why? What have you done?"

Or: "I hate you because you killed my dad."

But instead, a sarcastic thanks. Thanks for getting me caught. At least, that was the undertone the police investigators read into it.

In a cumulative assessment, as a county court would put it, several circumstances and strange details were incriminating for Sara. But to quote the legislative history: "A conviction may . . . not rest on an overall impression; an assessment must be made of individual proofs."

Martin also denied guilt after finding out that Therese had turned him in. He didn't seem to want to believe that she would betray him like that.

Excerpt from summary of interview 140621:

> Martin was told the police had interviewed Therese Tang, who described her meeting with Martin and their conversations.
>
> Therese first called Detective Martinsson to inform him that she had met with Martin; a decision was then made and a time scheduled for an interview.
>
> Martin was informed that Therese had had plenty of time to think about what to tell the police.
>
> Martin replied that he thought someone else had told the police this and that the police were making things up in saying it was Therese.
>
> Martin was then told it doesn't work that way. That the police do not make things up or say that someone said something they didn't.

Even so, Martin refused to accept it. After two more interviews, he stopped answering questions entirely and refused to cooperate with the interviewer. He would only sit in silence when brought to the interview room.

The investigators had to go back to the drawing board with the body, the blood, and the claims, to try to piece together the many circumstances that pointed to Martin and Sara being murderers.

It would have been an impossibility if not for Therese. Her efforts and the story she had coaxed out of Martin and partially recorded were the very foundation of the prosecutor's case.

When Therese took the stand, the day after the pathologist, the court janitor had to hand out tickets for the long line of spectators hoping to observe the courtroom that day.

After a few hours spent on setting out the background, Therese got to the material point in Martin's narrative: "It just all came rushing out of him. He told me that on a previous occasion, Sara had tried to do it with a forestry machine when they were out working, that it was supposed to look like an accident. But that she had been unable to follow through for emotional reasons. After that, they started planning this. Sara wanted it to happen at night, but Martin thought the morning was better because then it would just look like farmwork. He told me he had dug the grave himself the day before. He claimed they decided Martin would come by in the morning and be let into the house. He went up to Göran, who was on his side facing the wall, slightly propped up in the bed. When Martin was about five feet away, Göran turned and was about to shout something, and then Martin fired."

She gave a precise and detailed account. Almost too good, the defense lawyers reckoned, trying to paint her as an overconfident witness. She was too sure of herself, Martin's lawyer argued. She wanted the suspects convicted at any cost, in order to gain renown and fame for having solved the Göran Lundblad murder. This, the lawyer implied, caused her to alter her story, whether consciously or unconsciously.

The court dismissed that statement, because the details of her testimony were established as early as the evening of June 19 and had provided the basis on which the police had built their entire investigation ever since.

Take, for example, the fact that cell-phone tracking showed that Martin's phone moved from Norra Förlösa via Trekanten to Kalmar and back again on the morning of Göran's death. This was not necessarily significant in its own right, but coupled with Therese's assertion that he had told her he'd thrown the empty shotgun shell in a lake outside Trekanten that morning, his phone's whereabouts took on new meaning.

The same thing was true of the fact that Martin's phone had been in contact with Sara's at 6:28 a.m. on the day of the murder. That could simply be a morning greeting, an early declaration of love, or a quick call to check in about something happening in their shared life later in the day.

But when combined with the information from Martin's confession to Therese about Sara spending that night at her father's house, and her letting Martin and his borrowed shotgun in, that phone call took on a graver significance as well.

Checking in, absolutely. Or was he actually checking that everything was as expected, that Göran wasn't on to them, that Sara's father was still in his bed, and that the execution could proceed as planned?

When Martin was confronted with the probative weight of the many puzzle pieces, something unexpected happened. Martin confessed to a crime.

Or, rather: his lawyer confessed for him. Not to the murder, but to being involved as an accessory. A different person, "the shooter," a close friend of Martin's, supposedly called him on the morning of the murder. Showed him a fait accompli—Göran, dead—and ordered him to help get rid of the body.

That fits with parts of his confession to Therese. He may have seen the body, with the dangling eye. Might have even taken part in wrapping the body in the tarpaulin, which leaked blood. Driven it to the grave. Maybe even helped clean up.

But the picture had already been set by Therese's testimony, which was well supported by the things the police had already uncovered.

Martin's new version didn't fit. Was "the shooter" supposed to have let himself in without a key, killed Göran, called Martin in, helped bury the body, and cleaned out the room without Sara noticing? Where was the call on Martin's cell-phone log from this mysterious friend?

It was so far-fetched that it needn't even be taken into consideration, according to the Kalmar County Court, which concluded:

> The circumstances that suggest that Sara Lundblad participated in the murder also strongly suggest that no one other than Martin Törnblad shot Göran Lundblad.

On January 20, 2015, the Norra Förlösa couple were given their sentence. Eighteen years in prison each, the longest determinate punishment Swedish law allows.

They escaped the indeterminate lifetime sentence because Göran Lundblad's death had been so quick. He hadn't had time to feel much fear, there was no drawn-out suffering before the shot was fired and his brain exploded. Given that, lifetime imprisonment was inappropriate, as established by the Supreme Court in 2013.

Even though the victim was a close relative, even though he was "defenseless" in his bed, and even though the murder was carefully planned, Göran Lundblad didn't suffer enough before he died, in the court's opinion, for his daughter and her partner to be sentenced to lifetime imprisonment.

The sentence of eighteen years was upheld by the appellate court to which all parties appealed, including the prosecutor, who wanted life. Almost three years after the murder, on June 4, 2015, the Supreme Court declined to grant a review permit. The case was, at long last, closed.

Since Sweden practices parole after two-thirds of a sentence served for good behavior, Martin and Sara can count on being released in the summer of 2026. That year, their son will turn thirteen and will have lived in foster care for the greater part of his life. Both his parents will be destitute.

Martin's father, Åke, went bankrupt shortly after his son's arrest. Because a killer may not inherit the estate of his or her victim, all of Göran Lundblad's possessions, including the expensive Mercedes, the pickup truck Sara used, everything—approximately fifty million kronor (six million dollars) in all—was awarded to younger sister Maria, the one who had called Missing People in October 2012 and set all the wheels in motion.

EPILOGUE

People usually don't speak much after a court session ends. When the presiding judge declares "thus, this trial is concluded" and, on occasion, underscores his or her point with a pounding of a gavel, there is rarely much to add.

The formal sentence is normally promulgated a couple of weeks later, and on that occasion, everything is so well rehearsed, structured, and formulaic that most people are cowed. Everyone gathers up their thoughts and belongings in silence. A couple of sighs, scattered exhalations. The rustle of clothes as people stand up.

When Therese Tang got up from her chair in the gallery after the final day of the Förlösa trial, it was with a strong sense of relief.

"It was a natural close to so many weeks of tension," she said. "It was like pulling out an enormous plug."

The autumn of 2014 had been filled with strange occurrences in the wake of all the attention surrounding the murder case. Almost every paper in the country published interviews with Therese alongside their reporting on the investigation into the murder of the wealthy farmer.

Therese was called "the murder witness" in the headlines, as well as on the radio and TV news. Not everyone liked it. Apart from the usual crop of emails and texts full of hate and sexual innuendo that every renowned or famous woman is forced to put up with, other, more inexplicable things happened.

Her car was vandalized, both when it was parked outside her house in Oskarshamn and down in Kalmar. All four tires punctured at once—not a coincidence. Twice, she came home to find dead animals by her front door. Her mailbox was broken, and someone left notes in it that read "I see you."

Anonymous Facebook users told her she was going to "burn in hell." In addition, someone seemed to be skulking around the neighborhood, spying on her. More than ten times, she noticed someone sneaking around her backyard, and on one occasion a man in a parked car stared up at the house through binoculars.

Was it jealousy, potentially insane people, or was it someone affected by the criminal investigation? A relative, friend, or acquaintance of Martin's or Sara's? There were many conceivable explanations, but no certainty, because no one was apprehended or formally placed under suspicion, despite Therese's reports to the police.

The most serious event happened on the way out to Göran's grave in the field, in November 2014. Therese was accompanied by journalist Anders Blank from local paper *Barometern*, a photographer, and a couple of colleagues from Missing People. Martin and Sara had been coincidentally charged on the same day. On the way to the gravesite, they happened to meet Martin's younger brother, Mikael.

The young man was driving a small excavator and obviously had no intention of letting them pass, even though the small forest road they were on was a public highway. He threatened to hurt them if they continued down the road.

In the end, Anders Blank climbed out of the car to talk to the younger brother. After a brief conversation, the brother snapped. He turned the boom of his excavator around swiftly and hit Anders Blank with the large metal bucket. Not with full force in the head; that would have been the end of the journalist. Instead, the bucket struck him around his elbow, but with enough force to throw him several yards into the undergrowth.

Everything was filmed with a cell phone from inside the car—which turned out to be crucial evidence in the subsequent assault case against Mikael Törnblad. This time, the situation was resolved without serious injury, despite shouting, yelling, and threats from the young man in the excavator. The news team turned around, reported the matter to the police, and after a process that ended up taking more than a year and a half, Martin's brother was finally convicted of both assault and intimidation in December 2015.

The "murder witness" could not, in other words, simply do her duty. After contacting the police, giving a statement, and subsequently testifying in court, she could not go on with her life as though nothing had happened.

Feelings are, of course, stirred up when relatives are tried for murder. Therese stayed in close contact that autumn with Sara's half sisters Eleonora and Maria.

"They were the ones I spent the most time with during the trial," Therese said. "I did what I could to support them. Asked how they were doing, explained the process, and answered their questions as best I could. On the day of the closing statements, I had lunch with them and their mother, Irina. They had made me a flower arrangement and little Santa Claus cards with lovely messages. It made me cry."

Throughout the trial, Maria and Eleonora tried to leave through the back door to avoid the press, as Therese used the main exit and answered questions from the gathered media. On the final day, it was no different. Therese was greeted by a wall of reporters, cameras, and microphones before she could make it to the car where Anders Lindfors was waiting with Eleonora, Maria, and Therese's husband, Richard, in the backseat.

"We dropped Eleonora and Maria off at their hotel and drove north," Therese explained. "I was pretty drained mentally, felt both empty and at the same time overfilled with impressions and feelings, now that everything was coming to an end."

A couple of months from then, in the spring, Therese would receive an invitation from the Norra Förlösa Road Association. They wanted her to join them at a pizzeria in Oskarshamn. Ten or so Förlösa residents would be gathering there to toast her accomplishment and honor the dead.

"They said they wanted to thank me for not having to feel afraid anymore," Therese said. "They finally had peace of mind. They gave me flowers, and they had also started a collection to help me. They knew I was struggling financially, so they gave me a couple of thousand-krona notes as well; it was incredible to be met with so much love."

After the trial was over, Therese drove homeward through the winter gloom on the afternoon of December 12, 2014, talking quietly to her husband and Anders Lindfors about the tribulations of the past several months. They rolled north along E22, toward the house in Oskarshamn, past Lindsdal Junction and the exit for Norra Förlösa.

Four days later, on December 16, Swedish State Television aired the show *Crime of the Week*. The show usually draws over a million viewers every Tuesday night. This was the final episode of the season, and in Therese's house a handful of people had gathered in front of the TV to watch.

The Lundblad family was visiting—Eleonora, Maria, and Irina—and Anders had come as well.

Just a few hours earlier, Kalmar County Court had remanded Martin and Sara into custody until their sentencing. It was unusual for a court to require several days to come to a decision about detention.

It usually implies that the court doesn't consider the case entirely clear-cut.

One of the segments of that evening's episode was about the evidence archive in the basement of the Örebro Police Station. "It can make cold cases hot again," said host Camilla Kvartoft.

On the show that night, criminologist and author Leif G. W. Persson, for his part, promised to tell the story of the "priest poisoner" Anders Lindbäck, Sweden's first serial killer, who in the nineteenth century murdered three members of his congregation by putting arsenic in the communion wine.

But the program's main story was about something closer in both time and space to the people in Therese's living room: the Göran Lundblad case.

After a run-through of known facts, interviews with Detective Martinsson, and a segment where Therese talked about Martin's confession, the program went back to the studio.

Camilla Kvartoft: This afternoon, we found out the twenty-three-year-old and the twenty-six-year-old have been remanded in custody until their sentencing, which won't happen until January. How do you interpret that?

Leif G. W. Persson: I interpret that as they're going to be found guilty of this murder. Otherwise they would probably have let them out, at least her.

CK: So the story Therese was able to tell the police was enough?

LGWP: Yes, that's right. This is in fact Therese's case, if I can be a bit ironic about the local plods. Without her, this would have remained a mystery.

"We had dinner together that night as well," said Therese. "We cried and hugged a lot. It felt like they were finally able to close the books on their missing father."

As that evening drew to a close, tears were dried. They all knew this was the end, but smiles and promises of friendship were exchanged between the Lundblad family members who were still alive and free, and Therese Tang, the investigator who had gone with her gut, who had stayed with the chase to the end.

Aside from the gravestone, the only enduring physical memory of Göran Lundblad is a light-gray rectangular patch in a field just north of Kalmar, in the dark heart of Småland.

AFTERWORD

This book constitutes one of many possible versions of a long and complex history and a gruesome crime.

The dramatized sections of the book are based on my own research into the facts, on published sources recounting situations and contexts, and on interviews.

Concretely, the material is drawn from:

- The police investigation and sentences in case B2149-14, heard in the Kalmar County Court, and case B380-15, heard in the Göta Court of Appeals.
- Previously sealed documentation from the police investigation in the same cases.
- Other legal documentation, such as relevant police logs.
- Audio recordings and transcripts of the trials. I'd like to take this opportunity to thank lawyer Sofi Sundbom, who runs the online blog rättegång.se. Her recordings and transcripts have been immensely helpful.
- Articles, news reporting, and documentaries in newspapers and on television and radio.
- Interviews with approximately ten people—witnesses and other people affected by the events—during 2016.

- Interviews with Therese Tang, 2015–2017.
- Other published sources—audio, images, and text—of interest to the investigation, such as text-message exchanges and Facebook conversations. The majority of this material was provided by Therese Tang.

In my rendition, tense and word order have on occasion been changed to achieve a better flow, provide a more coherent context, and adhere more closely to the conventions of written prose.

The following people's names have been changed: Tiina Nieminen; Irina; and Doris, Henry, and Johan Nydahl.

Both Sara Lundblad and Martin Törnblad have, since they were incarcerated, worked on appealing their convictions and having them overturned. Sara maintains her innocence. Martin has from the high-security prison facility in Kumla made some new claims about "the shooter," but this has so far led to no tangible results.

In other words, the story of the murder of Göran Lundblad and its aftermath continue. For the people who loved him, it will never end.

Joakim Palmkvist, Malmö, 2018

ACKNOWLEDGMENTS

There are many people for me to thank for helping to bring this book into existence, but none more than Therese Tang, who cut through the veils of secrecy, took personal risks, and brought an impossible case to justice. There are more cases out there, Therese! Go get 'em!

I also owe the greatest of thanks to my Swedish publisher and good friend Martin Kaunitz. Without his guidance and laughter none of my books would have come true.

Martin, the world is not enough.

Publisher and editor Elin Sennerö was also instrumental in the making of this book. Elin, all my very best to you and your family.

My deepest gratitude and respect to each and every person who chose to talk to me and share their experiences and knowledge.

Among them, of course, the people of Norra Förlösa, in the dark heart of Sweden.

ABOUT THE AUTHOR

Photo © 2017 Sofia Runarsdotter

Joakim Palmkvist worked for over two decades as a journalist and is one of Sweden's most experienced and well-known crime reporters. He has interviewed some of the country's most notorious criminals and lives under a protected identity after publishing accounts about the mafia and extremist groups on both the right and the left. Palmkvist lives in Malmö.

ABOUT THE TRANSLATOR

Photo © 2018 Sean McCreery

Agnes Broomé is a literary translator and preceptor in Scandinavian at Harvard University. She has a PhD in translation studies, and her translations include August Prize–winner *The Expedition* by Bea Uusma.